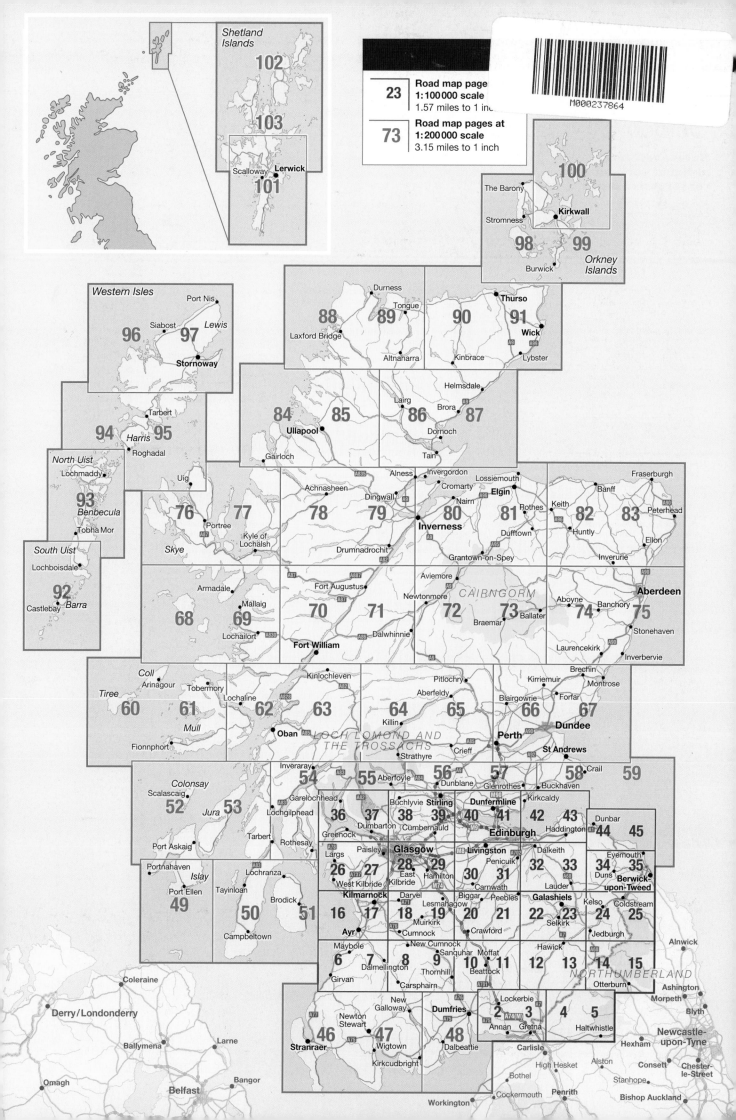

# Best places to visit

## Outdoors

### Nature reserves, national parks and conservation areas

#### Aberdeen and Moray

**Cairngorm National Park** *Braemar, Aberdeenshire.* The Cairngorm National Park covers 2375 square miles of the Highlands, Moray and Aberdeenshire. It holds more than a quarter of Scotland's remaining native woodland and is home to over a quarter of Scotland's threatened species. 📞 01479 873535 🖥 www.cairngorms.co.uk **73 C6**

**Forvie National Nature Reserve** *Collieston, Aberdeenshire.* The Ythan estuary, riverside, sand dunes, coastal heath and seacliffs make this a rich area for a variety of plants and wildlife. As well as breeding terns, this reserve supports Britain's biggest colony of breeding eider duck and attracts large groups of geese and waders in winter. No entry to tern breeding area from April to August. 📞 01358 751330 🖥 www.nnr-scotland.org.uk **83 F7**

**Fowlsheugh** *Crawton, Aberdeenshire.* In spring and summer the cliffs are crammed with breeding fulmars, guillemots, herring gulls, kittiwakes, puffins, razorbills and shags. From May to July, boat trips from Stonehaven take visitors in the evening to watch the nesting seabirds. 📞 01346 532017 🖥 www.rspb.org.uk **75 D5**

**Loch of Strathbeg** *Crimond, Aberdeenshire.* Pink-footed geese and whooper swans winter here regularly, while summer breeders include lapwings, redshanks, common and Sandwich terns. 📞 01346 532017 🖥 www.rspb.org.uk **83 C7**

**St Cyrus National Nature Reserve** *St Cyrus, Aberdeenshire.* The cliffs and dunes of St Cyrus support a range of plants, including some you would not expect to find this far north. These provide suitable habitat for a rich variety of insects, particularly moths and butterflies. Breeding birds include terns, stonechats and whin-chats, as well as fulmars on the cliffs. No access to tern breeding area April to August. 🖥 www.nnr-scotland.org.uk **67 A7**

#### Argyll, Bute, Stirling, Trossachs

**Flanders Moss National Nature Reserve** *Thornhill, Stirling.* This reserve is a remnant of one of the largest lowland bog areas in Britain. Its colourful sphagnum mosses support a variety of insects in summer and birdlife, including birds of prey in the autumn. The viewing tower provides the best overview. Visitors should keep to the circular path. 📞 (SNH) 01786 450362 🖥 www.nnr-scotland.org.uk **56 C1**

**Loch Gruinart** *Aoradh, Islay, Argyll and Bute.* Hundreds of lapwings, redshanks and snipe breed by the loch in spring, while hen harriers nest up on the moorland in early summer. Corncrake can be heard at night during the summer. Large numbers of barnacle and white-fronted geese winter here, while golden eagles and peregrine falcons can be seen hunting all year. 📞 01496 850505 🖥 www.rspb.org.uk **52 F2**

**Loch Lomond and the Trossachs National Park** *Aberfoyle, Stirling.* Scotland's first national park opened in July 2002. It contains a wide variety of special habitats and large amounts of protection for wildlife. It is divided into four areas: Lomond, which centres on the Loch and Ben Lomond and is good for watersports among other activities; the Trossachs, which includes Queen Elizabeth Forest Park and Loch Katrine and is an excellent place for scenery and walking; Breadalbane, which has spectacular scenery and some good hillwalking; and Argyll, which has extensive forests and sea lochs. 🖥 www.lochlomond-trossachs.org **55 B8**

**Moine Mhor National Nature Reserve** *Bellanoch, Argyll and Bute.* This waterlogged system of pools and bogs is home to curlews and hen harriers, as well as a wide range of dragonflies in summer. The best views over the reserve are from the Crinan Canal, near Bellanoch, or the ancient hill fort of Dunadd. Stay on the paths. 🖥 www.nnr-scotland.org.uk 📞 01546 603611 **53 C8**

**Staffa National Nature Reserve** *Staffa, Argyll and Bute.* The distinctive hexagonal rock columns of this uninhabited island are formed from basalt, just like those of the Giant's Causeway on the opposite side of the Irish Sea. In spring and early summer, the cliffs and grassy clifftops provide nesting sites for guillemots, puffins and razorbills, as well as other seabirds. Tour boats operate from Mull and Iona. See also Fingal's Cave. 📞 (NTS) 01681 700659 🖥 www.nts.org.uk 🖥 www.nnr-scotland.org.uk **61 D6**

**Taynish National Nature Reserve** *Tayvallich, Argyll and Bute.* This ancient deciduous woodland lies on a scenic peninsula overlooking Loch Sween. Its dripping ferns and mosses, mixed with marshland and grassland, support more than 300 plant species and 20 kinds of butterfly in early summer. 📞 01546 603611 🖥 www.nnr-scotland.org.uk **53 D7**

**The Oa (Upper Killeyan)** *Port Ellen, Islay, Argyll and Bute.* Choughs and, sometimes, golden eagles can be seen from the coast, while Greenland white-fronted geese use the bog in winter. 📞 01496 300118 🖥 www.rspb.org.uk **49 B2**

#### Glasgow and the Clyde

**Baron's Haugh** *Motherwell, North Lanarkshire.* More than 170 species of birds have been recorded in this small urban nature reserve. Kingfishers can be seen by the river and whooper swans winter on the meadows. 📞 0141 3310993 🖥 www.rspb.org.uk **29 C5**

**Clyde Valley Woodlands National Nature Reserve** *Lanark, South Lanarkshire.* This reserve features steep gorges with woodland typical of the Clyde Valley, including ash, oak and wych elm. Birdlife includes flycatchers, redstarts and warblers during the breeding season. The steepness of the terrain means that the paths can be dangerous when wet. 📞 (SNH) 01698 421668 🖥 www.nnr-scotland.org.uk **29 E8**

**Lochwinnoch** *Renfrewshire.* In winter the large variety of wildfowl on the loch includes goosanders, while in spring lapwings display and sedge warblers can be heard singing. 📞 01505 842663 🖥 www.rspb.org.uk **27 C6**

#### Perth, Angus, Dundee and Fife

**Ben Lawers National Nature Reserve** *Milton Morenish, Perth and Kinross.* This reserve, on the north side of Loch Tay, has a unique range of mountain plants because the soils are unusually rich at high altitude, supporting a superb collection of arctic-alpine plants that flower in early to mid-summer. Work is being undertaken to restore the natural montane willow scrub. There is a nature trail and ranger-led walks are available. Birds that can be seen in season include curlew, dipper, ptarmigan, raven and red grouse. 📞 (NTS) 01567 820988 🖥 www.nts.org.uk 🖥 www.nnr-scotland.org.uk **64 D4**

**Isle of May National Nature Reserve** *Isle of May, Fife.* As well as containing one of the largest puffin colonies in Scotland, together with guillemots and razorbills, this tiny island in the Firth of Forth has a lighthouse, a 12th-century chapel and a bird observatory. Access is by boat from Anstruther Easter. The reserve is closed during the autumn seal pupping season. 📞 (SNH) 01334 654038 🖥 www.nnr-scotland.org.uk **58 C4**

**Loch Leven National Nature Reserve** *Kinross, Perth and Kinross.* Loch Leven is Scotland's largest lowland freshwater loch. Among the wildfowl that depend on it are up to 20,000 pink-footed geese in winter. See also Loch Leven Nature Reserve. 🖥 www.nnr-scotland.org.uk 📞 01577 864439 **57 B6**

**Loch Leven Nature Reserve** *Loch Leven NNR, Kinross, Perth and Kinross.* Thousands of ducks overwinter here, along with greylag and pink-footed geese and whooper swans. The wet grassland provides a haven for nesting ducks, lapwings, redshanks and snipe. Birds that breed in the woodland on Vane Hill include great spotted woodpeckers, tree pipits and willow warblers. Nature trails. See also Loch Leven National Nature Reserve. 📞 01577 862355 🖥 www.rspb.org.uk **57 B6**

**Loch of Kinnordy** *Kinnordy, Angus.* The lochs, mires and fens of the reserve are surrounded by farmland. On the reserve, wildfowl, wading birds and ospreys visit regularly in the spring and summer, when black-necked grebes may also occur. In winter, the reserve is full of wildfowl. 📞 01577 862355 🖥 www.rspb.org.uk **66 B3**

**Tentsmuir National Nature Reserve** *Tayport, Fife.* The dunes and beach on the south side of the mouth of the Tay Estuary form an important roosting and feeding area for huge numbers of waders and wildfowl, especially in the winter for the latter, as well as a place for more common and grey seals to rest. In summer, the grasslands behind the dunes are a haven for butterflies. 📞 01382 553704 🖥 www.nnr-scotland.org.uk **67 E4**

#### South of Scotland

**Caerlaverock National Nature Reserve** *Bankend, Dumfries and Galloway.* Thousands of wildfowl, including barnacle geese from the Arctic, winter on the estuary and feed on the tidal saltmarsh. 📞 0300 067 3200; Wildfowl and Wetlands Trust 01387 770200 🖥 www.wwt.org.uk 🖥 www.nnr-scotland.org.uk **2 F2**

**Grey Mare's Tail Nature Reserve** *Moffat, Dumfries and Galloway.* The spectacular 200ft waterfall is formed by the Tail Burn dropping from Loch Skene. The surrounding reserve is rich in wild flowers and a herd of wild goats can sometimes be seen in the area. 📞 07713 786230 🖥 www.nts.org.uk **11 B7**

**Ken-Dee Marshes** *Glenlochar, Dumfries and Galloway.* In winter, many wildfowl, including white-fronted geese, can be seen on the wetlands, while in spring, pied flycatchers and redstarts arrive to breed in the woodlands. Red kites hunt in the area and mammals present include red squirrels and otters. 📞 01556 670464 🖥 www.rspb.org.uk **48 C1**

**Mull of Galloway** *Drummore, Dumfries and Galloway.* Thousands of gannets, guillemots, puffins and razorbills nest on the cliffs between April and July. 📞 01988 402130 🖥 www.rspb.org.uk **46 F3**

**St Abb's Head National Nature Reserve** *St Abbs, Scottish Borders.* The stunning cliff supports large breeding colonies of fulmars guillemots, kittiwakes, puffins, razorbills and shags in May–July. In spring and high summer the grasslands are full of flowers, which in summer attract large numbers of butterflies. In autumn and spring large numbers of migrant birds pass close to the cliffs. Nature centre, guided walks. 📞 (NTS) 01890 771443 🖥 www.nts.org.uk 🖥 www.nnr-scotland.org.uk **35 A7**

---

**Shetland Islands**

**Orkney Islands**

**1** South of Scotland
**2** Glasgow and the Clyde
**3** Edinburgh and East Central Scotland
**4** Perth, Angus, Dundee and Fife
**5** Argyll, Bute, Stirling, Trossachs
**6** Aberdeen and Moray
**7** The Highlands
**8** Western Isles, Orkney and Shetland

▼ **Glen Affric** Scottish Viewpoint / Alamy

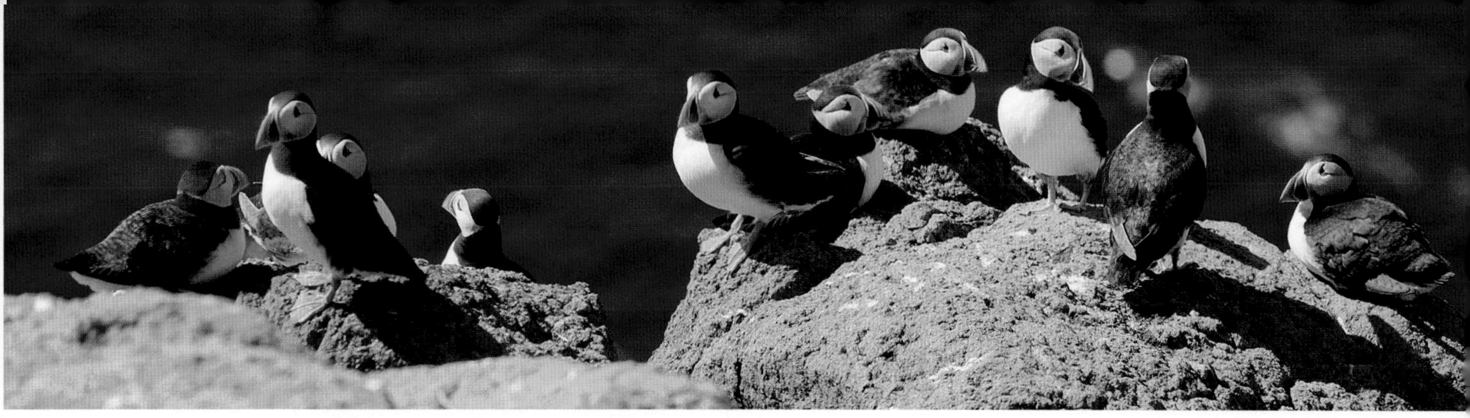

**Whitlaw Mosses National Nature Reserve** *Selkirk, Scottish Borders.* These four low-lying areas contain a variety of wetland habitats including moss carpets, swamps of sedges, willow scrub, meadows and grasslands. The fragile surfaces are easily damaged and look deceptively solid. Keep to the firm ground. 0300 067 3200 www.nnr-scotland.org.uk **23 D6**

**Wood of Cree** *Minnigaff, Dumfries and Galloway.* The Wood of Cree is the largest ancient wood in southern Scotland. In spring, migrant redstarts and pied flycatchers arrive from Africa. Otters can sometimes be seen. 01988 402130 www.rspb.org.uk **47 B5**

## The Highlands

**Abernethy National Nature Reserve** *Nethy Bridge, Highland.* The largest remnant native Scots pinewood in Britain, Abernethy Forest offers a unique mix of woodland and northern bog (keep to the tracks). Birds include capercaillie, crossbill, crested tit, goldeneye and osprey, which breed in the wide variety of habitats. See also Loch Garten. 01479 810477 www.nnr-scotland.org.uk **72 A5**

**Beinn Eighe National Nature Reserve** *Kinlochewe, Highland.* Among Beinn Eighe's wonderful mountain scenery, overlooking Loch Maree, are some of the few remaining fragments of ancient pinewood in Scotland. The wildlife includes golden eagles, pine martens and red deer, as well as a wide variety of dragonflies over the bogland. The visitor centre provides information on the various woodland and mountain trails. 01445 760254 www.nnr-scotland.org.uk **78 B1**

**Ben Wyvis National Nature Reserve** *Garve, Highland.* Animals that are found in the area include red and roe deer, pine martens and golden eagles. The habitats vary from the moss-covered upper slopes to the dwarf shrub heath and boglands lower down that support plants like dwarf birch, cloudberry and dwarf cornel. Some areas may be closed for deer stalking between August and October. 01479 810447 www.nnr-scotland.org.uk **79 B6**

**Corrieshalloch Gorge National Nature Reserve** *Braemore, Highland.* This spectacular, mile-long gorge, a box canyon, is 200ft deep. The river that carved this channel, the Abhainn Droma, plunges over the Falls of Measach. These can be seen from the suspension bridge, built by John Fowler – a co-designer of the Forth Bridge. The gorge is home to a rich variety of liverworts and mosses. 0844 493224 www.nts.org.uk **85 F6**

**Corrimony** *Highland.* Set in a superb landscape, this reserve has conifer plantations, native woodland and open moorland. In summer, Loch Comhnard has breeding common sandpipers, curlews and greenshanks, with ospreys and red-throated divers sometimes seen. Goldeneyes and whooper swans are among the winter visitors. Black grouse can be seen in the birchwoods, while the pinewoods have breeding bullfinches, spotted flycatchers and wood warblers. 01463 715000 www.rspb.org.uk **79 E5**

**Craigellachie National Nature Reserve** *Aviemore, Highland.* Scenic trails through the mature birchwood that cloaks the lower slopes of the hill of Craigellachie provide fine views across Aviemore and Strathspey to the Cairngorms. Peregrines nest on the cliff between April and July, while spring is the best time to see the woodland flowers. www.nnr-scotland.org.uk 01479 810477 **72 A3**

**Culbin Sands** *Nairn, Highland.* Culbin Sands is one of the largest shingle and sand dune bars in Britain. Bar-tailed godwits, knot and oystercatchers can be seen at high tide. In winter, large numbers of sea ducks are visible offshore. 01463 715000 www.rspb.org.uk **80 C3**

**Fairy Glen** *Rosemarkie, Highland.* A small area of broadleaved woodland in a pretty, steep-sided glen with a fast-flowing stream. Dippers can be seen in the stream. 01463 715000 www.rspb.org.uk **80 C2**

**Forsinard Flows** *Highland.* The blanket-bog peatlands of Forsinard are at the heart of the Flow Country. Breeding birds including dunlin, golden plovers and merlins. Visitor centre, bog pool trail and guided walks. 01641 571225 www.rspb.org.uk **90 D2**

**Glen Affric National Nature Reserve** *Cannich, Highland.* Glen Affric is among the most beautiful glens and has one of the largest remaining ancient pinewoods in Scotland. Wildlife present includes some of Scotland's most elusive species – black grouse, capercaillies, crested tits, crossbills golden eagles, otters, red-throated divers and pine martens. Activities include hillwalking, mountain biking on forest tracks and open water canoeing. (FCS) 01463 791575 www.nnr-scotland.org.uk http://scotland.forestry.gov.uk **78 F3**

**Glen Roy National Nature Reserve** *Roybridge, Highland.* The famous 'Parallel Roads' of Glen Roy were created during the last ice age when glaciers dammed the end of the glen and created a succession of lakes in it. The shorelines of these form the 'Roads' on the hillsides that can be seen from the viewpoint. 01397 704716 www.nnr-scotland.org.uk **71 D5**

**Glenborrodale** *Highland.* An ancient oakwood on the north shore of Loch Sunart. In spring, wood warblers, redstarts and spotted flycatchers nest. Otters and seals can be seen in the loch. 01463 715000 www.rspb.org.uk **62 A1**

**Handa Island** *Scourie, Highland.* This internationally important nature reserve, is a mass of red Torridon sandstone. In summer it has breeding populations of razorbills, guillemots and puffins. There are also remnants of the cottages of the crofters who lived on the island until the 19th century. A walk around the island offers views across the Minch and of the Great Stack rock formation. Access is by public transport, on foot and then ferry. www.scottishwildlifetrust.org.uk **88 D3**

**Insh Marshes National Nature Reserve** *Kingussie, Highland.* This is one of Europe's most important wetlands, primarily because about half of all British goldeneyes breed here, as do substantial numbers of wigeon. Waders that visit the site include curlews, lapwings, oystercatchers, redshanks and snipe. In winter, the flooded marshes are home to large groups of whooper swans and greylag geese. (RSPB) 01540 661518 www.nnr-scotland.org.uk www.rspb.org.uk **72 B2**

**Loch Fleet National Nature Reserve** *Golspie, Highland.* This tidal basin is home to common seals, and waders and wildfowl are easy to spot on the mudflats. The sand dunes, coastal heath and pinewood plantations are rich in wild flowers. Among the annual highlights are the ospreys that can be seen fishing in early to mid-summer. www.scottishwildlifetrust.org.uk www.nnr-scotland.org.uk **86 D5**

**Loch Garten** *Boat of Garten, Highland.* In summer, ospreys can be seen from the osprey centre, which also has a video feed of the nest. In April and early May, male capercaillies display (lek) around dawn. Other rarities include crested tits, Scottish crossbills and red squirrels. Visitor centre. See also Abernethy Forest National Nature Reserve. 01479 831476 www.rspb.org.uk **72 A4**

**Loch Ruthven** *East Croachy, Highland.* This lovely loch is the most important site in the UK for Slavonian grebes. Ospreys can be seen in summer and hen harriers and peregrines can also sometimes be spotted. 01463 715000 www.rspb.org.uk **80 F1**

**Rum National Nature Reserve** *Kinloch, Rum, Highland.* The spectacular Isle of Rum is home to otters, red deer, sea eagles and a mountaintop colony of Manx shearwaters. Access is via ferry from Mallaig. www.nnr-scotland.org.uk 01687 462026 **68 C3**

## The Outer Islands

**Birsay Moors** *Finstown, Mainland, Orkney.* In the summer, hen harriers, short-eared owls and Arctic skuas nest on the moorland. The Orkney vole is also common on the reserve. 01856 850176 www.rspb.org.uk **98 A4**

**Brodgar** *Hestwall, Mainland, Orkney.* Snipe can be heard drumming in the summer, and other breeding waders include curlews, dunlin, lapwings, oystercatchers and redshanks. Wildfowl present on the reserve in summer includes, gadwalls, wigeon, shovelers and teal. See also Ring of Brodgar. 01856 850176 www.rspb.org.uk **98 B3**

**Copinsay** *Skaill, Orkney.* The cliffs of this uninhabited island are home to a huge colony of breeding seabirds, including fulmars, guillemots, kittiwakes, puffins and razorbills. 01224 624824 www.rspb.org.uk **100 C2**

**Cottascarth and Rendall Moss** *Finstown, Mainland, Orkney.* Hen harriers, merlins and short-eared owls can be seen, while nearby Rendall Moss is great for breeding curlews. 01856 850176 www.rspb.org.uk **98 B4**

**Fair Isle** *Stoneybreck, Shetland.* This isolated island is home to around 70 people. It has a bird observatory, which is open to the public in summer, and the Shetlands council and National Trust for Scotland encourage traditional crofting practices and conservation. Chiefly famous for its traditional knitted garments, additional crafts now include traditional wooden boat building, fiddle making and the manufacture of stained glass windows. Accessible in summer by boat from Grutness, on Shetland or flights from Tingwall (Lerwick) airport and Kirkwall, Orkney. www.fairisle.org.uk www.nts.org.uk 0844 4932238 **101 E4**

**Fetlar** *Houbie, Shetland.* In summer, the breeding birds include nine-tenths of all British red-necked phalaropes, as well as arctic and great skuas, red-throated divers and whimbrels. 01957 733246 www.rspb.org.uk **102 D6**

**Hermaness National Nature Reserve** *Burrafirth, Unst, Shetland.* National Nature Reserve overlooking Muckle Flugga, the cliffs and stacks of Herma Ness are a haven for more than 100,000 seabirds, including over 50,000 nesting puffins and 30,000 gannets, while the inland moors hold the third largest colony of great skuas in the world. The walk to the cliffs takes three to four hours. www.nnr-scotland.org.uk **102 B6**

**Hobbister** *Kirkwall, Mainland, Orkney.* Hen harriers, red-throated divers and short-eared owls breed on the moorland in early summer, while black guillemots and red-breasted mergansers can be seen from the coast. 01856 850176 www.rspb.org.uk **98 C4**

**Hoy** *Rackwick, Orkney.* The reserve is a mixture of moorland and cliffs and includes the Old Man of Hoy rock stack. Dunlin, golden plovers, great skuas and red grouse breed on the moor and guillemots, kittiwakes and razorbills on the cliffs. See also Old Man of Hoy. 01856 850176 www.rspb.org.uk **100 B2**

**Marwick Head** *Marwick, Mainland, Orkney.* Thousands of pairs of seabirds crowd onto the cliffs during the breeding season. Among the coastal specialities in the grasslands on the cliff top are sea campion, spring squill and thrift. 01856 850176 www.rspb.org.uk **98 A3**

**Monach Isles National Nature Reserve** *Monach Isles, Western Isles.* Breeding birds in the summer include terns and black guillemots and there is a rich variety of plants on the machair, but these islands are primarily known for the internationally important colonies of Atlantic grey seals that breed here in the autumn. (SNH) 01870 620 238 www.nnr-scotland.org.uk **93 B1**

**Mousa** *Shetland.* Many of the island's 12,000 storm petrels nest near Mousa broch, and arctic skuas, arctic terns, black guillemots, great skuas, oystercatchers and ringed plovers also breed. Common seals breed on the shoreline. Harbour porpoises, minke whales and orcas can sometimes be seen en route to the island. 01950 460800 www.rspb.org.uk **101 D3**

**North Hill** *Papa Westray, Orkney.* The cliffs house breeding guillemots, kittiwakes and razorbills, with arctic skuas and arctic terns nests, eiders, oystercatchers and ringed plovers. Contact the warden before any visit. 01856 850176 www.rspb.org.uk **100 A2**

**Noss National Nature Reserve** *Noss, Shetland.* Some 45,000 guillemots, 7000 pairs of gannets and thousands of fulmars, kittiwakes and puffins breed on the ledges of this island's cliffs. Seals are often seen in the surrounding seas and great skuas over the moorland. 01595 693345 www.nnr-scotland.org.uk **101 E2**

**Noup Cliffs** *Westray, Orkney.* More than 44,500 guillemots and 12,700 pairs of kittiwakes breed on these lonely cliffs, as well as good numbers of fulmars and razorbills. 01856 850176 www.rspb.org.uk **100 B1**

**Sumburgh Head** *Sumburgh, Mainland, Shetland.* The cliffs attract thousands of breeding birds, including fulmars, guillemots and puffins. Gannets can be seen offshore, and occasionally whales and dolphins. 01950 460800 www.rspb.org.uk **101 F3**

**Trumland** *Brinian, Rousay, Orkney.* The heather moorland of this reserve provides ideal nesting grounds for hen harriers, merlins and red-throated divers. 01856 821395 www.rspb.org.uk **100 D2**

▲ **Puffins on the Isle of May** Alamy

# Country and forest parks

## Aberdeen and Moray

**Aden Country Park** *Mintlaw, Aberdeenshire.* Some 230 acres of woodlands, a large lake and a variety of wildlife. (park management) 01771 624378, (ranger service) 01771 622857 www.adencountrypark.org.uk **83 D6**

## Argyll, Bute, Stirling, Trossachs

**Argyll Forest Park** *Lochgoilhead, Argyll and Bute.* The Argyll Forest Park occupies 24,000 hectares (60,000 acres) of southern Argyll. Activities available include rock climbing, hill walking, boating and hiking. Among the wildlife that may be seen in the sea lochs are sea otters, sharks and grey seals. http://scotland.forestry.gov.uk 0845 3673787 **54 C4**

**Queen Elizabeth Forest Park** *David Marshall Lodge, near Aberfoyle, Stirling.* Nestling between the eastern shore of Loch Lomond and the Trossachs, 45,000 acres of woodland, moorland and mountainside have been reserved for walkers and hikers; also Go Ape high wire forest adventure. 01877 382383 http://scotland.forestry.gov.uk **55 B8**

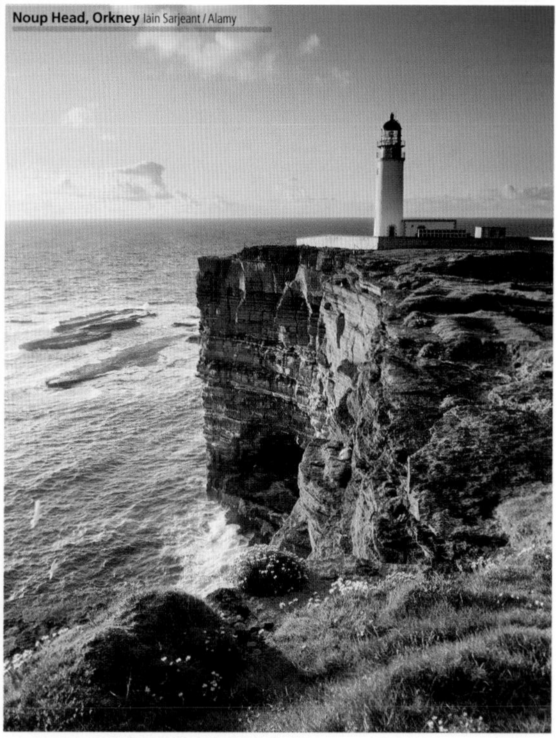

**Noup Head, Orkney** Iain Sarjeant / Alamy

### Glasgow and the Clyde

**Calderglen Country Park** *Strathaven Road, East Kilbride, South Lanarkshire.* As well as miles of nature trails, this country park has a children's zoo with exotic animals, adventure play areas and a visitor centre. ☎01355 236 644
🖳www.slleisureandculture.co.uk **28 D4**

**Gleniffer Braes Country Park** *Glenfield Road, Paisley, Renfrewshire.* A large area of woodland and moorland with an adventure playground.
🖳www.renfrewshire.gov.uk
☎0330 300 0380 **27 B8**

**Strathclyde Country Park** *336 Hamilton Road, Motherwell, North Lanarkshire.* Centred on Strathclyde Loch, this park consists of 1100 acres of mature woodland, wetland, wildlife areas and open parkland. See also activities. ☎01698 402060
🖳www.northlanarkshire.gov.uk **29 C5**

### Perth, Angus, Dundee and Fife

**Crombie Country Park** *Monikie, Broughty Ferry, Dundee City.* Woodland country park with guided nature trails, interpretation of forestry in the area as far back as 2000 BCE, an orienteering course, a children's play area. ☎01241 860360
🖳www.angus.gov.uk **67 D4**

**Gartmorn Dam Country Park** *Sauchie, Clackmannanshire.* This local nature reserve and Site of Special Scientific Interest includes the oldest man-made reservoir still working in Scotland, built by the 6th Earl of Mar in 1713 to provide water to drive the pumps in his nearby coal mines. There are extensive footpaths, links to national cycleways and horse riding routes.
🖳www.clacksweb.org.uk **40 B2**

▼ **The walkway to the second chamber of Smoo Cave** Scottish Viewpoint / Alamy

### South of Scotland

**Galloway Forest Park** *New Galloway, Dumfries and Galloway.* Britain's largest forest park covers more than 300 square miles with habitat ranging from forest, moorland and loch to mountains and beaches. There are extensive walking trails and cycle trails, horse riding, fishing, a wide variety of wildlife, forest drives, and stunning views. ☎0300 067 6800
🖳http://scotland.forestry.gov.uk **47 B8**

## Other natural features

### Argyll, Bute, Stirling, Trossachs

**Fingal's Cave** *Staffa, Argyll and Bute.* The uninhabited isle of Staffa inspired Mendelssohn to compose his 'Hebridean Overture', of which the most famous movement is named after this cave. The hexagonal shape of the rocks that make up its walls, floor and roof occurred when Tertiary basalt lava flows shrank and cracked as they cooled after a volcanic eruption.
☎01681 700659 🖳www.nts.org.uk **61 D6**

**Mackinnon's Cave** *Balnahard, Mull, Argyll and Bute.* Accessible only at low tide, this is the largest sea-cave in the Hebrides. The grisly legend asserts that evil spirits once devoured a group of people here.
🖳www.isle-of-mull.net/attractions/geology/mackinnons-cave **61 D7**

### Edinburgh and East Central

**Arthur's Seat** *Holyrood Park, Edinburgh, City of Edinburgh.* At 823 ft high, this extinct volcanic plug looms over the city.

The hike to the top affords spectacular views. ☎0131 6528150
🖳www.historicenvironment.scot **42 F1**

#### The Highlands
**Falls of Shin** *Lairg, Highland.* Between June and September, these falls are one of the best places to watch salmon going upriver to spawn. ☎01863 766554
🖳http://scotland.forestry.gov.uk **86 D2**

**Smoo Cave** *Durness, Highland.* A 200ft long complex of three caves etched into the limestone cliffs by the stream and the sea. The central cave is crossed by rubber dinghy.
🖳www.smoocave.org **89 B6**

## Parks and gardens

### Aberdeen and Moray

**Cruickshank Botanic Garden** *St Machar Drive, Aberdeen, Aberdeen City.* Pretty displays of shrubs, alpine and herbaceous plants, with water and rock gardens. There is also a small zoological museum.
🖳http://abdn.ac.uk/botanic-garden/ **75 B6**

**Pitmedden Garden** *Ellon, Aberdeenshire.* The centrepiece of this garden, known as the Great Garden, was originally laid out in 1675. The parterres were relaid in the 1950s with designs that may have been used in the gardens of Holyrood House and the original owner's coat of arms. The gardens include a visitor centre, woodland walks, a herb garden and a small museum devoted to farming life. ☎01651 842352
🖳www.nts.org.uk **83 E6**

### Argyll, Bute, Stirling, Trossachs
**Achamore House Gardens** *Ardminish, Gigha, Argyll and Bute.* Sir James Horlick, one of the world's greatest gardeners, created this landscape filled with azaleas, rhododendrons, camellias, hydrangeas and roses. ☎(at Gigha Hotel) 01583 505254
🖳www.gigha.org.uk **50 B2**

**Ardencraig Gardens** *Rothesay, Bute, Argyll and Bute.* In summer the gardens and hothouses are overflowing with flowering plants. Also has aviaries with exotic birds. ☎01700 504644 🖳www.exploreargyll.co.uk **54 F3**

**Ardkinglas Woodland Garden** *Cairndow, Argyll and Bute.* One of Scotland's best collections of conifers, with spectacular views over Loch Fyne and rhododendrons in flower in June. ☎01499 600261
🖳www.ardkinglas.com **54 A4**

**Arduaine Garden** *Arduaine, Argyll and Bute.* This outstanding garden, with an important collection of rare trees and shrubs, lies on a promontory bounded by Loch Melfort and the Sound of Jura, and benefits from the warmth brought by the Gulf Stream. Among the seasonal highlights are rhododendrons, azaleas and magnolias. ☎01852 200366 🖳www.nts.org.uk **53 A7**

**Ascog Fernery and Gardens** *Ascog Hall, Ascog, Argyll and Bute.* Restored Victorian conservatories, containing a wide range of ferns, including one that is alleged to be

▲ **Pitmedden Gardens, Aberdeenshire**
DG Farquhar / Alamy

more than 1000 years old. ☎01700 503461
🖳www.ascogfernery.com **54 F4**

**Benmore Botanic Gardens** *Benmore, Argyll and Bute.* An offshoot of Edinburgh's Royal Botanic Gardens, with masses of rhododendrons and azaleas flowering in late spring. Among the trees from all over the world is an avenue of giant redwoods. ☎01369 706261 🖳www.rbge.org.uk **36 C1**

**Crarae Gardens** *Crarae, Argyll and Bute.* Beautiful gardens overlooking Loch Fyne, with panoramic vistas, spectacular waterfalls, rhododendrons in late spring and various walking trails. ☎01546 886614 🖳www.nts.org.uk **54 C2**

### Edinburgh and East Central
**Holyrood Park** *Queen's Drive, Edinburgh, City of Edinburgh.* The former royal hunting ground occupies 650 acres, and includes moorland, a loch and the towering 'Arthur's Seat'. ☎0131 6528150
🖳www.historicenvironment.scot **42 F1**

**Royal Botanic Gardens** *Inverleith Row, Edinburgh, City of Edinburgh.* One of the most beautiful botanic gardens in Britain, spread across 70 acres and dating from the late 17th century. Highlights include the Glasshouse Experience, the Palm House and the Chinese Garden. ☎0131 248 2909
🖳www.rbge.org.uk **41 E8**

### Glasgow and the Clyde
**Glasgow Botanic Gardens** *Great Western Road, Glasgow, City of Glasgow.* An extensive collection of herb gardens and tropical plants, founded in 1871.
🖳www.glasgowbotanicgardens.com
☎0141 2761614 **28 A2**

### Perth, Angus, Dundee and Fife
**Branklyn Garden** *116 Dundee Road, Perth, Perth and Kinross.* A small garden holds a magnificent collection of alpines and rhododendrons as well as peat-garden and herbaceous plants from all over the world. It was founded in 1922 and now belongs to the National Trust for Scotland. ☎01738 625535 🖳www.nts.org.uk **66 E1**

### South of Scotland
**Dawyck Botanic Garden** *Drumelzier, Scottish Borders.* The collection – an offshoot of the Royal Botanic Garden in Edinburgh – includes conifers, and flowering shrubs. ☎01721 760254
🖳www.rbge.org.uk **21 B7**

**Harestanes Visitor Centre** *Bonjedward, Scottish Borders.* Trails and guided walks, Discovery room with wildlife displays.
🖳www.scotborders.gov
☎01835 830306 **24 E1**

**Kailzie Gardens** *Kirkburn, Scottish Borders.* Series of formal walled Victorian gardens, with woodland and waterside walks, as well as waterfowl and owl collections. ☎01721 720007
🖳www.kailziegardens.com **22 B1**

◀ **Benmore Botanic Gardens, Argyle and Bute** DGFarquhar / Alamy

**Logan Botanic Garden** *Port Logan, Dumfries and Galloway.* The mild climate of south western Scotland allows this beautiful annexe of the Royal Botanic Garden in Edinburgh to grow a larger range of plants from temperate regions, such as palms and tree ferns. 01776 860231 www.rbge.org.uk **46 E2**

### The Highlands

**Inverewe Gardens** *Poolewe, Highland.* This extensive garden was created on an area of bare rocks on this treeless, barren peninsula in the 1860s. It now holds more than 100 acres of one of the greatest exotic plant collections in the world. Sheltered from the winds by extensive belts of trees, it benefits from the warmth of the Gulf Stream. www.nts.org.uk 01445 712952 **84 E2**

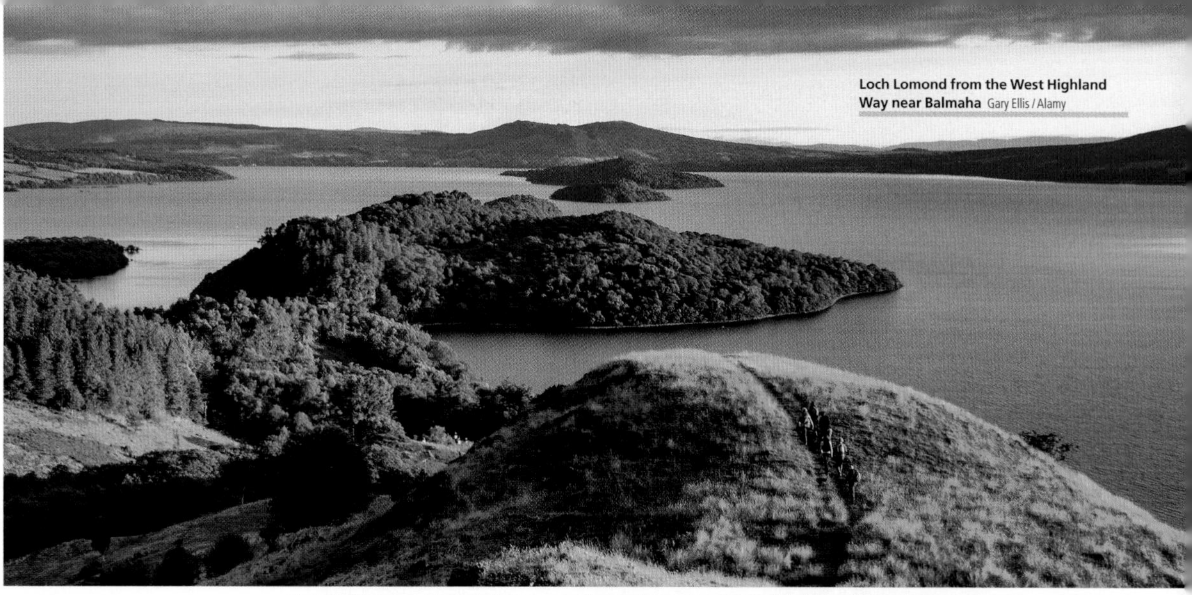

Loch Lomond from the West Highland Way near Balmaha Gary Ellis / Alamy

## Boat trips

### Argyll, Bute, Stirling, Trossachs

**Staffa Boat Trips** *Fionnphort, Mull, Argyll and Bute.* Boat trips to Fingal's Cave on Staffa. Weather permitting, the boat sails right into the cave, allowing passengers to land. 01681 700358 www.staffatrips.co.uk **61 E6**

**Sea Life Surveys and Eco-cruz** *Ledaig, Mull, Argyll and Bute.* Research vessels that take passengers while conducting surveys of the area's dolphins and whales. www.sealifesurveys.com 01688 302916 **62 D4**

**SS Sir Walter Scott** *Trossachs Pier, Loch Katrine, Aberfoyle, Stirling.* A small steamship that makes trips across Loch Katrine, made famous by Scott's evocative poem, 'The Lady of the Lake'. www.lochkatrine.com/steamship.html 01877 376316 **55 B7**

**Turus Mara** *Penmore Mill, Dervaig, Isle of Mull, Argyll, PA75 6QS.* Boat trips to Fingal's Cave on Staffa, to the Trennish Isles or whale- and dolphin-watching. www.turusmara.com 0800 0858786 **61 B7**

### Edinburgh and East Central

**Maid of the Forth** *Hawes Pier, South Queensferry, City of Edinburgh.* Trips to see the birds and sealife of the islands in the Firth of Forth. 0131 3315000 www.maidoftheforth.co.uk **41 E6**

**Sula** *North Berwick, East Lothian.* The boat 'Sula' provides trips around Bass Rock from North Berwick harbour. Breeding birds that may be seen include fulmars, guillemots, puffins, razorbills and terns, as well as Scotland's second biggest gannet colony. www.sulaboattrips.co.uk 01620 880 770 **43 C7**

### Perth, Angus, Dundee and Fife

**May Princess** *Anstruther Easter, Fife.* This ferry runs daily boat trips to the nature reserve on the Isle of May from the lifeboat station. Also fast boat trips in the RIB 'Osprey'. 07957 585200 www.isleofmayferry.com **58 B3**

### The Highlands

**Aquaxplore** *Elgol, Skye, Highland.* Trips to otherwise inaccessible locations around Skye and neighbouring islands by rigid inflatable boat. 01471 866244 www.aquaxplore.co.uk **68 A5**

**Bella Jane Boat Trips** *Elgol, Skye, Highland.* Trips from Elgol to Loch Coruisk and the seal colony. www.bellajane.co.uk 01471 866244 **68 A5**

**Crannog Cruises** *The Town Pier, Fort William, Highland.* Short wildlife cruises on Loch Linnie. 01397 700714 www.crannog.net **70 E3**

**Ecoventures** *Harbour Workshop, Victoria Place, Cromarty, Highland.* Full-day trips to see the dolphins and seals in the outer regions of the Moray Firth. 01381 600323 www.ecoventures.co.uk **80 B2**

**Handa Island Ferry** *Tarbet, Scourie, Highland.* Trips run from the tiny hamlet of Tarbet to the internationally important wildlife reserve throughout the day during summer. 07780967800 www.handa-ferry.com **88 D3**

**Jacobite Cruises Loch Ness** *Tomnahurich Bridge, Glenurquhart Road, Inverness, Highland.* A range of cruises on Loch Ness, with options for visiting various attractions around the Loch. 01463 233999 www.jacobite.co.uk **79 D8**

**John O'Groats Wildlife Cruises** *Ferry Office, John O'Groats, Highland.* Half-day trips on the local ferry in high summer. Whales and dolphins are sometimes spotted and seabirds almost guaranteed. 01955 611353 www.jogferry.co.uk **91 A7**

**MV Shearwater** *The Harbour, Arisaig, Highland.* Boat trips run by Arisaig Marine between Arisaig and the nature reserve on Rum, as well as Eigg, Muck and Canna. Whales and porpoises are sometimes seen en route. 01687 450224 www.arisaig.co.uk **69 D6**

**Sea.fari Adventures** *Armadale Bay, Ardvasar, Skye, Highland.* Trips to view scenery and wildlife around the island. www.whalespotting.co.uk 01471 833316 **69 B6**

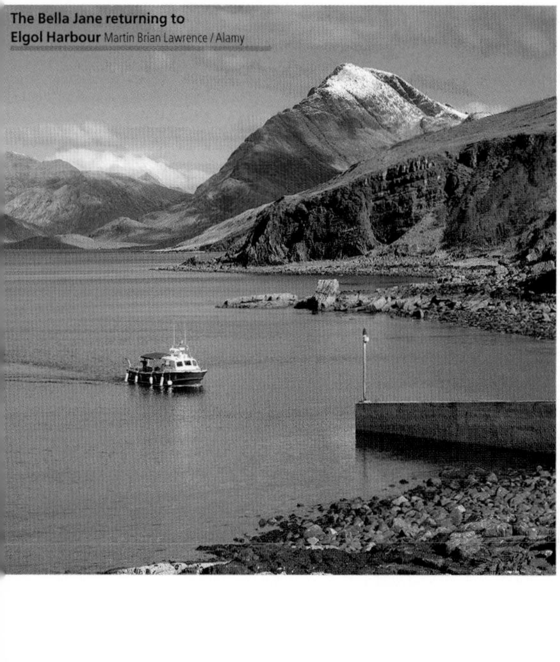

The Bella Jane returning to Elgol Harbour Martin Brian Lawrence / Alamy

# Walking, cycling and riding trails

### Aberdeen and Moray

**Moray Monster Trails** *Balnacoul, Fochabers, Moray* A winding woodland mountain bike trail with spectacular views over the nearby gorge, accessed from the Winding Walks car park. http://scotland.forestry.gov.uk **81 C8**

**Speyside Way** *Buckie, Moray* This challenging route follows the river Spey for 66 miles, south from the coast, via Craigellachie uphill to the ski resort of Aviemore. www.speysideway.org **82 B1**

**Winding Walks Forest Walks** *Balnacoul, Fochabers, Moray* Waymarked paths of varying degrees through mature conifer and beech woodland, near a steep gully. http://scotland.forestry.gov.uk **81 C8**

### Argyll, Bute, Stirling, Trossachs

**An Caisteal** *Crianlarich, Stirling* The hike to the top of this 3265 ft peak from the layby 2 miles from Crianlarich takes around 5 hours there and back. Tyndrum TIC 01838 400246 **64 E1**

**Ben Cruachan Walk** *Lochawe, Argyll and Bute* The challenging hikes on this ben take between 6 and 9 hours from Cruachan Dam Visitor Centre. **63 E6**

**Ben Lui** *Tyndrum, Stirling* One of the more popular walks on this mountain goes up the south-eastern ridge from Cononish Farm and takes 7 hours up and back. Tyndrum TIC 01838 400246 **63 D8**

**Campsies Fells Trail** *Stirling, Stirling* A local trail that links villages in the region, such as Fintry and Gargunnock, with open-country and forest paths. Stirling TIC 01786 475019 **39 B6**

**Cruach Tairbeirt** *Arrochar, Argyll and Bute* A waymarked 2 mile forest walk on the flanks of Cruach Tairbeirt from Arrochar and Tarbet railway station. The climb to the viewpoints is fairly easy, but allow at least 2 hours. http://scotland.forestry.gov.uk **55 B5**

**Rob Roy Way** *Drymen, Stirling* An unmarked, unofficial path from Drymen to Loch Tay and then north-east along Strathtay. Its 80 miles includes woodlands, heaths and remote moorland. **37 C8**

**The Trossachs Trail** *Brig o'Turk, Stirling* Not a single route but a network of interlinking pathways in an area roughly bounded by Callander in the East, Doune and Aberfoyle in the south, Loch Lomond in the west and the Crianlarich Hills in the north. Among the good starting points is Brig o'Turk. **55 B8**

**West Island Way** *Port Bannatyne, Bute, Argyll and Bute* This relatively easy route leads for 30 miles from Kilchattan Bay round the Isle of Bute via Port Bannatyne across varied scenery including seashore, moorland, forest and farmland. **54 F3**

### Glasgow and the Clyde

**Clyde Walkway** *New Lanark, South Lanarkshire* A 40 mile route tracing the river Clyde downstream from the spectacular Falls of Clyde at New Lanark to where it meets the river Kelvin. **19 A8**

**Glasgow to Gourock** *Gourock, City of Glasgow* A 14 mile cycle route that runs to the west of Glasgow via Paisley, Kilmacolm and Greenock along minor roads and a disused railway line. **36 E3**

**Kelvin Allander Walkway** *Glasgow, City of Glasgow* This 9 mile gentle route follows the rivers Kelvin and Allander from the Tall Ship in Glasgow Harbour through Kelvingrove Park and Maryhill to Milngavie, where the West Highland Way starts. **28 A2**

**West Highland Way** *Milngavie, East Dunbartonshire* This hike stretches 95 miles from Milngavie to Fort William, via Loch Lomond, Rannoch Moor and Glen Nevis. The path itself is not difficult and passes through some of Scotland's most spectacular scenery, using old drove roads, a military road built to help in moving troops during the suppression of the Highlands during the 18th century and old railway lines. **38 F2**

### Perth, Angus, Dundee and Fife

**Dollar Glen** *Dollar, Clackmannanshire* A waymarked path through this spectacular wooded glen provides a beautiful approach to Castle Campbell. **56 C4**

**Fife Coastal Path** *North Queensferry, Fife* A 78 mile route running along the north shore of the Firth of Forth between North Queensferry and Newport on Tay via Crail and St Andrews. As well as coastal paths, it takes in some pretty villages and seaside towns. **41 D6**

**Loch Leven** *Leven, Fife* The views from the 20-mile circuit of roads around the loch are stunning. **58 B1**

### South of Scotland

**Berwickshire Coastal Path** *St. Abbs, Scottish Borders* A 15 mile path that leads along the east coast from Berwick-upon-Tweed, just over the English Border to St Abbs. **35 A7**

**Cock of Arran Coast Walk** *Lochranza, Arran, North Ayrshire* This 8 mile route runs along the north-east coast between Lochranza and Sannox. The route takes about 4 to 5 hours to complete. **51 A5**

**Goat Fell** *Brodick, Arran, North Ayrshire* There are several routes to the summit of Arran's highest mountain (874 m), including from Brodick itself to the south and Corrie to the east. Most of the routes take about 8 hours. **51 C6**

**Isle of Arran Coastal Way** *Brodick, Arran, North Ayrshire* The coastal paths make a 60 mile circuit around the island. The north of the island has steeper climbs, but these provide magnificent views. In some stretches, demanding paths have road-based alternatives. **51 C6**

**Newton Stewart to Glenluce** *Newton Stewart, Dumfries and Galloway* A 50 mile route through farmland and pretty villages, along the coast of the Machars peninsula. **47 C6**

**The Pilgrims Way** *Newton Stewart, Dumfries and Galloway* A 25 mile route between Newton Stewart to the Isle of Whithorn near the tip of the Machars peninsula. It is associated with St Ninian, who introduced Christianity to Scotland and ends at the ruined 13th-century chapel dedicated to the saint. **47 C6**

**St Cuthbert's Way** *Melrose, Scottish Borders* This 60 mile route links sites associated with St Cuthbert, from Melrose to Holy Island in Northumberland. It crosses the Eildon Hills and follows the course of the Tweed and then, once over the border, traverses the Cheviot Hills to Fenwick. Part of its course follows Roman Dere Street. **23 C6**

**Southern Uplands Way** *Portpatrick, Dumfries and Galloway* This scenic coast-to-coast route runs for 210 miles and is demanding in places. It starts in Portpatrick on the west coast and its often remote track goes via Sanquar, Moffat and Melrose to Cockburnspath a few miles south of Dunbar. **46 D2**

**Tweed Cycle Way** *Biggar, Scottish Borders* This route runs from Biggar along the Tweed Valley to Berwick-upon-Tweed just over the English border. **20 B4**

### The Highlands

**Ben More** *Crianlarich, Highland* Allow at least 6 hours for the strenuous hike to the summit and back from Benmore Farm. Tyndrum TIC 01838 400246 **64 E1**

**Ben Nevis Summit** *Fort William, Highland* One route to the summit starts from the Glen Nevis Visitor Centre and uses a zig-zagging pony path to reach the summit. Whether returning via the same route, or descending via the Allt a'Mhuilinn, the walk takes about 8 hours. Fort William TIC 01397 701801 **70 E3**

**Cairn Gorm High Circuit** *Aviemore, Highland* A 7 mile circular route from the ski-area car park at Aviemore up to the summit of Cairn Gorm and back, via the rim of coire an t-Sneachda, Cairn Lochan and the ridge via Lurcher's Gully back to the car park. Aviemore TIC 01479 810930 **72 A3**

**Cape Wrath Trail** *Fort William, Highland* This 300 mile route runs almost parallel to the 'North to the Cape' route. However, leads via Kintail, Torridon, Dundonnel and Assynt, including Beinne Eighe and Lurg Mór on the way. **70 E3**

**Great Glen Cycle Route** *Fort William, Highland* This 50 mile route is mainly off road and links Fort William and Inverness, going through a variety of spectacular scenery and forestry. Fort William TIC 01397 701801 **70 E3**

**Great Glen Way** *Fort William, Highland* This 73 mile walking route, like the cycle route, runs from Fort William to Inverness, but follows a slightly different path. It goes along Glen Mor, follows the north-west shores of Loch Lochy and Loch Ness and then the course of the Caledonian Canal. Much of the walk is along towpaths and broad forest paths, with a few more challenging sections. **70 E3**

**Lairig Ghru trail** *Aviemore, Highland* A demanding 24 mile hike from Aviemore, over the Lairig Ghru Pass to Braemar **72 A3**

**North to the Cape** *Fort William, Highland* This trail leads 200 miles from Fort William to Cape Wrath, via Knoydart, Eas a Chùluinn and some of the Monros of Benn Eighe National Nature Reserve. It is extremely challenging in places. **70 E3**

## Animal attractions

### Aberdeen and Moray

**Doonies Farm** *Coast Road, Nigg, Aberdeen City.* One of the largest collections of rare-breed farm animals, including horses, goats, cattle, sheep, pigs and poultry. Children's play area. 🖥 www.dooniesfarm.co.uk 📞 01224 875879 **75 B6**

**▲ Bottlenose dolphins breaching in the Moray Firth** *Charlie Phillips / Alamy*

**Macduff Marine Aquarium** *11 High Shore, Macduff, Aberdeenshire.* This aquarium concentrates on the sealife of the Moray Firth, with rays, native fish, crustaceans and touch tanks. 🖥 www.macduff-aquarium.org.uk 📞 01261 833369 **82 B4**

**North East Falconry Centre** *Broadland, Carnie, Huntly, Aberdeenshire.* Daily demonstrations of falconry, with flying eagles and falcons. There are also owls in the collection. 🖥 www.huntly-falconry-centre.com 📞 01466 760328 **82 E2**

### Argyll, Bute, Stirling, Trossachs

**Blair Drummond Safari and Adventure Park** *Blair Drummond, Stirling.* The animal collection includes chimpanzees, elephants, monkeys, lemurs, zebras, bears, giraffes, ostriches, rhinoceroses, camels, bison, wallabies and penguins. Sea lion displays take place regularly and other attractions include a pets farm, boating and an adventure playground. 📞 01786 841456 🖥 www.blairdrummond.com **56 C2**

**Scottish Sea Life and Marine Sanctuary** *Barcaldine, Argyll and Bute.* On the southern shore of Loch Creran, this centre has plenty of sea creatures, including stingrays that can be stroked. Children can dip in the rock pools and learn how orphaned seal pups are rescued and returned to the wild. 🖥 www.sealsanctuary.co.uk/oban1.htm 📞 01631 720386 **62 C4**

### Edinburgh and East Central

**Edinburgh Butterfly and Insect World** *Dobbies Garden World, Lasswade, Midlothian.* Breeding butterflies from around the world, in enclosures that visitors may walk through. Small animals include, leaf-cutting ants, beetles, scorpions, locusts, spiders, and grasshoppers, while among the larger specimens are terrapins, snakes, an iguana and some quail. 🖥 www.edinburgh-butterfly-world.co.uk 📞 0131 6634932 **32 A2**

**Edinburgh Zoo** *134 Corstorphine Road, Edinburgh, City of Edinburgh.* The collection holds more than 1500 animals, including endangered species such as snow leopards, white rhinos and pygmy hippos. Not forgetting the two most famous residents, Tian Tian and Yuan Guang, a pair of giant pandas on loan from China. 🖥 www.edinburghzoo.org.uk 📞 0131 3349171 **41 F8**

**Scottish Seabird Centre** *North Berwick, East Lothian.* The chief feature of this centre is the close-up views of the birdlife of nearby Bass Rock, obtained via a live link to cameras there. There are also games for children and exhibits on Scotland's different seabirds. 📞 01620 890202 🖥 www.seabird.org **43 C7**

### Perth, Angus, Dundee and Fife

**Deep Sea World** *Forthside Terrace, North Queensferry, Fife.* Attractions include sharks, piranhas, an underwater tunnel, touch pools with rays and snake-handling sessions. 📞 01383 411880 🖥 www.deepseaworld.com **41 D6**

**St Andrews Aquarium** *The Scores, St Andrews, Fife.* This popular attraction holds seals, sharks, exotic fish, crustaceans, rays, octopuses, seahorses and touchpools. 🖥 www.standrewsaquarium.co.uk 📞 01334 474786 **67 F5**

**Scottish Deer Centre** *Rankeilour, Cupar, Fife.* The centre has red, fallow and sika deer, as well as reindeer, wolves and falconry displays, strenuous guided nature trails and a play area. 📞 01337 810391 🖥 www.tsdc.co.uk **57 A8**

### The Highlands

**Black Isle Wildlife and Country Park** *North Kessock, Drumsmittal, Highland.* Wildlife, as well as goats, rabbits, pot-bellied pigs, cattle and rare-breed sheep. 📞 01463 731656 🖥 www.blackislewildlifepark.org **80 D1**

**Cairngorm Reindeer Centre** *Glenmore, Highland.* A herd of reindeer can be seen here in the winter. 📞 01459 861228 🖥 www.cairngormreindeer.co.uk **72 A4**

**Chanonry Point** *Fortrose, Highland.* This spit is an excellent site for seeing some of the Moray Firth's dolphins chasing fish at high tide. **80 C2**

**Craig Highland Farm** *Woodside, Plockton, Highland.* Set on the shore of Loch Carron, this farm has rare and traditional breeds of sheep and chickens, as well as rabbits, pigs, geese and ponies on the farm. In the surrounding area there is a chance of seeing seals, otters and pine martens. 🖥 http://craighighlandfarm.co.uk 📞 01599 544 205 **77 E8**

**Dolphins and seals of the Moray Firth** *North Kessock, Highland.* More than 100 bottle-nosed dolphins live in the Moray Firth. At the visitor centre in North Kessock, visitors can listen in to the dolphins' calls. Among the best viewing points is nearby Kessock Bridge **80 D1**

**Eilean Bàn** *Kyle of Lochalsh, Highland.* Island wildlife sanctuary under the Skye Bridge. Once the home of Gavin Maxwell, author of 'Ring of Bright Water', this sanctuary is particularly associated with otters. Guided tours must be prebooked at the Bright Water Visitor Centre in Kyleakin (📞 01599 530040). 🖥 www.eileanban.org **77 F7**

**Highland Wildlife Park** *Kincraig, Highland.* This extensive park is devoted to the native fauna of the Highlands, from the whole range of habitats. Forest specialities include polecat, wildcat, red squirrel and capercaillie, while arctic fox and snowy owl prefer tundra; otters and beavers are wetland species and tawny owls, badgers and black grouse inhabit the woodlands. Some species are extinct in the wild, or have only been reintroduced in limited areas: these include lynx, white-tailed sea eagle, wolf and chough. In the reserve, exotic but rare, animals such as moufflon, Przewalski's horse, Soay sheep and European bison are held. 🖥 www.highlandwildlifepark.org.uk 📞 01540 651270 **72 B3**

**Loch Ness Exhibition Centre** *Drumnadrochit, Highland.* This exhibition explores the history of Nessie through eyewitness accounts and the research of various expeditions to locate the monster. 📞 01456 450573 🖥 www.lochness.com **79 F7**

## Beaches and resorts

### Aberdeen and Moray

**Cullen** *Moray.* The sands of Cullen Bay are sheltered from the wind benefit from the warm waters of the Gulf Stream, which finishes its journey in the Moray Firth. **82 B2**

**Fraserburgh Bay** *Fraserburgh, Aberdeenshire.* The bay, with good sandy beaches, lies to the east of the fishing town and is relatively sheltered. **83 B6**

### Argyll, Bute, Stirling, Trossachs

**Rothesay** *Bute, Argyll and Bute.* A handsome Victorian resort with a pier, palm-tree lined promenade and 1920s Winter Gardens. Attractions include Rothesay Castle, Bute Museum, St Mary's Chapel, Ardencraig Gardens and Ascog Fernery and Gardens. **54 F3**

### Edinburgh and East Central

**North Berwick** *East Lothian.* An attractive Victorian seaside resort, with long sandy beaches, golf courses and a small harbour. The beach of Milsey Bay is particularly good. Local attractions include boat trips to Bass Rock, The Scottish Seabird Centre, the Auld Kirk and Dirleton Castle. **43 C7**

### Perth, Angus, Dundee and Fife

**Anstruther Easter** *Fife.* This summer resort used to be an important centre of the herring-fishing industry. Among the best of the beaches is Billow Ness beach. Attractions and excursions include the tiny village of Cellardyke, with traditional stone

Loch Carron at Plockton *Andrew Hopkins / Alamy*

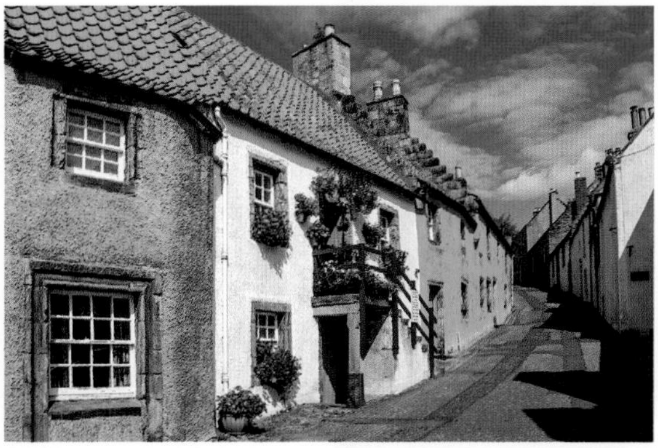

▲ **Culross** John Peter Photography / Alamy

houses and an old harbour, 'The Scottish Fisheries Museum', and boat trips on the 'May Princess' to the 'Isle of May **58 B3**

**Arbroath** *Angus.* A busy resort, once an important hub of the haddock fishing and smoking industries. The long, sandy beach is south of the town. Other attractions include the ruins of Arbroath Abbey, the Signal Tower, in the old shore station of the Bell Rock lighthouse, housing a local history museum, and the red sandstone church of St Vigeans about a mile north of the town. There are good walks along the clifftops north of the town. **67 C6**

**Broughty Ferry** *Dundee, Dundee City.* Set against the backdrop of an attractive suburb of Dundee, this stretch of sandy beach looks across the Firth of Tay to Tentsmuir Forest. **66 D4**

**Crail** *Fife.* As well as many beaches, natural bathing facilities are available at Roome Bay. Lobster and crab boats still work from the harbour, which is surrounded by old fishing cottages, many of which are lived in by members of the thriving artists' colony. Great views of the harbour can be obtained from Castle Walk. There is also a Crail Museum and Heritage Centre **58 B4**

**Earlsferry and Elie beaches** *Earlsferry, Fife.* A series of beautiful golden-brown sandy beaches and sheltered coves overlooking the outer Firth of Forth. **58 C2**

**Lunan Bay** *Angus.* Almost two miles of fine, sandy beaches overlook Lunan Bay a few miles from Montrose. **67 B6**

**Montrose** *Angus.* A wide expanse of golden sand, backed by sand dunes, stretches along the coast north of the town. **67 B7**

**St Andrews** *Fife.* The West Sands lie north of the city centre, backed by a series of some of the most famous golf courses in the world. **67 F5**

### South of Scotland

**Coldingham Bay** *Coldingham, Scottish Borders.* This tiny, sandy beach has a thriving surfing community and some of the best cold-water diving in Europe. **35 A7**

### The Highlands

**Achmelvich** *Highland.* A semicircular bay with brilliant white sands and blue water, looking out towards the distant Isle of Lewis. **84 A4**

**Brora Beach** *Brora, Highland.* North of the little village of the same name on the east coast lies a two-mile stretch of good, sandy beach. **87 C6**

**Dornoch** *Highland.* A pleasant seaside resort, famous for its golf course, Dornoch's beaches overlook Dornoch Firth. Dornoch Cathedral is also worth a visit. Seals can sometimes be seen lounging on the sandbars beyond the south beach. **86 E4**

**Embo Beach** *Embo, Highland.* Facing onto the North Sea, the sands of Embo Beach are a good area for envigorating walks. **86 D5**

**Gairloch** *Highland.* There are several good beaches near this small resort, of which Big Sand is best sheltered fom the wind. There are also some excellent coastal walks. The Gairloch Heritage Museum has a range of displays about aspects of life here. **84 F2**

**Gruinard Beach** *Little Gruinard, Highland.* A sheltered beach overlooking the bay of the same name and looking over Gruinard Isle towards the Summer Islands. **84 E3**

**Morar beach** *Morar, Highland.* Part of the stretch of beaches known as the Silver Sands of Morar that circle a narrow bay. **69 C6**

**Portmahomack** *Highland.* A broad area of sand stretches west of the town. The Tarbat Discovery Centre, in Tarbat church, has Pictish and early Christian archaeological finds from the area. To the north-east of the town, Tarbat Ness provides good walks to the lighthouse. **87 E6**

# Towns and villages

### Aberdeen and Moray

**Fordyce** *Aberdeenshire.* A well-preserved historic village. There are rich canopied tombs in the medieval St Tarquin's church. **82 B2**

### Argyll, Bute, Stirling, Trossachs

**Blairlogie** *Stirling.* An attractive little village with a ruined 17th-century church, Logie Auld Kirk, surrounded by orchards. **39 A7**

**Inveraray** *Argyll and Bute.* An 18th-century planned town in a stunning setting overlooking Loch Fyne. It is stuffed with Georgian buildings, a Neoclassical church and a Georgian Jail. Excellent views can be obtained from the bell tower of All Saints Church **54 B3**

**Luss** *Argyll and Bute.* Attractive conservation village with lovely views over Loch Lomond. The church has some good Victorian stained glass. **37 B6**

**Port Charlotte** *Islay, Argyll and Bute.* Founded in 1828 by Walter Frederick Campbell, Port Charlotte is Islay's prettiest village, with white-washed cottages overlooking Loch Indaal. The Wildlife Information Centre is a good source of information about the island's flora and fauna. **49 A2**

**Tarbert** *Argyll and Bute.* The pretty harbour front of this fishing village is best seen from the ruins of Robert the Bruce's ruined castle. **54 F1**

**Tobermory** *Mull, Argyll and Bute.* An attractive fishing village at the northern tip of the island, with brightly coloured houses perched between the bay and the steep cliffs. Among the attractions are the Mull Museum and the Tobermory Distillery. **61 B8**

### Edinburgh and East Central

**Aberlady** *East Lothian.* Pretty conservation village with Gothic-style cottages, fine medieval glass in the church and a small nature reserve on the silted-up site of the old harbour. **43 D5**

**Cramond** *City of Edinburgh.* A pretty village in the western outskirts of Edinburgh, overlooking the Forth. It also has a Roman fort, a medieval bridge and tower house and a 17th-century church. Depending on the tide, Cramond Island can be reached across a causeway. **41 E7**

**Dirleton** *East Lothian.* Reputed to be the prettiest village in Scotland. Castle and garden. **43 D6**

**Haddington** *East Lothian.* A compact country town, with some fine architecture from the 17th–19th centuries. In Court Street, the Town House was built by William Adam in 1748 and there are other stylish buildings in this area of the town. St Mary's Church, in Church Street, is an architectural mixture with several interesting tombs. **43 F6**

**North Berwick** *East Lothian.* A charming seaside town set in an attractive coastal setting, looking out on Bass Rock. There are fragments of the Auld Kirk near the harbour and a small local museum on School Road. **43 C7**

### Glasgow and the Clyde

**Biggar** *South Lanarkshire.* A pleasant town in a rural setting, and dominated by Tinto Hill. A large number of museums includes the Moat Park Heritage Centre, Brownsbank Cottage, Biggar and Upper Clydesdale Museum, Greenhill Covenanters' Museum, the Puppet Museum and the Biggar Gasworks Museum. **20 B4**

### Perth, Angus, Dundee and Fife

**Comrie** *Perth and Kinross.* This pretty conservation village suffers more earth tremors than anywhere else in the British Isles because it is sited directly above the Highland Boundary Fault. **40 C4**

**Crail** *Fife.* An attractive fishing village, with cobbled streets, grander merchants' houses and the 12th-century St Mary's Church. **58 B4**

**Culross** *Fife.* A former royal burgh maintained by the National Trust for Scotland. Many of the houses are 17th century. Attractions include Culross Palace, Culross Abbey, the Town House and the Study. **40 C3**

**Dunfermline** *Fife.* The centre of the town has quaint narrow cobbled streets and some fine late 19th-century Gothic Revivial buildings. The dominant abbey ruins include a palace, Abbot House, built into them at a later date. **41 C5**

**Falkland** *Fife.* The village of Falkland grew up around Falkland Palace and has many well-preserved 17th- and 18th-century buildings. **57 B7**

**Kirriemuir** *Angus.* The centre of town is a maze of narrow, winding passages with picturesque shopping streets. Attractions include Barrie's Birthplace, a small aviation museum that also houses a camera obscura. **66 B3**

### South of Scotland

**Dumfries** *Dumfries and Galloway.* One of the towns associated with the poet Robert Burns, who spent the last 30 years of his life here. As well as the Burns sites, Mid Steeple is worth a look as is the Devorgilla Bridge, built in 1341. **48 B3**

**Jedburgh** *Scottish Borders.* The most prominent feature of this pleasant old market town is the ruined abbey. The 19th-century Jedburgh Castle Jail is built on the site of the 12th-century castle and has displays on the history of prison life. **24 E2**

**Kirkcudbright** *Dumfries and Galloway.* An attractive small town on the river Dee with colourful houses, and a thriving artistic colony. MacLellan's Castle is a 16th-century tower house at the end of the high street. **47 D8**

**Melrose** *Scottish Borders.* Dominated by the ruined abbey, this pretty little town also has a tiny ecclesiastical museum in the Commendator's House, an archaeological museum in the Trimontium Exhibition off Market Square and the charming Priorwood Garden. **23 C6**

**Peebles** *Scottish Borders.* A handsome town on the River Tweed. The Old Parish Church on the High Street has some interesting features. On the same street there is a small museum, the Tweedale Museum and Gallery. **21 A9**

### The Highlands

**Dornoch** *Highland.* Cathedral, fortified 16th-century Bishop's Palace, Witch's Stone commemorating the last witch burned in Scotland, in 1722. **86 E4**

**Plockton** *Highland.* A picturesque village overlooking Loch Carron, it was transformed from a sleepy hamlet to a fishing village in the late 18th century. **77 E8**

**Rosemarkie** *Highland.* A pretty village on the coast of the Black Isle. The Groam House Museum has a good collection of carved Pictish standing stones. **80 C2**

# Buildings

## Castles and palaces

### Aberdeen and Moray

**Braemar Castle** *Braemar, Aberdeenshire.* This romantic castle dates from 1628. After being requisitioned as a government garrison after the 1745 rebellion, it became a family residence. Highlights include the dungeon and the remarkable, star-shaped defensive walls. It has now been leased to the local community. ☎01339 741219 www.braemarcastle.co.uk **73 C6**

**Brodie Castle** *Brodie, Forres, Moray.* The oldest part of the building is a typical 'Z'-shaped Scottish tower house, which dates from 1567 with additions from the 17th and 19th centuries. The collection includes a good range of paintings, fine furniture and porcelain. The rooms are known for their panelling and beautiful plasterwork. The parkland includes a woodland walk and a wild garden. ☎01309 641371 www.nts.org.uk **81 C4**

**Castle Fraser, Garden and Estate** *Sauchen, Inverurie, Aberdeenshire.* This impressive castle, although looking like a medieval French chateau, is one of the fortress-like Castles of Mar. It was built between c.1575 and 1636. The interior was remodelled in 1838 and some rooms still have decoration and furnishings dating from that period. The extensive grounds include an 18th-century walled garden that has been remodelled to create a formal area. ☎01330 833463 www.nts.org.uk **74 A4**

**Craigievar Castle** *Alford, Aberdeenshire.* A beautiful pink tower house, lavishly decorated with turrets and substantially as it was on its completion in 1626. Nearly all of its rooms have contemporary decorative plaster ceilings, and there is a good collection of furniture collected over the centuries. Guided tours of castle. Gardens open. ☎01339 883635 www.nts.org.uk **74 B2**

**Crathes Castle, Garden and Estate** *Banchory, Aberdeenshire.* In fact a late 16th-century tower house with a number of 'medieval features' added, Crathes castle has several remarkable painted ceilings of that date as well as family portraits and vernacular furniture. The walled garden is made up of eight areas and the yew hedge dates to 1702. There are several nature trails in the grounds. ☎0333 433 0701 www.nts.org.uk **74 C4**

**Drum Castle, Garden and Estate** *Banchory, Aberdeenshire.* The massive square keep of Drum Castle is one of the three oldest tower houses in Scotland, dating from the late 13th century and was given by Robert the Bruce to his armour bearer, William de Irvine, in 1323. The Jacobean mansion was added in 1619 and further extensions made in the 19th century. The house remained in the hands of the Irvines until 1976 when the National Trust for Scotland took over and contains a collection of portraits and good Georgian

**Dunnottar Castle** David Gowans / Alamy

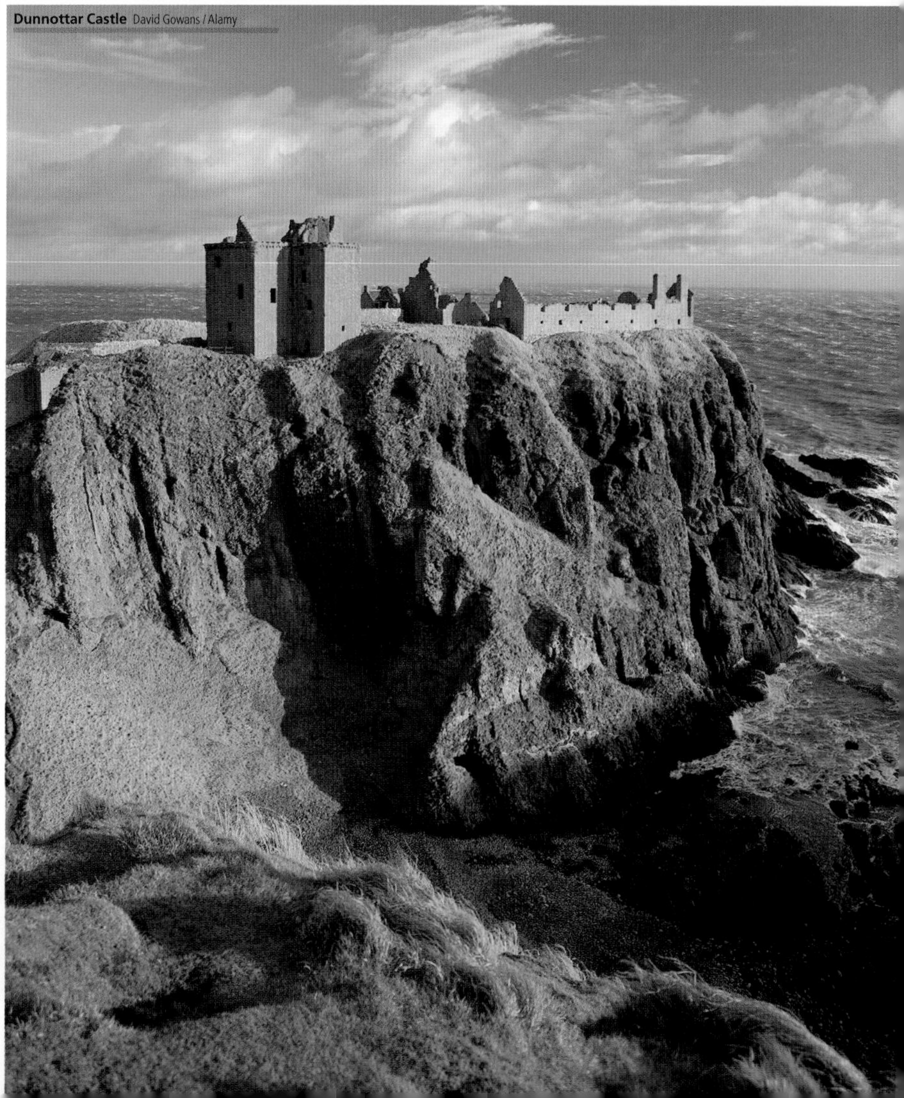

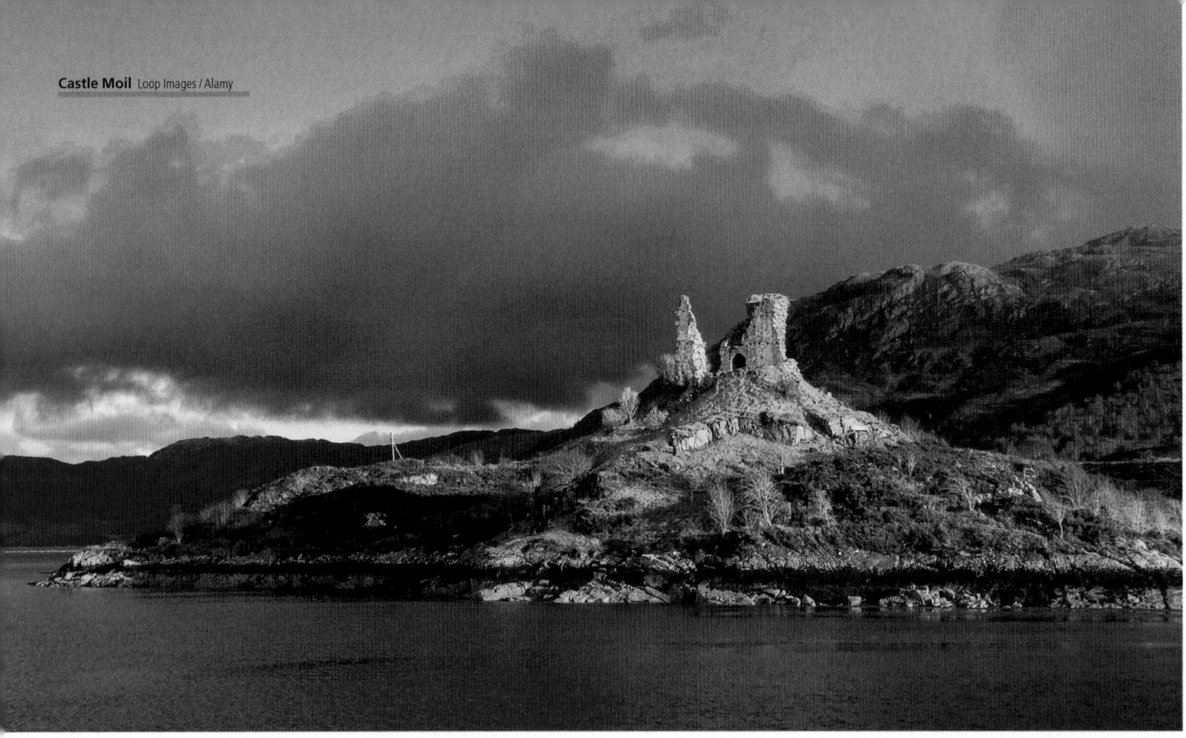
**Castle Moil** Loop Images / Alamy

furniture. The grounds contain the woods of Drum – remnant oak and pine woodland – and a garden of historic roses.
www.nts.org.uk **75 B4**

**Dunnottar Castle** *Stonehaven, Aberdeenshire.* Set high on a 160ft cliff above the sea, the ruins of this castle include a chapel from 1392. The original fortress was built in the 9th century and bloody episodes in the past include William Wallace's slaughter of the whole English Plantagenet garrison in 1297 and the torture of 165 Covenanters in 1685. The drawing room was restored in 1926. 01569 762173
www.dunottarcastle.co.uk **75 D5**

**Fyvie Castle** *Fyvie, Aberdeenshire.* The oldest of the five towers dates from the 13th century and the castle is a fine example of Scottish baronial architecture. The 17th-century morning room has beautiful contemporary panelling and a fine plaster ceiling, while later Edwardian remodelling includes a beautiful dining room. The collection includes 16th-century tapestries, paintings by Gainsborough, Raeburn and Romney and antique arms and armour. The grounds and Fyvie Loch were designed as a landscaped parkland around the beginning of the 19th century, replacing the original hunting grounds. The grounds include a restored racquets court, an ice house and a bird hide. 01641 891266
www.nts.org.uk **82 E4**

## Argyll, Bute, Stirling, Trossachs

**Duart Castle** *Craignure, Mull, Argyll and Bute.* Perched on a spit of rock, this was the head of the MacLeans from the 13th century. Having been burned down by the Campbells, it was confiscated by the government after the rebellion of 1745. It was brought back and restored by Fitzroy MacLean early in the 20th century. Highlights include the dungeons and ramparts. 01680 812309
www.duartcastle.com **62 D2**

**Dunstaffnage Castle** *Dunbeg, Argyll and Bute.* The 13th century castle lies on the site of the Scots court until Kenneth MacAlpin unified Scotland and moved the seat of power to Scone in the 10th century. It was captured by Robert the Bruce in 1309, then handed over to the Campbells in 1470. Flora MacDonald was held here temporarily, and the castle burned down in 1810. The curtain walls and battlements are substantially intact, making it fun for children to explore.
www.historicenvironment.scot
01631 562465 **62 D3**

**Inveraray Castle** *Inveraray, Argyll and Bute.* This greenish-grey castle is an early example of Gothic revival building and contains pictures, 18th-century French furniture and a vast collection of arms and armour. www.inveraray-castle.com
01499 302203 **54 B3**

**Skipness Castle and Chapel** *Skipness, Argyll and Bute.* The castle, of which a five-storey tower remains, once controlled shipping through Loch Fyne. The surrounding hamlet was originally a Norse settlement. Open Apr–Sep.
www.historicenvironment.scot **51 A5**

**Stirling Castle** *Upper Castle Hill, Stirling, Stirling.* This strategically placed castle had its heyday in the first half of the 16th century during the reigns of James IV and V, the latter of whom made the Renaissance-style additions to the medieval building. It later became the headquarters of the Argyll and Sutherland Highlanders, with pipe banners, regimental colours and silver. Some of the medals date as far back as the Battle of Waterloo. 01786 450000 (castle)
01786 475165 (museum)
www.stirlingcastle.gov.uk
www.argylls.co.uk (museum) **39 B6**

## Edinburgh and East Central

**Craigmillar Castle** *Craigmillar, City of Edinburgh.* Guarding the southern approach to Edinburgh, the first part of this now ruined, but extensive, castle was built in the late 14th century and enclosing walls were added during the early 15th century. The outer wall and moat were added in the 16th century. Most of the castle can be explored, including the tower and cellars. Mary Queen of Scots' brother and Lord Bothwell met here to plan her second husband's murder. 0131 6614445
www.historicenvironment.scot **42 F1**

**Dirleton Castle** *Dirleton, East Lothian.* This rose-tinted, fairy-tale castle dates back to the 13th century. Sacked by Cromwell's forces in 1650 and then further pulled down by the owners of the land to create a pretty folly. 01620 850330
www.historicenvironment.scot **43 D6**

**Edinburgh Castle** *Castlehill, Edinburgh, City of Edinburgh.* Attractions in this 800-year-old castle, perched high above the city on the plug of an extinct volcano, include the royal palace, the castle museum, the Scottish crown jewels, the Stone of Destiny, the Great Hall, the 12th-century St Margaret's chapel and the vaults under the castle. 0131 2259846
www.edinburghcastle.gov.uk **41 F8**

**Lauriston Castle** *2a Cramond Road South, Davidson's Mains, City of Edinburgh.* The centre of this mansion, which is set in its own parkland, is a 16th-century tower house. The rest of the building is neo-Jacobean. The collection includes fine furniture and Flemish tapestries.
www.edinburghmuseums.org.uk
0131 3362060 **41 F8**

**Linlithgow Palace** *Linlithgow, West Lothian.* Once one of the favourite palaces of Scotland's kings, this building was begun under James I in 1425 and continued for more than a century. Mary Queen of Scots was born here in 1542. Cromwell's troops were billeted here in the 1650s. Although it burned down in 1746, the pink walls still stand to as much as five storeys and much of the interior layout can still be seen. There is a small exhibition of architectural finds in the great hall. 01506 842896
www.historicenvironment.scot **40 E4**

**Palace of Holyroodhouse** *Canongate, Edinburgh, City of Edinburgh.* A royal palace built for James IV in 1498, remodelled in the 1560s and renovated in early 17th century for James VI. The tour includes Mary Queen of Scots' apartments. 0303 123 7306
www.royalcollection.org.uk **42 F1**

**Tantallon Castle** *Near North Berwick, East Lothian.* Ruined 14th-century castle, the ancient stronghold of the Douglases. It was destroyed by Cromwell in 1651 after a 12-day siege. The setting on the cliffs facing Bass Rock is dramatic, especially in windy weather. 01620 892727
www.historicenvironment.scot **43 C7**

## Glasgow and the Clyde

**Bothwell Castle** *Bothwell, Uddingston, South Lanarkshire.* The strategically located fortress is widely thought of as Scotland's finest 13th-century castle. The massive red sandstone ruins include the main keep. The walls are up to 16ft thick, which is why substantial parts of the building remain, despite its near 800-year history of sieges. www.historicenvironment.scot
01698 816894 **28 C4**

**Craignethan Castle** *Crossford, South Lanarkshire.* Rebuilt as the last great medieval castle in Scotland in 1530 for James V, this building has a feature unique in Scotland – a caponier – a vault wedged into the moat between the two sections of the castle allowing defenders to fire on attackers from behind 5ft thick walls. The tower house and its cellars are virtually intact. 01555 860364
www.historicenvironment.scot **29 E7**

## Perth, Angus, Dundee and Fife

**Aberdour Castle** *Aberdour, Burntisland, Fife.* The earliest part of the castle, the tower, dates from the 14th century, while the other parts were added in the 16th and 17th centuries, including the fine dovecot. 0131 668 8916
www.historicenvironment.scot **41 C7**

**Balhousie Castle** *Hay Street, Perth, Perth and Kinross.* See Black Watch Regimental Museum **66 E1**

**Blair Castle** *Blair Atholl, Pitlochry, Perth and Kinross.* Almost the archetypical Scottish castle, with whitewashed walls and turrets, Blair Castle dates originally from 1269. The contents are magnificent, incuding paintings, furniture, beautiful plasterwork. The military aspect is most obvious in the entrance hall where a wide range of weapons is on display, while the ballroom holds family portraits and a vast display of antlers and tapestry room contains rich Brussels tapestries and an ornate four-poster. The grounds are impressive, with woodland walks, as well as Highland cows and peacocks that add to the overall impression of grandeur. 01796 481207
www.blair-castle.co.uk **65 B7**

**Broughty Castle** *Castle Green, Broughty Ferry, Dundee City.* This fort protected the ferry crossing over the Tay estuary and was built in the 15th century. It was besieged by the English in the 16th century and attacked by Cromwell's troops in the 17th. In the mid-19th century it was restored as part of Britain's coastal defences. The museum now housed within it has displays on arms and armour, local history and whaling. Fine views over the Tay estuary and Fife can be obtained from the observation tower.
www.leisureandculturedundee.com
www.historicenvironment.scot
01382 436916 **66 D4**

**Castle Menzies** *Aberfeldy, Perth and Kinross.* Until the middle of the last century, this 16th-century Z-plan tower house was the seat of the Clan Menzies. It has now been restored by the Menzies Clan Society to what it would have looked like when first built. 01887 820982
www.menzies.org **65 C6**

**Castle of St Andrews** *The Scores, St Andrews, Fife.* Founded in 1200 as the palace of the bishops and archbishops of St Andrews, most of the remains date from the 14th and 16th centuries. Its history is full of betrayals, murders and sieges, especially at the time of the Reformation, including burnings at the stake. The secret passage dates from this period. 01334 477196
www.historicenvironment.scot **67 F5**

**Culross** *Culross, Fife.* The interior walls of this palace, built between 1597 and 1611 for Sir George Bruce, are covered in wooden panelling, painted with moral scenes and passages of both Scots and Latin. The house is set within peaceful walled gardens. 0844 4932189 www.nts.org.uk **40 C3**

**Falkland Palace, Garden and Old Burgh** *Falkland, Fife.* A country residence of the Stuart kings and queens when on hunting trips in the Fife forest. The palace was built between 1501 and 1541 by James IV and his son, James V, who died here after his defeat by the English at the battle of Solway Firth in 1542. Mary Queen of Scots spent time here, and Charles II stayed here before his coronation by the Covanenters at Scone in 1651. It was abandoned after the uprising of 1715 and not restored until the late 19th century. Externally, it is a beautiful example of early Renaissance architecture. Guided tours include the drawing room, the tapestry gallery and the chapel royal, which is still in use and the keeper's apartments in the gatehouse are also on display. The real (royal) tennis court – the oldest in Britain – was built in 1539. 01337 857397
www.nts.org.uk **57 B7**

**Glamis Castle** *Glamis, Angus.* Best known as the childhood home of the Queen Mother, Glamis was given to the Lyon family in 1372. Originally, it was a five-storey L-shaped castle and one of the settings for Macbeth. Features on the guided tour include the Victorian dining room with a fine plaster ceiling, the drawing room with beautiful early 17th-century plasterwork, the chapel, with idiosyncratic late 17th-century paintings, King Malcolm's Room, with leather panelling and an ornate carved wooden chimneypiece, the royal apartments, Duncan's Hall and a 15th-century crypt. The grounds include a formal Italian Garden and woodland walks. www.glamis-castle.co.uk
01307 840393 **66 C3**

**Kellie Castle and Garden** *Pittenweem, Fife.* The oldest part of the castle is believed to date from 1360, but the building was enlarged to its present form in about 1606, then deserted for more than two centuries. Sympathetically restored in around 1878, its plaster ceilings, painted panelling and furniture form a harmonious whole. The walled garden has been laid out to a late Victorian plan. 01333 720271
www.nts.org.uk **58 B3**

**Eilean Donan Castle reflected in Loch Duich** Deco / Alamy

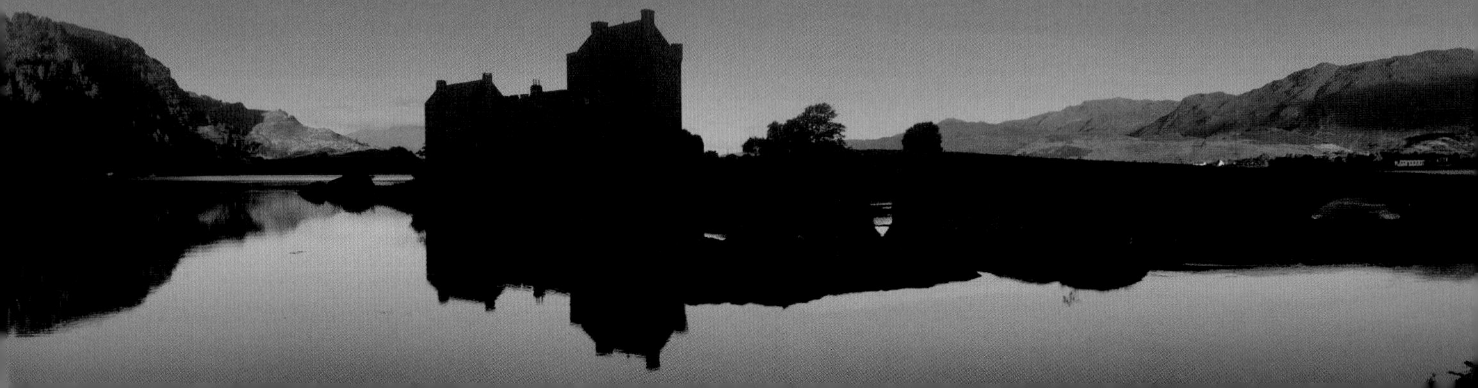

**Loch Leven Castle** *Castle Island, Kinross, Fife.* A fortress dating from the 14th century that belonged to the Douglas family. Mary Queen of Scots was imprisoned, and signed her abdication here before escaping and finally being captured in England. The tower s 14th century and the curtain wall dates from the 16th century. Access is by ferry from Kinross. 01577 862670 www.historicenvironment.scot **57 B6**

**Scone Palace** *Scone, Perth and Kinross.* The site of the first capital of United Scotland. The earliest part of the current palace dates to 1580 and the additions to 1803–8. Its contents include French furniture, 16th-century needlework including hangings embroidered by Mary Queen of Scots, china and ivories and good paintings. David Douglas, after whom the Douglas fir was named, was born here and there is a fine collection of rare conifers in the pinetum, including one Douglas fir grown from a seed he sent back from California. Highland cows and peacocks roam in the gardens. 01738 552300 www.scone-palace.co.uk **66 E1**

## South of Scotland

**Brodick Castle, Garden and Country Park** *Brodick, Arran, North Ayrshire.* This red sandstone castle dates from the 13th century, on the site of an earlier Viking fortress, with 17th- and 19th-century additions The collections include paintings, silver and antiques. The gardens were laid out in the 1920s and include specimens from the Himalayas, Chile, New Zealand and Tasmania. The woodland garden contains a fine collection of rhododendrons and the formal garden, which was originally laid out in 1710, has been restored as a Victorian garden. 01770 302202 www.nts.org.uk **51 C6**

**Caerlaverock Castle** *Dumfries, Dumfries and Galloway.* This unusual castle was built in the late 13th century, and first saw action during the Wars of Independence when it was besieged by Edward I in 1300. In 1312, it was attacked by the Scots and in 1356–7 by the English again. Its triangular form, with defensive towers, was strong: during the Civil War it was besieged for 13 weeks before being forced to surrender. Inside is an unexpected building, the Nithsdale Lodging, a Renaissance façade with mythological and heraldic scenes. Sadly it was destroyed by the Covenanters within a few years. 0131 668 8800 www.historicenvironment.scot **48 C4**

**Culzean Castle and Country Park** *Maybole, South Ayrshire.* One of Scotland's most impressive stately homes. Its strategic site, looking over the Firth of Clyde towards Arran, has been associated with the Kennedy family since the 12th century. Although the current castle suits its position by looking defensive on the outside, inside it is a grand neoclassical house. It was built by Robert Adam between 1772 and 1790 and is notable for the oval staircase, some of the plasterwork, the saloon, family portraits and furniture. Guided tours are available. The extensive country park includes woodland trails, a camellia house, lakes, clifftop views and a walled garden. The Gas House has an exibition on coal gas lighting. 0844 4932149 www.nts.org.uk **6 B3**

**Drumlanrig Castle** *Thornhill, Dumfries and Galloway.* The home of the dukes of Buccleuch and Queensberry, Drumlanrig was built between 1679 and 1689. The collection includes paintings by Leonardo da Vinci, Rembrandt and Holbein, among others, and relics of Bonnie Prince Charlie. Children's playground, crafts centre and gardens. 01848 331555 www.drumlanrigcastle.co.uk **9 E8**

**Dundonald Castle** *Dundonald, South Ayrshire.* Robert II built this castle in the 1370s, incorporating part of an earlier building, making it the first home of a Stuart king. He used the castle as a summer residence until his death in 1390. It has an unpleasant dungeon, and the commanding views over Kilmarnock show the importance of this strategic location. 01563 851489 www.dundonaldcastle.org.uk **17 C6**

**Floors Castle** *Kelso, Scottish Borders.* Designed by William Adam in 1721 and remodelled in the 19th century by William Playfair. Substantial collection of French and English furniture, porcelain, paintings by Canaletto, Reynolds and Gainsborough. Walled garden and garden centre. www.roxburghe.net 01573 223333 **24 C3**

**Thirlestane Castle** *Lauder, Scottish Borders.* Country house with a late 16th-century keep, beautiful late 17th-century plaster ceilings, historic toy collection and exhibition of life in the Scottish Borders from prehistoric times onwards. www.thirlestanecastle.co.uk 01578 722430 **33 E6**

## The Highlands

**Castle Moil** *Kyleakin, Skye, Highland.* A small ruined medieval castle, perched on a jagged knoll overlooking Loch Alsh. **77 F7**

**Cawdor Castle** *Cawdor, Highland.* Although built two centuries too late, Cawdor will always be associated with the Shakespearian story of Macbeth's murder of Duncan, it represents the idea of a perfect medieval castle, with turrets, dungeons, gargoyles, a drawbridge, fortified walls and hidden passageways. The interior contains a great deal of fine furniture. The grounds include a woodland and nature trails. www.cawdorcastle.com 01667 404401 **80 D3**

**Dunrobin Castle** *Golspie, Highland.* The home of the Earls of Sutherland, this 'castle' was remodelled in 1845 by Charles Barry in the Scottish Baronial style. The French feel extends to the extensive gardens, which are loosely based on the designs for those at Versailles. There are 189 rooms, which were created by the Scottish architect Robert Lorimer after a fire in 1915. 01408 633177 www.dunrobincastle.co.uk **87 C5**

**Dunvegan Castle and Garden** *Dunvegan, Skye, Highland.* Dunvegan has been the main stronghold of the Macleod chiefs for almost eight centuries, but this mock fortress dates from the 1840s. It includes several relics, including the 'fairy flag' thought to protect Macleods from harm. The dining room has a display of old silver, while the dungeon is unpleasant. The castle lies on a rocky outcrop between the sea and several acres of beautiful gardens. www.dunvegancastle.com 01740 521206 **76 D2**

**Eilean Donan Castle** *Dornie, Skye, Highland.* Built on an offshore island in 1214 as a defence against the Danes, Eilean Donan was ruined in 1719 after Spanish Jacobite forces were defeated at the Battle of Glenshiel. It was restored by a member of the Clan MacRae and among its contents are Jacobite relics and a museum of clan warfare, as well as furniture from the 1650s and impressive interiors. 01599 555202 www.eileandonancastle.com **77 F8**

**Kinloch Castle** *Kinloch, Rum, Highland.* Guided tours of the castle are timed to coincide with ferry arrivals. Despite the appearance of the turreted exterior, it was complete in 1900 as part of a sporting estate. It has an Edwardian interior and furnishings appropriate to the upper-class life of the time. www.isleofrum.com/isleofrumheritag.php **68 C3**

**Urquhart Castle** *Drumnadrochit, Highland.* Standing above Loch Ness, this is one of the largest castles in Scotland. It was fought over for centuries, with parts being rebuilt as necessary. By 1600 it had been abandoned and was finally blown up in 1689 to prevent it being used by the Jacobites. Most of the existing buildings date from after the 16th century. www.historicenvironment.scot 01456 450551 **79 F7**

## The Outer Islands

**Bishop's Palace** *Broad Street, Kirkwall, Mainland, Orkney.* The 12th-century palace was built for Bishop William the Old and the round tower was added in the 16th century. www.historicenvironment.scot 01856 871918 **99 B5**

**Earl's Palace** *Watergate, Kirkwall, Mainland, Orkney.* Started in 1607 for Earl Patrick Stewart, the son of Mary Queen of Scots' illegitimate half-brother, the palace was the most accomplished example of Renaissance architecture in Scotland at the time. Even though he was using forced labour, he ran out of money and it was never completed. Although roofless, many details remain, including ornate windows, the grand entrance, and the magnificent central hall. The Earl was imprisoned in 1609 and executed in 1615. 01856 871918 www.historicenvironment.scot **99 B5**

# Houses

## Aberdeen and Moray

**Haddo House** *Ellon, Aberdeenshire.* A magnificent Palladian mansion, designed in 1732 by William Adam for William, 2nd Earl of Aberdeen. The interior is predominantly 'Adam Revival': this refurbishment was carried out in about 1880 for John, 7th Earl and 1st Marquess of Aberdeen. The contents include fine paintings, furniture and objets d'art. The extensive grounds were created in the early 19th century and hold deer, otters and red squirrels. 01651 851440 www.nts.org.uk **83 E5**

## Argyll, Bute, Stirling, Trossachs

**Argyll's Lodging** *Upper Castle Wynd, Stirling, Stirling.* This romantic building has served as both a home and a military hospital. The kitchen is the oldest part of the building, and dates to the early 16th century, while the rest of this impressive, turreted town house has been restored to look as it did when new in the 1680s. The drawing room still has the 9th Duke of Argyll's chair of state and is hung with antique tapestries. Combined tickets with Stirling Castle, from where they should be purchased. Guided tours available. 01786 450 000 www.historicenvironment.scot **39 B6**

**The Hill House** *Upper Colquhoun Street, Helensburgh, Argyll and Bute.* The best-preserved, and very popular, example of Charles Rennie Mackintosh's domestic architecture. It was commissioned in 1902 by the publisher Walter Blackie to include all the decorative schemes and furniture. Some of the fabric designs and one of the overmantels were by Mackintosh's wife, Margaret. 01436 673900 www.nts.org.uk **36 D4**

## Edinburgh and East Central

**Dalmeny House** *Queensferry, Edinburgh, City of Edinburgh.* The first neo-Gothic stately home in Scotland, Dalmeny House was built in 1815 by William Wilkins for the fourth Earl of Rosebery. Portraits include examples by Gainsborough, Lawrence, Raeburn, Millais and Reynolds. The collection includes important 18th-century French furniture and some memorabilia of Napoleon. Guided tours by prearrangement only, in June and July. 0131 3311188 www.dalmeny.co.uk **41 E7**

**The Georgian House** *7 Charlotte Square, Edinburgh, City of Edinburgh.* Robert and James Adam, furniture 18th century, Hepplewhite, Chippendale and Sheraton. It is laid out as it may have been when it was newly built. A working barrel organ plays a selection of Scottish airs. In the basement are the original wine cellar and a kitchen. 0131 226 3316 www.nts.org.uk **41 F8**

**Gladstone's Land** *477B Lawnmarket, Edinburgh, City of Edinburgh.* 17th-century Edinburgh tenement building, which would have been occupied by several merchant families. Completed in 1620, the six-storey building's ground floor has been restored to its original form as an arcaded booth. Inside, rooms have been redecorated and furnished in late 17th-century style and several have painted ceilings. 0131 226 5856 www.nts.org.uk **41 F8**

**Hopetoun House** *Old Philipstoun, West Lothian.* A Robert Adam-designed, 18th century masterpiece, notable for its gardens based on those at Versailles. The interior is filled with paintings and statues and 18th-century furniture. Formal gardens, nature trail, deer parks, stables museum. 0131 3312451 www.hopetoun.co.uk **40 E5**

**John Knox House** *43–45 High Street, Edinburgh, City of Edinburgh.* Home of the first Moderator of the Presbyterian Church of Scotland, John Knox, contains memorabilia and 15th-century interiors. **41 F8**

## Glasgow and the Clyde

**David Livingstone Centre** *165 Station Road, Blantyre, Glasgow, City of Glasgow.* The explorer and missionary David Livingstone was born in this tenement in 1813. The Livingstone family's rooms show the harshness of life for mill-workers while the other 23 tenements have displays on his missionary work and his adventures. 01698 536061 www.nts.org.uk **28 A2**

**Holmwood** *63 Netherlee Road, Cathcart, Glasgow, City of Glasgow.* A rare classical building by the Glasgow architect Alexander 'Greek' Thomson in 1857–8 for James Couper, a paper mill owner. The dining room has a frieze with scenes from the Iliad. The original highly imaginative decorative scheme for the house has been revealed by a recent renovation. 0141 571 0184 www.nts.org.uk **28 A2**

## Perth, Angus, Dundee and Fife

**Alloa Tower** *Alloa Park, Alloa, Clackmannanshire.* The mid 15th-century tower remains from the ancestral home of the earls of Mar and Kellie. The 6th earl partially restored and updated it before his exile after the 1715 Jacobite uprising. Among the rare medieval survivals are the timber roof structure and groin vaulting. The collection includes paintings by Jamesone, David Allan and Raeburn. 01259 211701 www.nts.org.uk **40 B1**

**House of Dun** *Montrose, Angus.* A Palladian mansion designed by Robert Adam for the Laird of Dun in 1730. The ornate relief plasterwork in the main rooms is full of Jacobite symbolism, and the restored interior has an extensive collection of period furniture and objects. Among the attractions in the courtyard is a gamekeeper's workshop. 01674 810264 www.nts.org.uk **67 B6**

**JM Barrie's Birthplace** *9 Brechin Road, Kirriemuir, Angus.* J M Barrie (1860–1937), the author of 'Peter Pan', was born here. The upper floors are furnished as they may have been at that time. The adjacent house, No 11, houses an exhibition about Barrie's literary and theatrical works. 01575 572646 www.nts.org.uk **66 B3**

## South of Scotland

**Abbotsford House** *Melrose, Scottish Borders.* Built in 1822, this is the house Sir Walter Scott lived in for the last 10 years of his life. Contains relics associated with the poet and some of his collections, including Napoleon's pen case, Rob Roy's sword and a lock of Bonnie Prince Charlie's hair. The library contains more than 9000 of his books. Gardens, grounds and private chapel. www.scotsabbotsford.co.uk 01896 752043 **23 C6**

**Bowhill House** *Selkirk, Scottish Borders.* Built in the 18th to 19th centuries, this country house contains antique French furniture, works of art by painters including Gainsborough, Reynolds, Canaletto and Claude. Among other exhibits is the shirt that the Duke of Monmouth, an illegitimate son of Charles II, wore to his execution. Also has a country park with an adventure playground and a Victorian kitchen. www.bowhillhouse.co.uk 01750 22204 **22 D4**

**Broughton House and Garden** *12 High Street, Kirkcudbright, Dumfries and Galloway.* An 18th-century town house, to which the Glasgow School of Art painter E A Hornel added an art gallery, a library, a studio and a sheltered Japanese garden. An extensive collection of paintings includes Hornel's own bright, colourful depictions of his native Galloway. 01557 330437 www.nts.org.uk **47 D8**

**Burns House** *Burns Street, Dumfries, Dumfries and Galloway.* The poet's home for the last three years of his life, with some of his possessions and furniture. 01387 255297 www.dumfriesmuseum.demon.co.uk **48 B3**

**Ellisland Farm** *Dumfries, Dumfries and Galloway.* Built by Robert Burns in 1788 as a working farm, Ellisland also houses a small museum dedicated to the poet with such personal effects as his pistol, sword, flute and fishing rod, as well as 18th-century farming implements. While here, Burns composed well over 100 songs and poems, including Auld Lang Syne. 01387 740426 www.ellislandfarm.co.uk **48 A3**

**Manderston House** *Duns, Scottish Borders.* Originally a Georgian building, but expanded between 1871 and 1905 into a large country house partly in the earlier, Neoclassical style of Robert Adam. The interior is lavishly decorated and furnished and includes decorative plaster ceilings and a silver staircase. Other features of interest are the biscuit-tin museum, the extravagant marble dairy (complete with cloisters), the tower house folly and 50 acres of gardens and woodland. 01361 883450 www.manderston.co.uk **34 D5**

**Mellerstain** *Gordon, Scottish Borders.* Thought by many to be Scotland's finest mansion, Mellerstain was started by William Adam, who built two wings and completed by his son, Robert in 1778. It has collections of antique furniture, paintings and impressive classical interior. 01573 410225 www.mellerstain.com **24 B1**

**Paxton House** *Berwick-upon-Tweed, Northumbria.* Designed by John and James Adam, Paxton is a Palladian mansion with a classicly serene exterior and simple interior with plasterwork by Robert Adam. The picture gallery houses paintings on loan

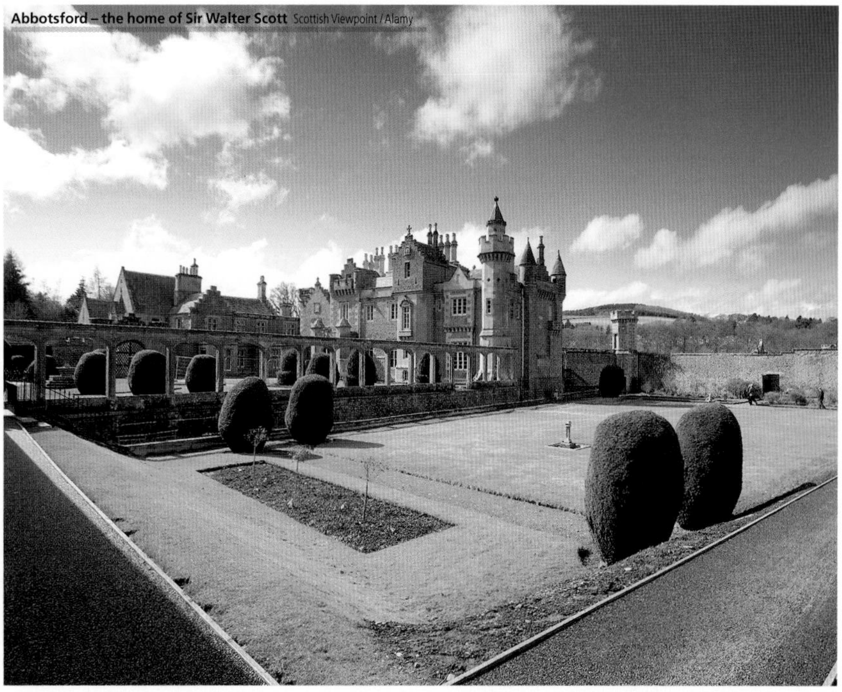

**Abbotsford – the home of Sir Walter Scott** Scottish Viewpoint / Alamy

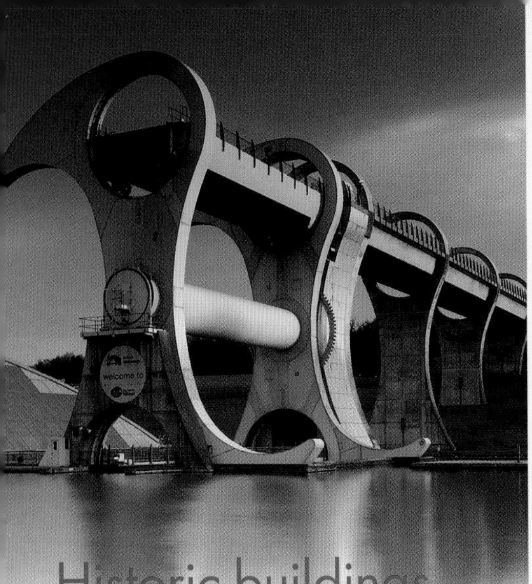

# Historic buildings

## Argyll, Bute, Stirling, Trossachs

**Bonawe Iron Furnace (industrial)** *Taynuilt, Argyll and Bute* The best preserved 18th-century charcoal-fired ironworks in Scotland with an exhibition. At its height this site employed more than 600 people. 01866 822432 www.historicenvironment.scot **63 D5**

**Cruachan power station** *Dalmally, Argyll and Bute* At the northern end of Loch Awe, Cruachan is one of Scotland's first hydroelectric powerstations and has been operational since 1966. Guided tours (advance booking recommended) and visitor centre with interactive displays. 0141 6149105 www.visitcruachan.co.uk **63 E6**

**McCaig's Tower** *Pulpit Hill, Oban, Argyll and Bute* A replica of the Colosseum in Rome, built by John Stuart McCaig between 1897 and 1900. It served both as a memorial to his family and a means of creating work during an economic downturn. Although it is not finished, its walls reach as much as 12 metres (40 feet) and it provides excellent views. **62 E3**

## Edinburgh and East Central

**Falkirk Wheel** *Lime Road, Tamfourhill, Falkirk* Built to reconnect the Forth and Clyde and Union canals, the Falkirk Wheel is the world's first rotating boat lift. It rises to 34.5 m, a height that would have required 11 locks, moving 600 tonnes of water to that height in 4 minutes. The visitor centre has an interactive exhibition and a viewing gallery. Boat trips on the wheel can be prebooked. 08700 500 208 www.scottishcanals.co.uk/falkirk-wheel **39 D8**

**Outlook Tower and Camera Obscura** *Castlehill, Edinburgh, City of Edinburgh* The camera obscura (a series of mirrors and lenses) at the top of this tower throws images of nearby streets and buildings and the people in them onto a horizontal circular screen. 0131 2263709 www.camera-obscura.co.uk **41 F8**

**The Pineapple** *Dunmore, Airth, Falkirk* Folly, garden of Dunmore House, near Falkirk 1761, 45 feet-high summer house heated with hot air circulated through cavities in the wall (just like the Romans). 01383 880359 www.nts.org.uk **40 C1**

**Scottish Parliament Visitor Centre** *George IV Bridge, Edinburgh, City of Edinburgh* This centre explains the way the new Scottish parliament works. The debating chamber is open to the public when parliament is not sitting. 0131 348 5200 www.visitparliament.scot **41 F8**

## Perth, Angus, Dundee and Fife

**Camera Obscura** *Kirrie Hill, Kirriemuir, Angus* J M Barrie presented his home town with this cricket pavilion and the Camera Obscura within it in 1930. It offers views of Strathmore and the surrounding glens. 0844 493 2142 www.nts.org.uk **66 B3**

**Earthquake House** *Comrie, Perth and Kinross* Britain's first seismometer was set up in Comrie in 1840 and moved here in 1874 to record the incidence of tremors that still occur on the Highland Boundary Fault. There are now modern seismometers installed as well as a model of the original and they can all be viewed from outside. **65 C5**

**Mill of Benholm** *Benholm, Angus* A working watermill, the only surviving one the area. It is fed from the millpond above. The current mill is at least 300 years old but there is thought to have been a mill on this site for 800 years. 01561 362466 http://millofbenholm.org.uk **75 F5**

**Secret Bunker** *Underground Nuclear Command Centre, Crown Buildings, near Anstruther Easter, Fife* A labyrinth of tunnels that would have become Scotland's administrative centre in the wake of a nuclear attack. Rooms open include dormitories, canteen, communications, the chapel and the command centre. There are also guided tours and two cinemas. 01333 310301 www.secretbunker.co.uk **58 B3**

## South of Scotland

**Smailholm Tower** *Gordon, Scottish Borders* A restored 16th-century peel tower that provides excellent views over the countryside and contains a display on the ballads and legends of the borders. 01573 460 365 www.historicenvironment.scot **24 C1**

## The Outer Islands

**Barony Mills** *Birsay, The Barony, Mainland, Orkney* A working watermill dating from 1873, with its integral kiln for drying bere, the type of barley grown in the region. 01856 721439 www.birsay.org.uk/baronymill.htm **98 A3**

**Churchill Barriers (military/maritime)** *St Mary's, Mainland, Orkney* The four concrete and stone barriers were built between Mainland, Lamb Holm, Glims Holm, Burray and South Ronaldsay during World War II to protect the Royal Navy's ships in Scapa Flow, after HMS 'Royal Oak' was torpedoed in 1939. **99 C5**

**Click Mill** *Dounby, Mainland, Orkney* A horizontal watermill that provided a means of grinding enough flour for 2–3 families. The functioning mechanism can be seen beneath the building. www.historicenvironment.scot **98 A4**

◄ **Falkirk Wheel** Keith Fergus / Alamy ▼ **Earthquake House** Simon Whaley / Alamy

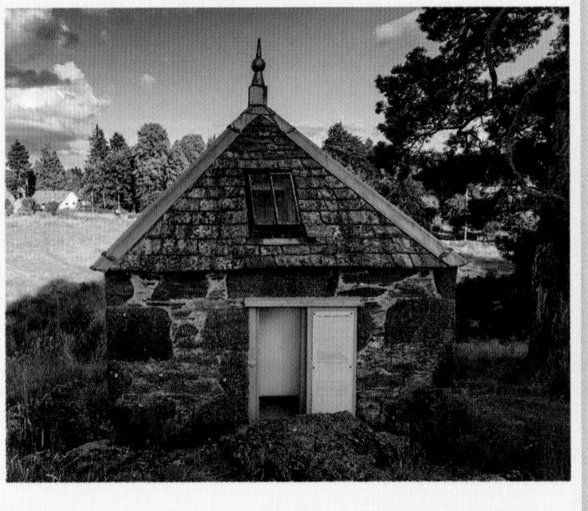

from the National Gallery of Scotland. The grounds are extensive and were designed by an assistant of Capability Brown. Other attractions include a Victorian boathouse with a salmon-netting museum, an adventure playground, Highland cattle, Shetland ponies, woodland walks and a hide from where red squirrels can be watched. www.paxtonhouse.co.uk 01289 386291 **35 D7**

**Thomas Carlyle's Birthplace** *The Arched House, Ecclefechan, Dumfries and Galloway.* The tiny house where the historian and essayist Thomas Carlyle was born in 1795 holds a collection of his belongings and letters. Built by his father and uncle in about 1791, the house, with its central passage, is representative of the local artisan dwelling of that period. 01576 300666 www.nts.org.uk **2 D4**

**Traquair House** *Innerleithen, Scottish Borders.* The oldest continually inhabited house in Scotland, home to a branch of the Stuart family since 1491. At least 27 monarchs are said to have visited and the family have particular associations with the Jacobite uprisings. The collections on display include paintings, manuscripts, glass, embroidery and silver. There is also a priest's hole and a hidden priest's room, as well as a bedspread said to have been embroidered by Mary Queen of Scots. The grounds include woodland walks, a maze, a brewery and craft workshops. The Bear Gates were last used by Bonnie Prince Charlie and the then owner swore they would never be opened again until there was another S tuart on the throne. 01896 830323 www.traquair.co.uk **22 B2**

# Monuments and ancient sites

## Argyll, Bute, Stirling, Trossachs

**Campbeltown Cross** *Off Main Street, Campbeltown, Argyll and Bute.* A 14th-century carved cross, brought from Kilkivan in the 17th century. Among the carvings are figures of saints, including St Michael slaying the dragon. **50 D3**

**Kildalton Cross** *Kildalton, Kintour, Islay, Argyll and Bute.* One of the finest Celtic crosses in Scotland, carved in the late 8th century, stands in the churchyard of the ruined medieval church. It has representations of the Virgin and Child, saints and biblical scenes. **49 A4**

**Kilmartin valley** *Kilmartin, Argyll and Bute.* More than 150 ancient sites in Kilmartin valley include Temple Wood stone circle, cairns at Ballymeanoch, Ri Cruin, Nether Largie and Dunchraigaig, an Iron Age hillfort at Dunadd, standing stones at Nether Largie, Ballymeanoch, where there is also a henge as well as numerous carved stones. Some of the finds from the area are on view in Kilmartin House Museum. 01546 510278 www.kilmartin.org **53 C8**

**Wallace Monument** *Manor Powis, Stirling.* A 216ft high monument, built in the Scots baronial style in the form of a medieval tower. Abbey Craig is where Wallace surveyed the ground before the battle of Stirling Bridge. At the tower's top is a representation of the Crown Royal of Scotland. A 16ft tall bronze statue of William Wallace is set about 32ft up on one corner of the building. Highlights inside include the Wallace Sword, a 700-year-old two-handed broadsword. At the top of the tower is a parapet offering views across the Forth valley and to Stirling. 01786 472140 www.nationalwallacemonument.com **39 A7**

## Edinburgh and East Central

**Caiy Stane** *Caiystane View, Oxgangs Road, Edinburgh, City of Edinburgh.* A 10ft high prehistoric stone, also known as the Kel Stone or General Kay's Monument, with markings known as cup-marks carved into it, is thought to mark the site of an ancient battle. **41 F8**

**Rough Castle** *Bonnybridge, Falkirk.* One of the forts that were built at 2-mile intervals along the entire length of the Antonine Wall, built by the Emperor Antonious Pius in AD 142 between the firths of Clyde and Forth. Rough Castle is the best-preserved part of the wall. www.historicenvironment.scot **39 D7**

**Scott Monument** *East Princes St Gardens, Edinburgh, City of Edinburgh.* Gothic monument to Sir Walter Scott. At its centre is a statue of the poet and his dog, Maida, with his heroes carved as small figures. Visitors can climb 287 steps to the top of the 200ft monument for amazing views. 0131 5294068 **41 F8**

## South of Scotland

**Auchagallon stone circle** *Auchagallon, North Ayrshire.* A Bronze Age cairn surrounded by a ring of 15 standing stones, overlooking Machrie Bay. www.historicenvironment.scot **50 C4**

**Burns Monument and Gardens** *Alloway, South Ayrshire.* A Greek-style monument containing manuscripts, books and relics associated with Robert Burns. The gardens are full of rare shrubs from the Himalayas. www.burnsmuseum.org.uk 01292 443700 **17 F5**

**Machrie Moor Standing Stones** *Balmichael, Arran, North Ayrshire.* A complex of six stone circles of different sizes and architecture, cairns, ruined huts and isolated standing stones. The different styles of the circles suggest that they were built at different times. Among the theories about their construction is that four of them align with the midsummer sunrise so they may be a form of calendar for agricultural purposes. **51 C5**

## The Highlands

**Clava Cairns** *Newlands, Highland.* One of the best-preserved Bronze Age burial sites in Britain, the complex consists of two passage graves, both aligned with the midwinter sunset, a ring cairn and other smaller circles. Each monument is surrounded by a stone circle and they all date to about 3000 BCE. 01667 400232 (for access) www.historicenvironment.scot **80 D2**

**Glenfinnan Monument** *Glenfinnan, Highland.* Set at the head of Loch Shiel in superb Highland scenery, this monument was erected in 1815 by Alexander Macdonald of Glenaladale in tribute to the clansmen who fought and died in the cause of Bonnie Prince Charlie in the 1740s. 01397 722250 www.nts.org.uk **70 D1**

**Grey Cairns of Camster** *Camster, Highland.* A series of burial chambers under long burial mounds set within bleak moorland. The chamber of the Round Cairn has a corbelled ceiling and the main chamber of the Long Cairn can also be entered. The mounds were built between 6000 and 4500 years ago. **91 D6**

**Monument to the Massacre of Glencoe** *Carnoch, Highland.* The monument commemorates the night in February 1692, Robert Campbell of the Argyll Campbells gave the order to kill all members of the Clan MacDonald because of their failure to swear an oath of allegiance to William III. Even in an age where murder was common, this was against the Highland rules of hospitality. **63 B6**

## The Outer Islands

**Blackhammer Cairn** *Brinian, Rousay, Orkney.* A restored Neolithic burial cairn, similar in shape and layout to the contemporary houses at the Knap of Howar site. 01856 751360 (for access) www.historicenvironment.scot **100 D2**

**Broch of Burroughston** *Edmonstone, Shapinsay, Orkney.* This Iron Age broch is one of the best preserved on Orkney and was occupied until Viking times. **99 A6**

**Broch of Gurness** *Aikerness, Westray, Orkney.* The best-preserved broch in Orkney. Built in the first century AD, this tower was originally 30ft high. The remains of small dwellings cluster between the broch and the outer defences, which consist of three ramparts and ditches. It is thought that as many as 40 families may have lived in these houses. 01856 751414 www.historicenvironment.scot **100 A2**

**Broch of Mousa** *Mousa, Shetland.* The walls of this large 2000-year-old broch stand to a height of more than 42ft, and

**The Wallace Monument, Stirling** David Robertson / Alamy

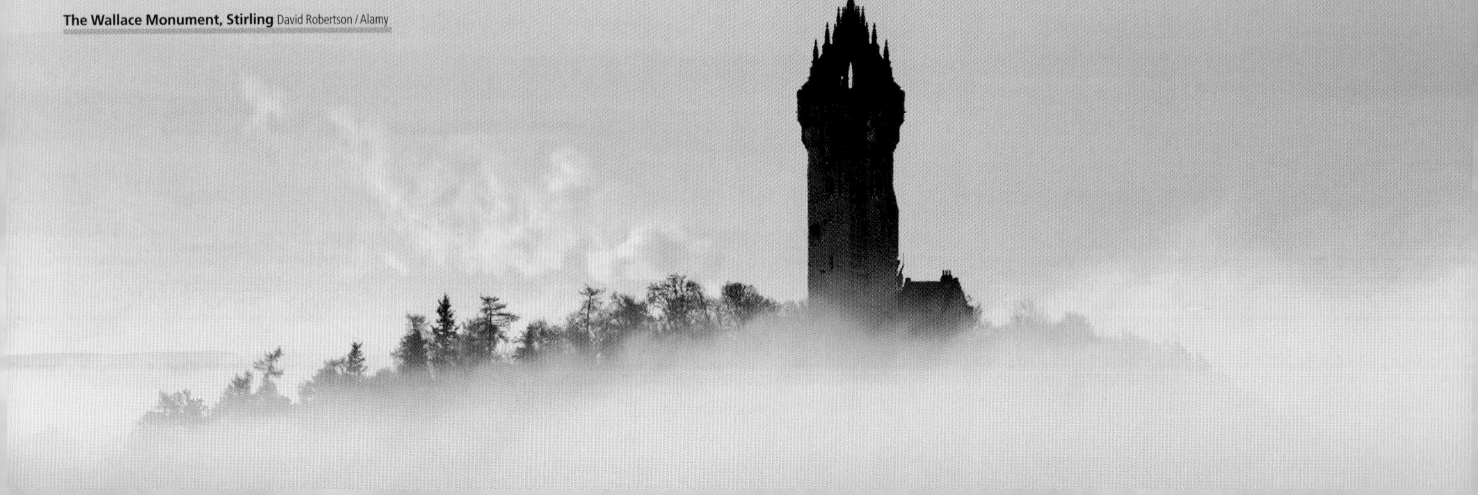

are substantially intact. The broch is double-skinned, with passages and galleries between the two skins giving access to all levels. 📞01856 841815 (Skara Brae) 📞ferry operator 07901 372339 🖥www.historicenvironment.scot **101 D3**

**Brough of Birsay** *The Barony, Mainland, Orkney.* The remains of Pictish and Norse settlements including farms, domestic buildings and a Norse cathedral from the early 12th century. Archaeologists have found evidence of metalworking on the site, and items are on display in the small museum. 📞01856 841815 (Skara Brae) 🖥www.historicenvironment.scot **98 A3**

**Calanais Standing Stones and Visitor Centre** *Calanais, Lewis, Western Isles.* A complex of standing stones. The main circle (Calanais) and the central megalith were erected about 5000 years ago and a chambered cairn inserted within the circle. The other rows and avenue were added over the following 2000 years. Callanish II is the remains of another circle with a cairn, Callanish III is another ring or ellipse and Callanish IV is another ring on the other side of the loch. There are also other settings of stones in the area. 📞01851 621422 🖥www.callanishvisitorcentre.co.uk **96 D5**

**Clickhimin Broch** *Lerwick, Mainland, Shetland.* The hugh circular broch, which was partially reconstructed in the 19th century, dominates the remains of the fort and houses. The site was a farm in the late Bronze Age and later developed into, first, a blockhouse fort and, second, a broch. Up to 60 people are thought to have lived in this settlement at its height. **101 B3**

**Cuween Hill Cairn** *Finstown, Mainland, Orkney.* A Neolithic burial chamber, probably associated with the Stonehall settlement and thought to date to about 3000 BCE, cut into solid rock at the top of Cuween hill. It has one main chamber with smaller chambers running off the walls. Visitors gain entrance to the tomb via a narrow passage that appears to be astronomically aligned. Excavations in the early 20th century revealed eight human and 24 dog skulls as well as ox bones. 📞01856 841815 (Skara Brae) 🖥www.historicenvironment.scot **98 B4**

**Dun Carloway Broch** *Dun Charlabhaig, Lewis, Western Isles.* One of the best preserved brochs in the Western Isles, with parts of the wall standing to nearly 32ft. It was built in the 1st century BCE. It is in a strong defensive position at the top of a steep hill, which would also have given the occupants a good view of anyone approaching. Several rooms on the ground floor and part of the stairway within the walls, which are 13ft thick at the base,

can be explored. 📞01851 643338 🖥www.historicenvironment.scot 🖥www.historicenvironment.co.uk/dounebroch.html **96 C4**

**Dwarfie Stane** *Whaness, Hoy, Orkney.* Unique in Britain, the Dwarfie Stane is a tomb carved into a large red sandstone block. It is thought to be Neolithic. The 3ft square entrance passage leads to two 'bed' spaces. 🖥www.historicenvironment.scot **98 C3**

**Jarlshof** *Sumburgh, Mainland, Shetland.* This large archaeological site, has remains dating back to the Stone Age, including a Bronze Age smithy, Iron Age houses, a broch, Picktish wheelhouses, Viking longhouses, and a ruined 16th-century laird's house. The buildings are open for visitors to explore inside. 📞01950 460112 🖥www.historicenvironment.scot **101 F3**

**Maes Howe** *Finstown, Mainland, Orkney.* Built about 3000 BCE, this beautiful chambered tomb is covered by a 114ft high earth mound. The entrance passage is in line with the midwinter sunset. Vikings raided the tomb in the 12th century and left a variety of graffiti on the walls. Guided tours, advance booking required. 📞01856 761606 🖥www.historicenvironment.scot **98 B4**

**Midhowe Broch** *Trumland, Westness, Rousay, Orkney.* An Iron Age broch perched on a small promontary and protected from the land side by two ditches and a stone wall. Parts of the tower stand to head height and there are remnants of later outbuildings. The interior divisions within the broch are of a later date. 🖥www.historicenvironment.scot 📞01856 841815 (Skara Brae) 📞ferry 01856 751360 **100 C1**

**Midhowe Chambered Cairn** *Trumland, Westness, Rousay, Orkney.* Protected under a large shed, this chambered tomb has been stripped of its soil so that visitors can see its complex structure from the walkways above. The main chamber is 75ft long and subdivided into 12 compartments with flat stones. 📞01856 841815 (Skara Brae) 📞ferry 01856 716360 🖥www.historicenvironment.scot **100 C1**

**Mine Howe** *Kirkwall, Mainland, Orkney.* Originally discovered in 1946, sealed, and then re-excavated in 2000, Mine Howe consists of a series of underground passages and chambers sunk into the top of a hill. There is also evidence of a surrounding ditch and nearby later settlement. The site has been dated to the Iron Age, but its function

remains a mystery. There is a small-scale reconstruction of part of the cairn nearby. 📞01856 861234 **99 B5**

**Quoyness Cairn** *Els Ness, Kettlehoft, Sanday, Orkney.* Constructed in about 2900 BCE and enclosed by an arc of eleven linked Bronze Age mounds, this Neolithic cairn appears to have been the heart of a sacred area. The central chamber is about 13ft high and reached through a 30ft long low entrance passage. The bones of at least ten adults and five children, as well as animal bones, stone and bone tools and carved stones were found in the main chamber and four of the six smaller chambers that open off it. 🖥www.historicenvironment.scot 📞01856 841815 (Skara Brae) 📞ferry 01856 872044 **100 C4**

**Ring of Brodgar** *Hestwall, Mainland, Orkney.* A 328ft stone circle, raised about 2500 BCE, with 36 of the original 60 massive stones still in situ, and surrounded by a masive ditch. 📞01856 841815 (Skara Brae) 🖥www.historicenvironment.scot **98 B3**

**Skara Brae** *Skaill, Mainland, Orkney.* This is one of the best-preserved prehistoric villages in Europe. Some of its fixtures, such as beds, have survived for 5000 years since it was abandoned. 📞01856 841815 🖥www.historicenvironment.scot **98 B3**

**Standing Stones of Stenness** *Finstown, Mainland, Orkney.* A prehistoric stone circle, dating to about 2500 BCE. Four of the twelve stones are still standing. 🖥www.historicenvironment.scot 📞01856 841815 (Skara Brae) **98 B4**

**Stone o' Setter** *Calfsound, Eday, Orkney.* A standing stone roughly 5m high, set in a spectacular landscape. Weathering has made it resemble a giant hand. **100 C3**

**Tomb of the Eagles** *Liddel, South Ronaldsay, Orkney.* A small cairn, in a dramatic setting, with a subdivided main chamber and three side chambers. Built in around 3000 BCE, it contained the remains of at least 340 people. Among the animal bones were those from white-tailed sea eagles and it is thought that the bird may have been significant to the people who built the tomb. There is a small 'hands-on' museum in the farmhouse. 🖥www.tomboftheeagles.co.uk **99 E5**

**Wideford Hill Cairn** *Kirkwall, Mainland, Orkney.* A large chambered cairn, with three concentric walls and three large cells running off the main chamber. The entrance passage is more than 16ft long. 📞01856 841815 (Skara Brae) 🖥www.historicenvironment.scot **99 B5**

# Religious buildings

## Aberdeen and Moray

**Cathedral Church of St Machar** *Church Square, Aberdeen, Aberdeen City.* This site was founded by St Machar, a follower of St Columba, in 580, although this fortified granite cathedral dates from the 15th century. The nave ceiling dates from 1520 and almost 50 different coats of arms from Scotland's nobles and bishops as well as Europe's royal houses make up its heraldic scheme. 📞01224 485 988 🖥www.stmachar.com **75 B6**

**Elgin Cathedral** *North College Street, Elgin, Moray.* This lovely ruin is the remains of a 13th-century building, which was burned down by the Wolf of Badenoch in 1390 as revenge for his excommunication for leaving his wife. There are several unusual medieval gravestones and a rare Pictish cross slab remains within the shell of the building. 📞01343 547171 🖥www.historicenvironment.scot **81 B7**

**King's College Chapel** *College Bounds, Aberdeen, Aberdeen City.* Finished in 1495, the chapel retains much of its original fittings and furniture, in particular the screens, stalls and ceiling are rare surviving examples of Scottish medieval wood carving. The stained glass is particularly fine. 🖥www.abdn.ac.uk/about/campus/kings-college-chapel-380.php 📞01224 272137 **75 B6**

**Pluscarden Abbey** *Kellas, Elgin, Moray.* One of only two working monasteries in Scotland, this Benedictine house was originally founded for a French order in 1230. The site includes the partially restored abbey, monastic buildings and church choir. Stained-glass workshops are also run by the monks. 🖥www.pluscardenabbey.org **81 C6**

**St Machar's Cathedral** *Aberdeen, Aberdeen City.* See Cathedral Church of St Machar **75 B6**

## Argyll, Bute, Stirling, Trossachs

**Balquhidder Church** *Balquhidder, Callander, Stirling.* A small church that holds an 8th-century stone called the St Angus' Stone, a 17th-century bell and some Gaelic bibles. Its chief claim to fame is the grave of Rob Roy, which lies in the churchyard. **56 B1**

**Cambuskenneth Abbey** *Cambuskenneth, Stirling.* The ruins of an abbey founded by David I in 1147. The only substantial remains are the 14th-century bell tower. King James III and his wife, Queen Margaret of Denmark are buried here, marked by a 19th-century monument. 🖥www.historicenvironment.scot **39 B7**

**Church of the Holy Rude** *St John Street, Stirling, Stirling.* This simple church is the site of the last coronation in Scotland, that of James VI in 1567. The stained glass is 19th-century. 🖥www.holyrude.org **39 B6**

**Dunblane Cathedral** *Cathedral Square, Dunblane, Stirling.* A superb, mainly 13th-century, Gothic church, with carved choir stalls, pews and screens, a hermit's cell, smart tombs and a Jesse Tree window. 🖥www.dunblanecathedral.org.uk 📞01786 825388 **56 B2**

**Holy Trinity Church** *12 Keir Street, Bridge of Allan, Stirling.* Built in 1860, this small church is interesting for its Charles Rennie Mackintosh designs and its stained glass windows. 01786 834155 **39 A6**

**Inchmahome Priory** *Port of Menteith, Stirling.* In spring and summer a ferry runs from Port of Menteith to the isle of Inchmahome, a beautiful ruined Augustinian priory in a lovely setting, with impressive tombs of important families from the surrounding area. 01877 385294 www.historicenvironment.scot **55 B8**

**Iona Abbey** *Baile Mor, Iona, Argyll and Bute.* A 13th-century Benedictine abbey, damaged during the Reformation but restored in the early 20th century and now home to a thriving religious community. Within the site are other structures, including the ruins of the Augustinian nunnery, St Martin and St John's crosses both from the 8th century, St Oran's chapel, and the infirmary museum. To the left of the abbey's entrance is St Columba's shrine, where the saint who founded the community in 563 may be buried. The island's cemetery surrounds St Oran's chapel and among the 60 kings said to be buried here are both Duncan and Macbeth. Many of the old grave slabs have been moved to the museum and the abbey's cloisters for safekeeping. www.iona.org.uk www.historicenvironment.scot 01681 700512 **61 E5**

**Macquarie Mausoleum** *Salen, Mull, Argyll and Bute.* The simple tomb, set in a clearing, of Lachlan Macquarie, governor of New South Wales from 1809–20. His predecessor Captain William Bligh had been unpopular because of his despotism, and the more liberal Macquarie is remembered by some as 'The father of Australia'. www.undiscoveredscotland.co.uk **61 C8**

## Edinburgh and East Central

**Holyrood Abbey** *Holyrood Palace grounds, Canongate, Edinburgh, City of Edinburgh.* The ruins of the old royal foundation include one of the west towers and the elaborate west doorway and one Romanesque doorway. It was sacked by the English in 1547, the whole eastern part of the building was pulled down during the reformation and Charles I's attempts at repair included a stone roof that collapsed in 1768, taking most of the rest of the building with it. www.historicenvironment.scot **41 F8**

**Rosslyn Chapel** *Roslin, Midlothian.* Properly known as the Collegiate Church of St Matthew, this is one of Scotland's most beautiful churches. It was built in the mid-15th century for William St Clair, 3rd Earl of Orkney. The interior is richly carved with vines and flowers, biblical figures, green men, moral tales and figures associated with Freemasonry and the Knights Templar, as well as cacti and corn, which were not known in Europe at that time, leading some people to speculate that St Clair's grandfather Prince Henry of Orkney had reached America a century before Columbus. A pair of carvings in the Lady Chapel ceiling is supposed to represent the apprentice who carved the beautiful apprentice pillar in the southeast corner and his master who murdered him in a fit of jealousy. 0131 4402159 www.rosslynchapel.com **32 B1**

**St Cuthbert's Kirk** *Dalmeny, Edinburgh, City of Edinburgh.* This Romanesque church has survived virtually intact. Of particular note are the beasts carved on the south doorway and the grotesques inside on the chancel arch and corbels. **41 F8**

**St Giles Cathedral** *High Street, Edinburgh, City of Edinburgh.* Gothic cathedral. Contents include the early 20th-century Thistle Chapel, which is dedicated to Scotland's highest order of chivalry and holds lovely stalls and heraldic stained-glass windows. 0131 2259442 www.stgilescathedral.org.uk **41 F8**

## Glasgow and the Clyde

**Cathedral of St Kentigern** *Cathedral Square, Glasgow, City of Glasgow.* Glasgow's Cathedral, also known as St Mungo's, is the only pre-Reformation cathedral in mainland Scotland to have survived virtually intact. St Kentigern (St Mungo) founded a monastic community here in the 5th century. The first stone church was consecrated in 1136, but burned down at the end of the 12th century. It was rebuilt as what is today known as the lower church. This was a medieval pilgrimage centre, focused on the shrine of St Kentigern. The upper church is a beautiful Gothic building, dating from the 15th century. The late 15th-century choir screen is a rare survival, and is decorated with figures depicting the seven deadly sins. www.historicenvironment.scot 0141 552 8198 **28 A2**

**Glasgow Cathedral** *Glasgow, City of Glasgow.* See Cathedral of St Kentigern. **28 A2**

**Paisley Abbey** *Abbey Close, Paisley, Renfrewshire.* Not particularly prepossessing from the outside, the abbey has a surprisingly pleasing interior. First built in 1163, rebuilt in the 14th-15th centuries and then restored in the 19th century, it is spacious and elaborately decorated. The stained glass, of various periods and styles, is particularly beautiful. The oldest item in the abbey is the 10th-century Celtic cross of St Barrochan. 0141 8897654 www.paisleyabbey.org.uk **27 B8**

**St Mungo's Cathedral, Glasgow** *Glasgow, City of Glasgow.* See Cathedral of St Kentigern. **28 A2**

## Perth, Angus, Dundee and Fife

**Arbroath Abbey** *Abbey Street, Arbroath, Angus.* William the Lion founded this monastery in 1178 and parts of the church and the domestic range remain. The church is chiefly famous as being the site where the Declaration of Arbroath was written in 1320. The declaration was a letter from eight earls and 31 barons to the pope, asking for support in their fight for Scottish independence from England. www.historicenvironment.scot 01241 878756 **67 C6**

**Balmerino Abbey** *Balmerino, Fife.* A Cistercian monastery, founded in 1229 and destroyed by the English in 1547. The ruined building may be viewed from the grounds, which contain many ancient trees, including a Spanish chestnut tree, which is more than 400 years old and one of the oldest in the country. 01721 722502 www.nts.org.uk **66 E3**

**Brechin Cathedral** *Church Square, Brechin, Angus.* Although the building is mainly the result of an early 20th-century reconstruction, the oldest part is the 104ft free-standing round tower, which was built in around 1000 and is one of only two of this type in Scotland and thought to be a place of sanctuary from Viking raids. The main door is set 6ft above the ground for the same reason. It has some lovely carvings including animals and saints, while there are several Pictish stones inside the church. www.brechincathedral.org.uk 01356 629360 **67 A5**

**Culross Abbey** *Culross, Fife.* Founded in 1217 by Malcolm, Earl of Fife. Although the Gothic nave is ruinous, the choir is still used as the town's parish church. www.historicenvironment.scot **40 C3**

**Dunfermline Abbey and Palace** *St Margaret's Street, Dunfermline, Fife.* The nave of this abbey remains from the mid-12th-century Romanesque building, while the flying buttresses, the shrine to the saint, the baptismal porch at the northwest and the flying buttresses are Gothic additions. Traces of the Celtic and 11th-century Culdee church can be seen through gratings in the nave floor. Of the many royal burials in the abbey, only those of St Margaret and Robert the Bruce have been located. A small part of the ruins of the royal palace lies next door. www.dunfermlineabbey.co.uk 01383 724586 **41 C5**

**Dunkeld Cathedral** *High Street, Dunkeld, Perth and Kinross.* The nave and clocktower of this partly ruined Gothic cathedral date from the 15th century while the choir, which is still in use as the parish church, was built in the previous century. Features of interest include an effigy of the Wolf of Badenoch and a 'lepers' peep' in the north wall, which allowed them to receive the sacrament without contaminating the rest of the congregation. The building suffered extensive damage during the Reformation and was restored in about 1600, but was burned during the battle of Dunkeld in 1689. www.dunkeldcathedral.org.uk **65 C8**

**Holy Trinity Church** *Off South Street, St Andrews, Fife.* The town church (or kirk), this medieval building was moved from its original site near the cathedral in 1410. Since then it suffered from alterations after the Reformation and an early 20th-century restoration, but the stained glass and carvings are well worth a visit. 01334 478 317 www.holyt.co.uk **67 F5**

**Kirk of St John the Baptist** *31 St John Place, Perth, Perth and Kinross.* Founded in 1126, the present church dates from the 15th century. An attractive building nestling in the middle of a network of cobbled streets, it was the venue in 1559 for John Knox's diatribe on idolatry, which helped to lead to the Reformation and the wholesale destruction of monasteries and religious art in Scotland. It was restored as a war memorial in the 1920s. www.st-johns-kirk.co.uk **66 E1**

**St Andrews Cathedral and Priory** *Off Pends Road, St Andrews, Fife.* Once the most important religious building in Scotland, this medieval cathedral took more than 150 years to build. There is a display of artefacts discovered within the building and grounds, as well as some early Christian and medieval monuments. 01334 472563 www.historicenvironment.scot **67 F5**

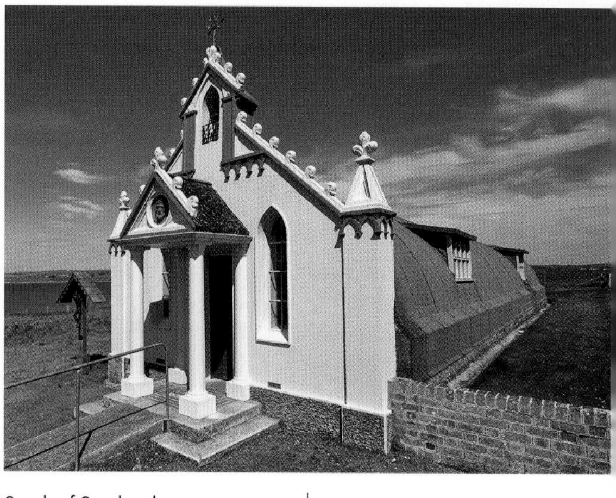

▲ **The Italian Chapel, Orkney**
Paul Williams / Alamy

## South of Scotland

**Crossraguel Abbey** *Maybole, South Ayrshire.* Substantial remains of a 13th-century Cluniac monastery. Some ornate carving remains in the apse of the abbey church, giving an indication of the richness of the building. More sculpture remains in the sacristy, including animals, humans and a green man. The chapter house, where the monks would meet to discuss abbey business, is substantially intact, as are the gatehouse and dovecote. The late 15th-century tower house was the abbot's residence 01655 883113 www.historicenvironment.scot **6 C4**

**Dryburgh Abbey** *Dryburgh, Scottish Borders.* A lovely ruined abbey set in a loop of the River Tweed. Its architecture is 'Transitional', with elements of Romanesque and Early Gothic. The poet, Sir Walter Scott is buried here. 01835 822381 www.historicenvironment.scot **23 C7**

**Dundrennan Abbey** *Kirkcudbright, Dumfries and Galloway.* The ruins of a beautiful Cistercian monastery, where Mary Queen of Scots spent her last night in Scotland before fleeing to England. www.historicenvironment.scot 01557 500262 **47 D8**

**Glenluce Abbey** *Glenluce, Dumfries and Galloway.* The ruins of this Cistercian abbey include a 15th-century chapter house with carved bosses and corbels including green men, cloisters and part of the complex water-supply system. 01581 300541 www.historicenvironment.scot **46 D3**

**Jedburgh Abbey** *Abbey Place, Jedburgh, Scottish Borders.* Partially restored ruined abbey, founded by King David I in 1138 and built in the Romanesque style. Visitor centre. www.historicenvironment.scot 01835 863925 **24 E2**

**Kelso Abbey** *Bridge Street, Kelso, Scottish Borders.* The earliest and probably the largest abbey in the Scottish Borders, Kelso was founded in 1128. It was repeatedly attacked by the English in the 16th century, but what does remain is some of the best Romanesque architecture in Scotland. **24 C3**

**Melrose Abbey** *Abbey Street, Melrose, Scottish Borders.* Ruined Cistercian abbey, built in the Perpendicular Gothic style. It was founded in 1136 and rebuilt by Robert the Bruce in the 14th century. A number of famous Scots are buried in the chancel. According to legend, the heart of Robert the Bruce was buried here and in 1997 a cask with a heart was excavated. It has since been reburied in the chapter house. Decorative, and often humourous, carvings survive in the chancel, including a gargoyle of a pig playing bagpipes on the roof. Fine stonework also survives in some of the window tracery, the pulpitum screen. www.historicenvironment.scot 01896 822562 **23 C7**

**St Michael's Parish Church** *Linlithgow, Scottish Borders.* One of Scotland's best examples of a parish church, despite severe damage in both the Reformation and Commonwealth periods. www.stmichaelsparish.org.uk **40 E4**

**Sweetheart Abbey** *New Abbey, Dumfries and Galloway.* The remains of a Cistercian abbey, founded in 1273. The roofless church survives but the monastic buildings have gone. There are traces of elaborate carving in some of the windows. The abbey's name comes from its founder, Devorgilla de Balliol, Lady of Galloway, who carried her husband's heart around in a casket for the last 22 years of her life. Her tomb is in the south transept. 01387 850397 www.historicenvironment.scot **48 C3**

## The Highlands

**Beauly Priory** *Beauly, Highland.* The ruins of this priory, one of only three built for the Valliscaulian order, date to 1230. The chapel of the holy cross, next to the north side of the nave, was added in the early 15th century. 01667 460 232 www.historicenvironment.scot **79 D7**

**Croick Church** *Croick, Highland.* This small chapel and its windswept churchyard sheltered 92 Highlanders in 1845 after their eviction from Glen Calvie to make way for the Duke of Sutherland's sheep. The chapel windows have graffiti scratched into them by the villagers. www.croickchurch.com **86 D1**

**Dornoch Cathedral** *Castle Street, Dornoch, Highland.* Originally founded in 1224, restored in the 19th century and returned to something approaching its original glory in the 20th century. The stained glass was donated by Andrew Carnegie. 01862 810296 www.dornoch-cathedral.com **86 E4**

**Fortrose Cathedral** *Fortrose, Highland.* The ruins of a beautiful early 13th-century cathedral, founded by King David I, situated in the middle of the pretty village green. 01667 460 232 www.historicenvironment.scot **80 C2**

▼ **Jedburgh Abbey** Jim Gibson / Alamy

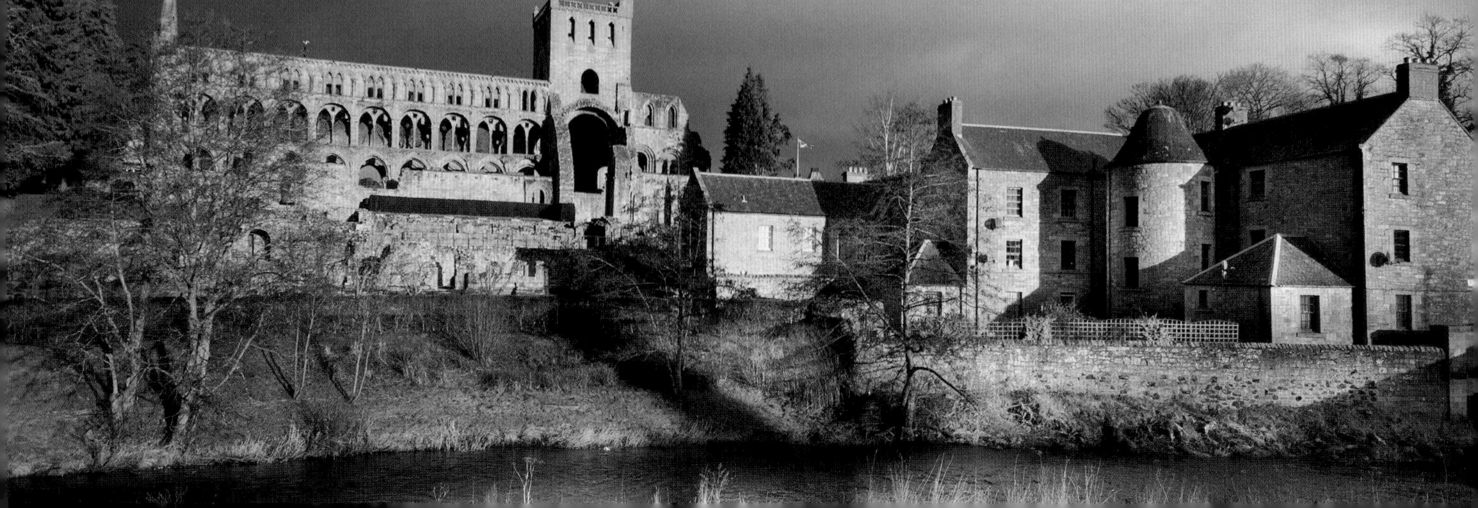

## The Outer Islands

**Italian Chapel** *St. Mary's, Mainland, Orkney.* A tiny chapel, adapted from two Nissen huts, created by Italian prisoners of war who were held here during World War II while working on the Churchill Barriers (see page X). The facade and trompe-l'oeil interior were restored in 1960 and the chapel is still regularly used for Mass. 01856 872856 http://businesses.orkney.com/b/italian_chapel1 **99 C5**

**St Magnus Cathedral** *Broad Street, Kirkwall, Mainland, Orkney.* Begun in 1137 by Earl Rognvald in honour of his uncle, St Magnus, the earliest part of Orkney's cathedral was built by masons who had previously worked on Durham Cathedral and is Romanesque in style. Later additions, such as the extended nave, are Gothic. There are interesting 17th-century tombs with skull-and-crossbones motifs and moralising texts. Among the monuments is that dedicated to the sailors who died when the Royal Oak was torpedoed in Scapa Flow in 1939. 01856 874894 www.stmagnus.org **99 B5**

# Museums and galleries

## Art and crafts

### Aberdeen and Moray

**Aberdeen Art Gallery** *Schoolhill, Aberdeen, Aberdeen City.* As well as a collection featuring the work of contemporary painters and a large number of portraits by Pre-Raphaelite artists, this gallery has a selection of modern ceramics, textiles and jewellery. 0300 200293 www.aagm.co.uk **75 B6**

**Duff House** *Banff, Aberdeenshire.* An elegant Georgian Baroque mansion, designed by William Adam and completed in 1737. It houses a collection of paintings on permanent loan from the National Gallery of Scotland and temporary exhibitions. www.duffhouse.org.uk **82 B3**

### Edinburgh and East Central

**Scottish National Gallery** *2 The Mound, Edinburgh, City of Edinburgh.* This gallery holds an extensive collection of paintings, including works by Botticelli, Raphael, Titian, El Greco, Velázquez, Rembrandt, Cézanne, Degas, van Gogh, Monet, Gauguin, Seurat and Renoir. www.nationalgalleries.org 0131 6246200 **41 F8**

**Scottish National Gallery of Modern Art** *Belford Road, Edinburgh, City of Edinburgh.* The main building, Modern One, holds the national collection of 20th-century art, including works by Pablo Picasso, Georges Braque, Henry Moore, Barbara Hepworth, Henri Matisse, Joan Miró, Max Ernst, Balthus, Roy Lichtenstein and David Hockney. Across the road, Modern Two houses an extensive collection of items donated by Sir Eduardo Paolozzi including works by Alberto Giacometti and Paolozzi himself. There are also sculptures in the grounds. 0131 62446200 www.nationalgalleries.org **41 F8**

**Scottish National Portrait Gallery** *1 Queen Street, Edinburgh, City of Edinburgh.* The collection includes portraits of famous people from the last four centuries of Scottish life, from the royal families to traditional heroes and modern actors. www.nationalgalleries.org 0131 6246200 **41 F8**

**Talbot Rice Gallery** *Old College, University of Edinburgh, Chambers Street, Edinburgh, City of Edinburgh.* Items from the university's art collection are housed here, including some old masters and works by 20th-century Scottish artists. There are also regular exhibitions of contemporary art. www.ed.ac.uk/talbot-rice 0131 6502210 **41 F8**

### Glasgow and the Clyde

**Burrell Collection** *2060 Pollokshaws Road, Glasgow, City of Glasgow.* Set within Pollok Country Park, this museum holds the fruits of more than 80 years collecting by Sir William Burrell, a wealthy ship owner. The broad range of artefacts includes, 19th-century French paintings, stained glass, Chinese ceramics, one of the original casts of Rodin's 'The Thinker', as well as furniture, textiles, 'objets d'art' and silver. www.glasgowlife.org.uk 0141 2872550 **28 B2**

**Hunterian Art Gallery** *22 Hillhead Street, Glasgow, City of Glasgow.* Part of the University of Glasgow, this gallery contains the second largest collection of works by James McNeill Whistler – some 60 in all – as well as works by Rembrandt, Rubens and 19th- and 20th-century Scottish artists. A reconstruction of Charles Rennie Mackintosh's house is reached through an extension and contains more than sixty original pieces of Mackintosh furniture and displays about the artist's home. www.gla.ac.uk/hunterian 0141 3304221 **28 A2**

**The Lighthouse** *11 Mitchell Lane, Glasgow, City of Glasgow.* State of the art exhibition centre that includes a Mackintosh Interpretation Centre, in which the artist's output is examined, and an IT area. www.thelighthouse.co.uk 0141 276 5360 **28 A2**

### South of Scotland

**Maclaurin Art Gallery and Rozelle House** *Monument Road, Rozelle Park, Ayr, South Ayrshire.* Good collection of contemporary art. Nature trail. www.south-ayrshire.gov.uk 01292 443708 **17 E5**

## Science and technology

### Aberdeen and Moray

**Aberdeen Science Centre** *The Tramsheds, 179 Constitution Street, Aberdeen, Aberdeen City.* A series of hands-on science exhibits that will occupy children of all ages. www.satrosphere.net 01224 640340 **75 B6**

### Argyll, Bute, Stirling, Trossachs

**Denny Tank** *Castle Street, Dumbarton, West Dunbartonshire.* This outpost of the Scottish Maritime Museum holds the world's oldest ship model experiment tank, where ship designers test models of ships before construction. The entire process is explained in a series of explanatory panels. www.scottishmaritimemuseum.org 01389 763444 **37 E7**

### Edinburgh and East Central

**Dental Museum** *Edinburgh, City of Edinburgh.* See Surgeons' Hall Museums **41 F8**

**Our Dynamic Earth** *107 Holyrood Road, Edinburgh, City of Edinburgh.* A fully interactive exploration of the geological and biological history of the Earth, including aquaria, audiovisual clips, simulations of different climates on Earth from tundra to rain forests. 0131 550 7801 www.dynamicearth.co.uk **41 F9**

**Surgeons' Hall Museums** *Nicolson Street, Edinburgh, City of Edinburgh.* Incorporating the Wohl Museum of Pathology, The Exhibition of the History of Surgery and Dental Museums, this specialist collection explores the development of surgical techniques over 500 years and houses wide collections of dental instruments and medical specimens. 0131 527 1711 https://museum.rcsed.ac.uk/ **41 F8**

### Glasgow and the Clyde

**Glasgow Science Centre** *50 Pacific Quay, Glasgow, City of Glasgow.* A science centre with interactive displays and a planetarium. www.glasgowsciencecentre.org 0141 4205000 **28 A2**

### Perth, Angus, Dundee and Fife

**Mills Observatory** *Glamis Road, Dundee, City of Dundee .* Britain's only full-time public observatory, it features a refracting telescope, small planetarium and displays of historic and modern equipment, pictures and models. www.leisureandculturedundee.com/mills-home 01382 435967 **66 D3**

### The Outer Islands

**Orkney Wireless Museum** *Kiln Corner, Junction Road, Kirkwall, Mainland, Orkney.* This museum is devoted to the wartime communications that operated at Scapa Flow in World War II. www.orkneywirelessmuseum.org.uk **99 B5**

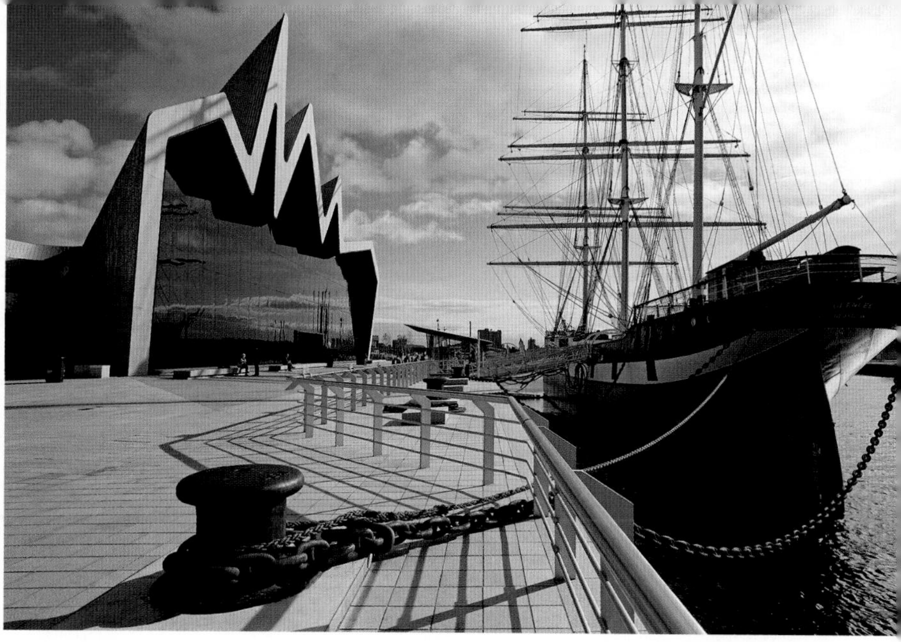

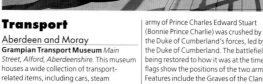

▲ **Tall ship *Glenlea* at the Riverside Museum, Glasgow** Findlay / Alamy

## Transport

### Aberdeen and Moray

**Grampian Transport Museum** *Main Street, Alford, Aberdeenshire.* This museum houses a wide collection of transport-related items, including cars, steam engines, trams and buses. 01975 562292 www.gtm.org.uk **74 A2**

### Argyll, Bute, Stirling, Trossachs

**Motoring Heritage Centre** *Main Street, Alexandria, West Dunbartonshire.* This factory used to be Scotland's largest motoring works, as well as its most palatial, and now houses a museum exploring Scotland's motoring heritage. www.motoringheritage.co.uk 01786 471744 **37 D6**

### Edinburgh and East Central

**National Museum of Flight** *East Fortune, East Lothian.* The old World War II aircraft hangars hold more than 50 vintage aircraft, among them a Tiger Moth, a Spitfire and a Vulcan, as well as a Concorde with an accompanying exhibition. 0300 123 6789 www.nms.ac.uk **43 E6**

**Myreton Motor Museum** *Aberlady, East Lothian.* A collection of vintage cars, military vehicles and motorbikes, as well as motoring memorabilia. www.myretonmotormuseum.co.uk 01875 870288 **43 E5**

### Glasgow and the Clyde

**Riverside Museum** *100 Pointhouse Place, Finnieston, Glasgow.* An enormous collection of cars, trains, trams, and other transport memorabilia. The Tall Ship is berthed alongside. 0141 2872720 www.glasgowlife.org.uk **28 A2**

## Military history

### Aberdeen and Moray

**Gordon Highlanders Museum** *St Lukes Viewfield Road, Aberdeen, Aberdeen City.* A museum devoted to one of Scotland's most famous regiments. 01224 311200 www.gordonhighlanders.com **75 B6**

### Argyll, Bute, Stirling, Trossachs

**Museum of the Argyll and Sutherland Highlanders** *Stirling, Stirling.* See Stirling Castle **39 B6**

### Edinburgh and East Central

**National War Museum** *Castlehill, Edinburgh, City of Edinburgh.* Set within Edinburgh Castle, this museum explores the last 400 years of war and military service, both within Scotland and as experienced by Scots serving abroad. 0300 123 6789 www.nms.ac.uk **41 F8**

### Perth, Angus, Dundee and Fife

**Black Watch Regimental Museum** *Balhousie Castle, Hay Street, Perth, Perth and Kinross.* This 16th-century castle houses weapons, uniforms, documents and medals showing the story of this famous regiment throughout their history. 01738 638152 www.theblackwatch.co.uk **66 E1**

### The Highlands

**Culloden** *Culloden Moor, Inverness, Highland.* The site of the end of the last Jacobite uprising. On 16 April, 1746, the army of Prince Charles Edward Stuart (Bonnie Prince Charlie) was crushed by the the Duke of Cumberland's forces, led by the Duke of Cumberland. The battlefield is being restored to how it was at the time and flags show the positions of the two armies. Features include the Graves of the Clans, the Well of the Dead, the Memorial Cairn, the Cumberland Stone and the Field of the English. Leanach Cottage, which survived the battle being fought around it, and outside which 30 Jacobites were burned alive, is open to the public. Guided tours of the battlefield are available and the visitor centre provides a background to the battle. 01463 796090 www.nts.org.uk **80 D2**

# Whisky

### Aberdeen and Moray

**Glenfarclas Distillery** *Ballindaloch, near Marypark, Moray* A small, independent distillery, founded in 1836 and still run by members of the same family. 01807 500257 www.glenfarclas.co.uk **81 E7**

**Glenfiddich Distillery** *Dufftown, Moray* Pre-booked guided tours of one of Scotland's most famous distilleries. www.glenfiddich.com **81 D8**

**Glenlivet Distillery** *Tomintoul, Moray* One of Scotland's most famous distilleries. 01542 783220 https://uk.theglenlivet.com/ **81 F6**

**Macallan Distillery** *Near Craigellachie, Moray* Prebooked guided tours around one of Speyside's best-known distilleries. www.themacallan.com **81 D7**

**Strathisla Distillery** *Seafield Avenue, Keith, Moray* Tours of the oldest working distillery in the Highlands, where Chivas Regal is made. 01542 783044 www.maltwhiskydistilleries.com **82 C1**

### Argyll, Bute, Stirling, Trossachs

**Ardbeg Distillery** *Ardbeg, Isle of Islay, Argyll and Bute* Prebooked guided tours around one of Islay's whisky distilleries. 01496 302244 www.ardbeg.com **49 B4**

**Bowmore Distillery** *School Street, Bowmore, Isle of Islay, Argyll and Bute* Guided tours of one of Islay's best-known distilleries. 01496 810671 www.bowmore.com **49 A3**

**Bunnahabhain Distillery** *Port Askaig, Isle of Islay, Argyll and Bute* Prebooked guided tours of one of Islay's distilleries. 01496 840646 **52 F4**

**Caol Ila Distillery** *Port Askaig, Isle of Islay, Argyll and Bute* Prebooked tours of one of Islay's distilleries. 01496 302769 www.discovering-distilleries.com/caolila **52 F4**

**Lagavulin Distillery** *Port Ellen, Isle of Islay, Argyll and Bute* Pre-booked, guided tours of one of Islay's whisky distilleries. 01496 302749 www.discovering-distilleries.com/lagavulin **49 B4**

**Laphroaig Distillery** *Laphroaig, Isle of Islay, Argyll and Bute* Guided tours around one of Scotland's most famous distilleries. Advance booking is required. 01496 302418 www.laphroaig.com **49 B3**

**Oban Distillery** *Stafford Street, Oban, Argyll and Bute* Guided tours and exhibition around a distillery that has been producing single-malt whisky since 1794. 01631 572004 www.discovering-distilleries.com/oban **62 E3**

**Tobermory Distillery** *Tobermory, Isle of Mull, Argyll and Bute* Prebooked tours around one of the oldest distilleries. www.tobermorydistillery.com 01688 302647 **61 B8**

### Edinburgh and East Central

**The Scotch Whisky Experience** *354 Castlehill, Edinburgh, City of Edinburgh* Dedicated to the history of Scotch whisky, exhibits in the centre explain how it is manufactured. Guided tours include tastings. 0131 2200441 www.scotchwhiskyexperience.co.uk **41 F8**

### Perth, Angus, Dundee and Fife

**Blair Athol Distillery** *Perth Road, Pitlochry, Perth and Kinross* Tours of one of Scotland's best known distilleries. Visitor centre. 01796 482003 www.discovering-distilleries.com/blairathol **65 B7**

**Glenturret Distillery** *The Hosh, Crieff, Perth and Kinross* Guided tours are available around Scotland's oldest distillery, which was founded in 1775. Museum of whisky. 01764 656565 www.famousgrouse.co.uk **65 E6**

### South of Scotland

**Isle of Arran Distillers** *Lochranza, Isle of Arran, North Ayrshire* Guided tours around Scotland's youngest distillery, which opened in 1995. 01770 830264 www.arranwhisky.com **51 A5**

### The Highlands

**Ben Nevis Distillery** *Lochy Bridge, Fort William, Highland* Visitor centre and tours around a small distillery at the foot of Ben Nevis. 01397 702476 www.bennevisdistillery.com **70 E3**

**Clynelish Distillery** *Brora, Highland* The northernmost distillery in mainland Scotland. Guided tours. 01408 623000 www.discovering-distilleries.com/clynelish **87 C6**

**Glenmorangie Distillery** *Tain, Highland* Guided tours and visitor centre located in one of the most famous distilleries. 01862 892477 www.glenmorangie.com **86 E4**

**Talisker Distillery** *Carbost, Isle of Skye, Highland* Prebooked visits to Skye's only distillery, which produces a peaty single malt. 01478 614308 www.discovering-distilleries.com/talisker **76 E3**

### The Outer Islands

**Highland Park Distillery** *The Hosh, Kirkwall, Mainland, Orkney* Tours around the world's northernmost distillery, showing the complete whisky-making process. 01856 874619 www.highlandpark.co.uk **99 C5**

**Fort George/Queen's Own Highlanders Regimental Museum** *Fort George, Inverness, Highland.* Set within the ramparts of Fort George, which was built after the battle of Culloden and which is still an active army base, this museum contains regimental exhibits from 1778 onwards. www.historicenvironment.scot 01667 460232 **80 C2**

**Queen's Own Highlanders Regimental Museum** *Inverness, Highland.* See Fort George **80 C2**

# Local history

## Aberdeen and Moray

**Elgin Museum** *High Street, Elgin, Moray.* This museum of local history also houses an assortment of anthropological items from around the world, Pictish exhibits and a good collection of fossils. 01343 543675 www.elginmuseum.org.uk **81 B7**

**Fraserburgh Heritage Centre** *Quarry Road, Fraserburgh, Aberdeenshire.* Exhibits include the history of the town, small boats and experiments into wireless communication conducted by Guglielmo Marconi in the town in 1904. www.fraserburghheritage.com 01346 512888 **83 B6**

**The Joiner's Workshop and Visitor Centre** *Fordyce, Aberdeenshire.* A small museum housing a collection of woodworking tools and machinery. Demonstrations. www.aberdeenshire.gov.uk **82 B2**

## Argyll, Bute, Stirling, Trossachs

**Auchindrain Folk Museum** *Auchindrain, Argyll and Bute.* A collection of about 20 thatched cottages furnished and decorated to show what life was like before the Highland Clearances. 01499 500235 www.auchindrain.org.uk **54 B3**

**Battle of Bannockburn Visitor Centre** *Glasgow Road, Whins of Milton, Stirling.* At the battle of Bannockburn, in 1314, Robert the Bruce of Scotland defeated the forces of Edward II of England, one in a series of battles that eventually led to Scottish independence. Audiovisual presentations and exhibits tell the story of the relationship between the two countries between the 13th and 17th centuries. 01786 812664 www.nts.org.uk **39 B6**

**Bute Museum** *Rothesay, Bute, Argyll and Bute.* A good collection covering the geology, natural history and archaeology of the island, including a lignite necklace thought to be more than 3500 years old. www.butemuseum.org 01700 505067 **54 F3**

**Dunblane Museum** *The Cross, Dunblane, Stirling.* A tiny museum, housed in a 17th-century building, with exhibits on both the history of the nearby cathedral and local archaeology. 01786 825691 www.dunblanemuseum.org.uk **56 B2**

**Iona Heritage Centre** *Baile Mor, Iona. Argyll and Bute.* A small museum on the social history of the last 200 years of life on the island, including the effects of the clearances in the 19th century, which halved the population of the island at a stroke. 01681 700576 **61 E5**

**Kilmartin House Museum** *Kilmartin, Argyll and Bute.* A small museum, housed in the old Manse, with explanations on the nature and use of crannogs (dwellings in lochs), henges and cairns, as well as axe-polishing and other activities. 01546 510278 www.kilmartin.org **53 C8**

**Mull Museum** *Main Street, Mull, Tobermory, Argyll and Bute.* This small museum houses exhibits relating to the history of the town and island, especially its fishing heritage. 01688 301100 www.mullmuseum.org.uk **61 B8**

**Museum of Islay Life** *Port Charlotte, Islay, Argyll and Bute.* A local museum that explores life on Islay from prehistoric times to the present. 01496 850358 http://islaymuseum.org **49 A2**

**Smith Art Gallery and Museum** *Dumbarton Road, Stirling, Stirling.* The history of Stirling, both royal and social, is explored in this museum, which was founded in 1874. Among its exhibits is the world's oldest known football, which is thought to date from the 1540s. 01786 471917 www.smithartgalleryandmusem.co.uk **39 B6**

## Edinburgh and East Central

**Museum of Edinburgh** *Huntly House, 142 Canongate, Edinburgh, City of Edinburgh.* Exhibits in this museum devoted to the history of Edinburgh include an original copy of the National Covenant, dating to 1638, and the bowl and collar of Greyfriars Bobby. www.edinburghmuseums.org.uk 0131 5294143 **41 F8**

**The People's Story** *163 Canongate, Edinburgh, City of Edinburgh.* This museum, housed in the late 16th-century Canongate Tolbooth, celebrates the social history of the inhabitants of Edinburgh from the late 18th century to the present, with an emphasis on the cultural displacements of the Industrial Revolution. www.edinburghmuseums.org.uk 0131 5294057 **41 F8**

## Glasgow and the Clyde

**North Lanarkshire Heritage Centre** *High Road, Motherwell, North Lanarkshire.* Multimedia exhibition on the history of Motherwell and the surrounding area. www.museumsgalleriesscotland.org.uk 01698 274590 **29 C5**

## Perth, Angus, Dundee and Fife

**Angus Folk Museum** *Kirkwynd Cottages, Kirkwynd, Glamis, Angus.* The Angus Folk Collection, the work of Jean, Lady Maitland, is housed in a row of early 18th-century cottages. 01674 810264 www.nts.org.uk **66 C3**

**Arbroath Signal Tower Museum** *Ladyloan, Arbroath, Angus.* Housed in the old signal tower from where messages were sent to the lighthouse on Bass Rock, this museum of local history covers subjects including textile and fishing. 01241 435329 www.angus.gov.uk **67 C6**

**Crail Museum and Heritage Centre** *62 Marketgate, Crail, Fife.* A small local museum with artefacts relating to the fishing and trading history of the East Neuk area of Fife. 01333 450869 wwwcrailmuseum.org.uk **58 B4**

**Kirkcaldy Galleries** *War Memorial Gardens, Kirkcaldy, Fife.* An exploration of the history of the town and the surrounding area, together with an art gallery. 01592 583206 www.onfife.com **42 B1**

**Meigle Sculptured Stone Museum** *Meigle, Perth and Kinross.* A small museum with a comprehensive collection of Pictish carved stones from the region. www.historicenvironment.scot 01828 640612 **66 C2**

**Perth Art Gallery and Museum** *George Street, Perth, Perth and Kinross.* This museum illustrates the town's history and has a good range of archaeological artefacts. A large section is devoted to the local whisky industry. 01738 632488 www.pkc.gov.uk **66 E1**

**Scottish Crannog Centre** *Kenmore, Perth and Kinross.* A museum devoted to the history of crannogs (loch-dwellings) with archaeological items from a nearby example, tours of a recreated crannog and demonstrations of Iron Age technology and crafts that visitors may try for themselves. 01887 830583 www.crannog.co.uk **65 C5**

## South of Scotland

**Dumfries Museum and Camera Obscura** *Church Street, Dumfries, Dumfries and Galloway.* This museum is devoted to southwestern Scotland's geology, archaeology and history. It is set in a converted 18th-century windmill and its camera obscura provides panoramic views of the town and countryside around. 01387 253374 www.dumfriesmuseum.demon.co.uk **48 B3**

**Isle of Arran Heritage Museum** *Brodick, Arran, North Ayrshire.* A museum of local history located in the former outbuildings of Brodick Castle and providing a good overview of life here since prehistoric times. Exhibits include a working kitchen, geological finds, a blacksmith's forge and 19th-century memorabilia. 01770 302636 www.arranmuseum.co.uk **51 C6**

**Jedburgh Castle Jail and Museum** *Castlegate, Jedburgh, Scottish Borders.* A Georgian prison, now a museum with displays about prison life through the ages. For a 19th-century building, the conditions are very comfortable, reflecting the influence of John Howard, the penal reformer, in the design. 01835 864750 www.scotborders.gov.uk **24 E2**

**Moffat Museum** *Church Gate, Moffat, Dumfries and Galloway.* Housed in a former bakery, this museum traces the history of Moffat and the surrounding region. www.moffatmuseum.co.uk 01683 220868 **11 C5**

**Stewartry Museum** *St Mary Street, Kirkcudbright, Dumfries and Galloway.* An idiosyncratic collection showing the history and culture of this part of Galloway. www.dumfriesmuseum.demon.co.uk 01557 331643 **47 D8**

## The Highlands

**Caithness Broch Centre** *The Old School House, Auckengill, Highland.* Small museum exploring the brochs of this part of Scotland and their long influence on the lives of the people of the region. 01955 631377 www.caithnessbrochcentre.co.uk **91 B7**

**Gairloch Heritage Museum** *Auchtercairn, Gairloch, Highland.* Arranged in a number of buildings this museum shows details of West Highland life from the time of the Picts to the present day. There are displays of activities such as butter-making and corn-grinding. 01445 712287 www.gairlochheritagemuseum.org **84 F2**

**Highland Folk Museum** *Kingussie Road, Newtonmore, Highland.* An 80-acre museum housed in several historic buildings that covers all the aspects of Highland life from the 1700s to the mid 19th century. www.highlifehighland.com 01540 673551 **72 C2**

**Laidhay Croft Museum** *Latheronwheel, Highland.* A small museum exploring the harsh life of crofters and clansmen in the area before the Highland Clearances. 07563 702321 http://laidhay.co.uk **91 E5**

**Timespan Heritage Centre** *Dunrobin Street, Helmsdale, Highland.* A heritage centre devoted to the history and people of this part of Sutherland, including crofting, the Vikings, the Highland clearances, witches, 19th- century sporting pursuits and the Kildonan gold rush. 01431 821327 www.timespan.org.uk **87 B7**

**West Highland Museum** *Cameron Square, Fort William, Highland.* This museum covers all aspects of local history, including the Jacobite Rising of 1745, the development of tartan, and social history. 01397 702169 www.westhighlandmuseum.org.uk **70 E3**

**Wick Heritage Museum** *19 Bank Row, Pultneytown, Wick, Highland.* The items in this museum include those from all aspects of the local fishing industry, with model boats, part of the old Noss Head lighthouse and hundreds of photographs from the 1880s. 01955 605393 www.wickheritage.org **91 C7**

## The Outer Islands

**Blackhouse Museum** *Arnol, Lewis, Western Isles.* A restored black house, showing how crofters lived in turf-roofed cottages, with people in one part and the animals in the other. 01851 710395 www.historicenvironment.scot **97 C6**

**Orkney Museum** *Tankerness House, Broad Street, Kirkwall, Mainland, Orkney.* Housed in a refurbished 16th-century merchant laird's house, this local museum shows life in the Orkneys over the last 5000 years. 01856 873535 www.orkney.gov.uk **99 B5**

**Shetland Crofthouse Museum** *Boddam, Mainland, Shetland.* This museum, housed in a 19th-century croft, portraits crofting life of the time with traditional furniture and fittings. 01950 460557 www.shetlandheritageassociation.com **101 E2**

**Shetland Museum and Archives** *Hay's Dock, Lerwick, Mainland, Shetland.* Explores the geology and history of the islands, with displays on the whaling, fishing and knitting industries. 01595 695057 www.shetlandmuseumandarchives.org.uk **101 B3**

**Tankerness House** *Kirkwall, Mainland, Orkney.* See Orkney Museum **99 B5**

**Unst Heritage Centre** *Haroldswick, Unst, Shetland.* This small museum, which is housed in the old school, concentrates on the history of the island, especially the herring-fishing industry. 01957 711528 www.unstheritage.com **102 B6**

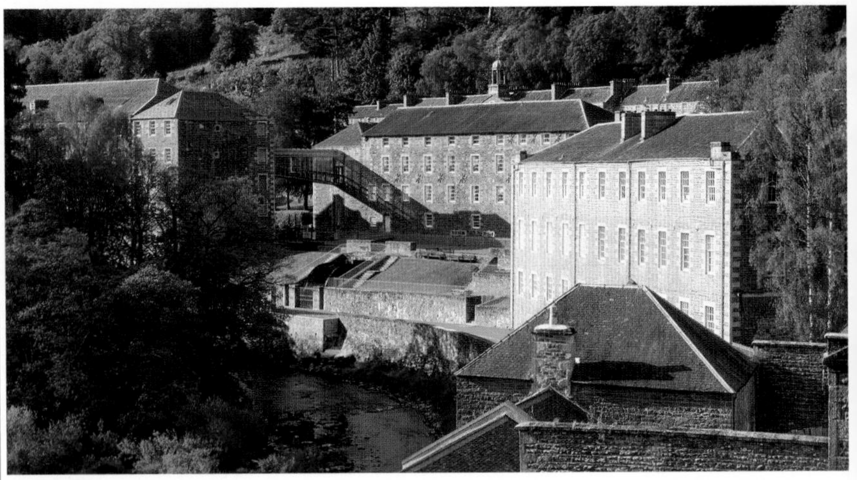

▲ **New Lanark World Heritage Village**
South West Images Scotland / Alamy

# Factories, mills and mines

## Edinburgh and East Central

**National Mining Museum Scotland** *Lady Victoria Colliery, Newtongrange, Midlothian.* Tours of a pithead, a mock-up of a working pitface and the winding engine, as well as displays on the history of coal-mining in Scotland. 0131 6637519 www.nationalminingmuseum.com **32 B2**

## Glasgow and the Clyde

**New Lanark World Heritage Village** *New Lanark Mills, Lanark, South Lanarkshire.* Restored warehouses and mill buildings house what was once the largest cotton-spinning complex in Britain with exhibitions on the work and workers at this model establishment. 01555 661345 01595 695057 www.newlanark.org **29 F8**

## Perth, Angus, Dundee and Fife

**Barry Mill** *Barry, Angus.* There has been a mill on this site since at least 1539, but the present meal mill dates from 1814. It operated until 1982, when it ceased production, but has since been restored to working order. 01241 856761 www.nts.org.uk **67 D5**

## South of Scotland

**Mill on the Fleet** *Gatehouse of Fleet, Dumfries and Galloway.* Local museum tracing the history of the cotton milling, shipbuilding, brewing and social history of this area of Dumfries and Galloway, set in a restored bobbin mill. 01557 814099 www.millonthefleet.co.uk **47 D8**

**The Scottish Crannog Centre, Loch Tay**
Scottish Viewpoint / Alamy

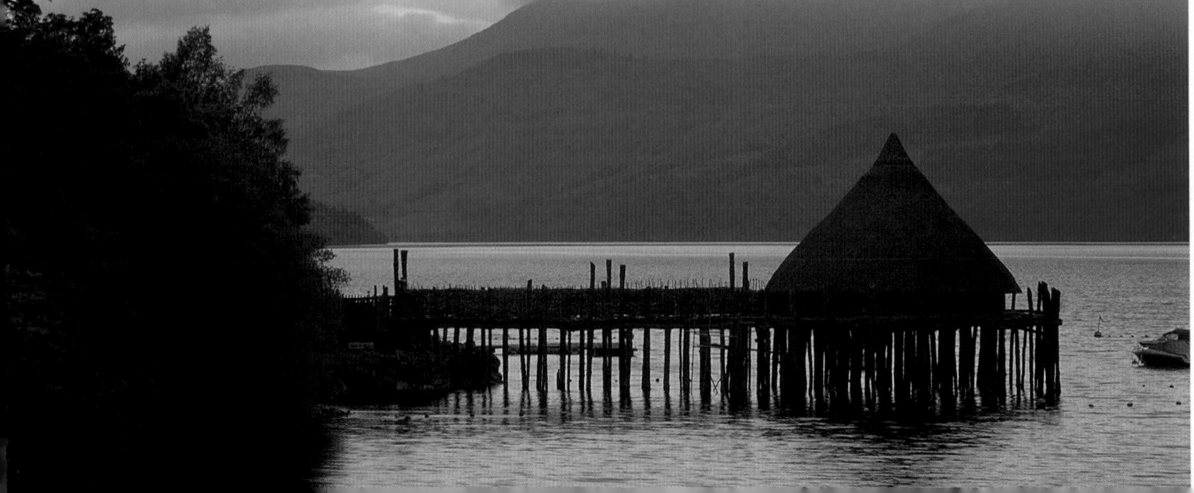

## The Highlands

**Aluminium Story Visitor Centre** *Linnhe Road, Kinlochleven, Highland.* Displays on how aluminium has been produced in the area for more than 90 years using hydro-electric power. ☎ 01955 831663 **63 A6**

## The Outer Islands

**Lewis Loom Centre** *3 Bayhead, Stornoway, Lewis, Western Isles.* Housed in a building known as the Old Grainstore, this weaving centre has demonstrations of the manufacture of Harris Tweed included in guided tours. ☎ 01851 704500 **97 D7**

# General museums

## Aberdeen and Moray

**Provost Skene's House** *Broad Street, Aberdeen, Aberdeen City.* Housed in a 16th-century private home, the oldest-surviving one in Aberdeen, this museum has archaeological exhibits, a costume gallery and a series of rooms showing changing interiors through the 17th, 18th and 19th centuries. The painted gallery has a cycle of 17th-century paintings depicting the life of Christ. ☎ 01224 641086 ⌨ www.aagm.co.uk **75 B6**

## Edinburgh and East Central

**Museum of Childhood** *42 High Street, Edinburgh, City of Edinburgh.* The collection includes antique toys and games, clothing, health and education. Video presentations and activity area. ☎ 0131 5294142 ⌨ www.edinburghmuseums.org.uk **41 F9**

**National Flag Heritage Centre** *Athelstaneford, East Lothian.* The exhibition in this redundant church traces the history of the Scottish flag, the saltire or flag of St Andrew, which originated near here. ⌨ http://scottishflagtrust.com **43 E6**

**National Museum of Scotland** *Chambers Street, Edinburgh, City of Edinburgh.* Exhibits include the decorative arts, geology, natural history, archaeology, ethnography, technology and science. The history of Scotland over the last 2.9 billion years is explored in modern galleries, including its role as an independent state before Union with England in the early 18th century and the Industrial Revolution. The collections of the former Royal Museum include an extraordinary range of items from all over the world: reliefs from the Assyrian royal palace of Nimrud, Buddhas from the far east, silverware, porcelain, fossils, classical Greek and Roman sculpture, scientific instruments, stuffed animals, a James Watt beam engine and Egyptian mummies. ☎ 0300 123 6789 ⌨ www.nms.ac.uk **41 F9**

**Writers' Museum** *Lady's Stair's House, off Lawnmarket, Edinburgh, City of Edinburgh.* Collections of manuscripts, letters and possessions of Robert Burns, Sir Walter Scott and Robert Louis Stevenson. ⌨ www.edinburghmuseums.org.uk ☎ 0131 5294901 **41 F8**

## Glasgow and the Clyde

**Hunterian Museum** *University of Glasgow, Main/Gilbert-Scott building, University Avenue, Glasgow, City of Glasgow.* Contains a wide range of zoological and archaeological specimens, including a dinosaur, large numbers of coins and an exploration of the Romans and Vikings in Scotland. The ethnographic part of the collection includes an exhibit on Captain Cook's voyages. ☎ 0141 3304221 ⌨ www.gla.ac.uk/hunterian **28 A2**

**Kelvingrove Art Gallery and Museum** *Kelvingrove Park, Glasgow, City of Glasgow.* The museum holds extensive collections on the natural history of Scotland, prehistoric and Roman Scotland, arms and armour, as well as antique musical instruments. ⌨ www.glasgowlife.org.uk ☎ 0141 276 9599 **28 A2**

**National Museum of Rural Life** *Kittochside, East Kilbride, South Lanarkshire.* An exhibition based within a working farm that continues to use traditional agricultural methods, this museum is divided into three principal sections: the Land Gallery, which explores how the Scots have used the land over the centuries and the effect of this on the landscape; the People's Gallery, which looks at the changing lives of farmers and their families over the last 400 years; and the Tools Gallery, which has an extensive collection of farming implements, ranging from early ploughs to a combine harvester. There is also an extensive collection of vintage agricultural machines. Visitors are encouraged to visit the 18th- century farmhouse where the cows are still milked by hand. Seasonal farming activities. ☎ 0300 123 6789 ⌨ www.nms.ac.uk **28 C3**

**St Mungo's Museum of Religious Life** *2 Castle Street, Glasgow, City of Glasgow.* This gallery has a collection of artworks representing figures from most of the world's major religions, including a controversial painting by Salvador Dalí – Christ of St John of the Cross – as well as statues of the Buddha and Hindu deities such as Ganesh. ☎ 0141 276 1625 ⌨ www.glasgowlife.org.uk **28 A2**

▼ *The Jacobite* steam train crossing Glenfinnan Viaduct *Blackout Concepts / Alamy*

# Family Attractions

## Aberdeen and Moray

**Alford Valley Railway** *Main Street, Alford, Aberdeenshire* A narrow-gauge train runs for about a mile from Alford Station to Murray Park, through the valley's wooded landscape. ☎ 07879 293934 ⌨ www.alfordvalleyrailway.org.uk **74 A2**

**Keith and Dufftown Railway** *Dufftown Station, Dufftown, Moray* Also known as the Whisky Line, this is an 11 mile route through beautiful countryside, providing views of wildlife, spectacular scenery. The diesel trains operate during summer weekends. ☎ 01340 821181 ⌨ www.keith-dufftown-railway.co.uk **81 E8**

## Edinburgh and East Central

**Bo'ness and Kinneil Railway** *Bo'ness Station, Union Street, Bo'ness, Falkirk* Steam trains run in the summer months. Railway exhibition at Bo'ness station. ☎ 01506 822298 ⌨ www.bkrailway.co.uk **40 D3**

**Brass Rubbing Centre** *Trinity Apse, Chalmers Close, High Street, Edinburgh, City of Edinburgh* Replicas of designs from the graves of such famous people as William Shakespeare are available for making brass rubbings. ☎ 0131 556 4364 ⌨ www.edinburghmuseums.org.uk **41 F8**

**Edinburgh Dungeon** *31 Market Street, Edinburgh, City of Edinburgh* Horror theme park exploring the more grisly side of Edinburgh's history. ☎ 0871 423 2250 ⌨ www.thedungeons.com **41 F8**

**The Real Mary King's Close** *Writer's Court, Edinburgh, City of Edinburgh* Visitor attraction reconstructing life in 17th-century Edinburgh, including a range of houses. ☎ 0131 225 0672 ⌨ www.realmarykingsclose.com **41 F8**

▼ **Cairngorm Funicular Railway** *Dominic Twist / Alamy*

## Glasgow and the Clyde

**Leadhills and Wanlockhead Railway** *The Station, Leadhills, South Lanarkshire* Diesel trains operate on this tourist railway between Leadhills and the disused lead mine at Wanlockhead, where there is a small museum and a beam engine. ⌨ www.leadhillsrailway.co.uk **9 A8**

**M&D's Scotland's Theme Park** *Strathclyde Country Park, 366 Hamilton Road, Motherwell, North Lanarkshire* The largest theme park in Scotland, with rides for both children and thrill-seekers, set among a large complex of attractions. ☎ 01698 333 777 ⌨ wwwscotlandsthemepark.com **29 C5**

## The Highlands

**Cairngorm Railway** *Cairngorm Mountain, Aviemore, Highland* The funicular railway journey from the Coire Cas car park lasts about 8 minutes, giving views up the mountains and over the Cairngorm plateau. There is a small mountain exhibition in the top station. ☎ 01479 861 261 ⌨ www.cairngormmountain.org **72 A4**

**Jacobite Steam Train** *Fort William Railway Station, Fort William, Highland* Return trips along the West Highland Railway between Fort William and Mallaig by steam train, through scenery incuding Loch Shiel, over the 21 arches of the Glenfinnan Viaduct and past the beautiful beaches of Morar. ☎ 01524 732100 ⌨ www.westcoastrailways.co.uk/jacobite/jacobite-steam-train-details.cfm **70 E3**

**Strathspey Steam Railway** *Dalfaber Road, Aviemore, Highland* This restored railway runs through Highland scenery between Aviemore and Broomhill via Boat of Garten. ☎ 01479 810 725 ⌨ www.strathspeyrailway.co.uk **72 A4**

**Treasures of the Earth** *Corpach, Fort William, Highland* A centre dedicated to crystals, rocks and gemstones, their properties, where they come from and how they are mined. Exhibits include a recreated mine which shows the conditions under which the miners work. ☎ 01389 772283 ⌨ www.treasuresoftheearth.co.uk **70 E2**

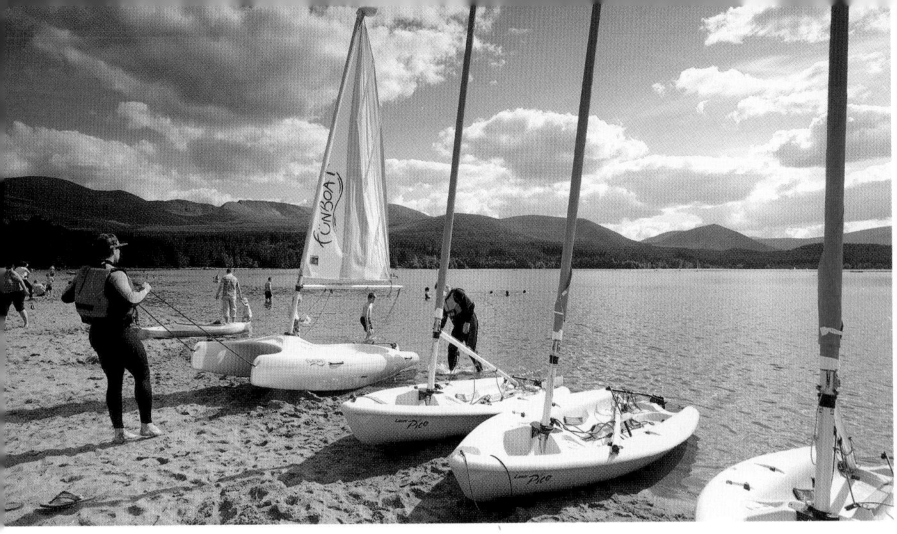


◀ **Loch Morlich Watersports Centre near Aviemore** Scottish Viewpoint / Alamy

### Perth, Angus, Dundee and Fife

**Andrew Carnegie Birthplace Museum** *Moodie Street, Dunfermline, Fife.* The small weaver's cottage where the 19th-century philanthropist was born has been converted into a museum, with an attached memorial hall. 01383 724302 www.carnegiebirthplace.com **41 C5**

**McManus Art Galleries and Museum** *Albert Square, Dundee, Dundee City.* Housed in an imposing, recently refurbished, Victorian building designed by Gilbert Scott, this museum explores Dundee's history, as well as holding collections of musical instruments, precious metalwork, sculpture, furniture and an extensive collection of 19th- and 20th-century paintings. 01382 307200 www.mcmanus.co.uk **66 D4**

### South of Scotland

**Mary Queen of Scots Visitor Centre** *Queen Street, Jedburgh, Scottish Borders.* The house where Mary Queen of Scots rested after an infamous visit to her lover, the Earl of Bothwell while still married to Henry, Lord Darnley. Contains paintings, engravings and articles relating to Mary's life. www.scotborders.gov.uk 01835 863331 **24 E2**

**Old Bridge House Museum** *Mill Road, Dumfries, Dumfries and Galloway.* Built in 1660, this house has been restored and furnished as it would have been in the second half of the 19th century, and is filled with an eclectic range of Victorian domestic articles. 01387 256904 www.dumfriesmuseum.demon.co.uk **48 B3**

**Robert Burns Birthplace Museum** *Murdoch's Lone, Alloway, South Ayrshire.* Museum and visitor centre based around the cottage in which the poet was born. www.burnsmuseum.org.uk 01292 443700 **17 F5**

**Robert Burns Centre** *Mill Road, Dumfries, Dumfries and Galloway.* A converted 18th-century watermill with exhibits about Robert Burns and the town of Dumfries. 01387 264808 **48 B3**

### The Highlands

**Inverness Museum and Art Gallery** *Castle Wynd, Inverness, Highland.* Exhibits on varied subjects including geology, wildlife and the history of weaponry. www.highlandlife.com 01463 237114 **80 D1**

# Sport

## Activity centres

### Edinburgh and East Central

**Beecraigs Country Park** *The Park Centre, Linlithgow, West Lothian.* Outdoor pursuits include, target and field archery, orienteering, canoeing and climbing, climbing and hillcraft, skiing and skiboarding. There is also a working deer farm with a red deer herd and a fishery. www.westlothian.gov.uk/beecraigs 01506 844516 **40 F3**

### Glasgow and the Clyde

**Strathclyde Country Park** *336 Hamilton Road, Motherwell, North Lanarkshire.* Activities available include: rowing, windsurfing, water skiing, dinghy sailing and canoeing (instruction provided on request), wayfaring and competitive orienteering. Mountain bikes can be rented. www.northlanarkshire.gov.uk 01698 402060 **29 C5**

### South of Scotland

**Galloway Activity Centre** *Parton, Castle Douglas, Dumfries and Galloway.* Offers courses in sailing, windsurfing, canoeing and powerboating, as well as such activities as quad biking, mountain biking, climbing and abseiling. 01556 502 011 www.lochken.co.uk **48 C1**

### The Highlands

**Monster Activities** *Fort Augustus, Highland.* In summer a wide range of outdoor activities is offered including mountain biking, abseiling, trekking, archery and knife throwing, as well as sailing, canoeing, kayaking, waterskiing, wakeboarding and white-water rafting. www.monsteractivities.com 07710 540398 **71 B5**

**Vertical Descents** *Inchree Falls, Onich, Highland.* Activities offered include canyoning, white-water rafting, rock climbing and abseiling, mountain biking, go-karting, archery and paintballing. www.verticaldescents.com 01855 821593 **70 E3**

## Climbing and caving

### Perth, Angus, Dundee and Fife

**The Mountaineering Council of Scotland** *The Old Granary, West Mill Street, Perth, Perth and Kinross.* Details of mountaineering clubs in Scotland. Publishes booklets on climbs and safety, and a newsletter. 01738 493942 www.mcofs.org.uk **66 E1**

## Cycling

### Aberdeen and Moray

**Alpine Bikes** *64–70 Holburn Street, Aberdeen, Aberdeen City.* Cycle hire within easy reach of the eastern Grampians and the Aberdeenshire coastline. 01224 212455 www.tiso.com **75 B6**

### Argyll, Bute, Stirling, Trossachs

**Brown's** *High Street, Tobermory, Mull, Argyll and Bute.* Cycle hire in a pretty town surrounded by beautiful landscapes. 01688 302020 www.brownstobermory.co.uk **61 B8**

**Finlay Ross General Store** *Baile Mor, Iona, Argyll and Bute.* Cycling is a good way to get around this small island to see the spectacular scenery. 01681 700357 **61 E5**

**Killin Outdoor Centre and Mountain Shop** *Main Street, Killin, Stirling.* Easy access to the area around Loch Tay as well as Glen Lochay and Glen Dochart. 01567 820652 www.killinoutdoor.co.uk **64 D3**

### Edinburgh and East Central

**Bike Trax** *13 Lochiun Place, Tollcross, Edinburgh, City of Edinburgh.* A convenient place on the outskirts of Edinburgh for hiring bicycles to explore the surrounding regions. 0131 2286333 www.biketrax.co.uk **41 F8**

### South of Scotland

**Alpine Bikes** *Peebles Road, Innerleithen, Arran, Scottish Borders.* Cycle hire in the beautiful surroundings of the Tweed Valley with a mixture of easy and more challenging places to cycle. 01896 830880 www.tiso.com **51 C6**

### The Highlands

**Alpine Bikes** *117 High Street, Fort William, Highland.* Ideally placed for cycling in both the flat areas around Loch Linnhe and more challenging areas in the hills. 01397 704008 www.tiso.com **70 E3**

**Barney's** *35 Castle Street, Inverness, Highland.* Inverness is a good base for cycling as it is close to Loch Ness, the Black Isle, the Moray Firth and the foothills of the mountains to the west. 01463 232249 **80 D1**

**Bothy Bikes** *Aviemore Shopping Centre, Grampian Road, Aviemore, Highland.* Hires out mountain bikes well suited to the challenging rides available in the Cairngorm National Park. 01479 810111 www.bothybikes.co.uk **72 A3**

**Island Cycles** *The Green, Portree, Skye, Highland.* Cycle hire within easy reach of Skye's scenic coastal roads. 01478 613121 www.islandcycles-skye.co.uk **76 D4**

**Skye Bicycle Hire** *Uig Campsite, Uig, Isle of Skye.* In the north of the island, Uig is located close to the stunning landscapes of both northern and western Skye. 01470 542714 www.uig-camping-skye.co.uk **76 B3**

### The Outer Islands

**AD Cycle Centre** *67 Kenneth Street, Stornoway, Lewis, Western Isles.* Cycling is the best way to get around Lewis and appreciate the landscape. 01851 704025 www.stornowaycyclehire.co.uk **97 D7**

**Cycle Orkney** *Tankerness Lane, Kirkwall, Mainland, Orkney.* Kirkwall is centrally placed on Mainland, giving easy access to a variety of rides through the rugged land. 01856 875777 www.cycleorkney.com **99 B5**

**Grantfield Garage** *Commercial Road, Lerwick, Mainland, Shetland.* Cycle hire giving access to Shetland's beautiful scenery. 01599 692709 www.grantfield-garage.co.uk **101 B3**

## Football

### Glasgow and the Clyde

**Celtic Football Club** *Celtic Park, Parkhead, Glasgow, City of Glasgow.* Guided tours and visitor centre with museum. 0871 226 1888 www.celticfc.net **28 A2**

**Hampden Stadium** *Hampden Park, Glasgow, City of Glasgow.* Scotland's national football stadium, which includes the Scottish Football Museum and guided tours. 0141 6204000 www.hampdenpark.co.uk **28 A2**

**Rangers Football Club** *Ibrox Stadium, 150 Edmiston Drive, Glasgow, City of Glasgow.* Tours of the stadium and trophy room. www.rangers.co.uk 0871 702 1972 **28 A2**

## Golf courses

### Edinburgh and East Central

**Muirfield** *Duncur Road, Gullane, East Lothian.* Built by Tom Morris in 1891, overlooking the Firth of Forth and home to the Honorable Company of Edinburgh Golfers. It is a par 70 links course, has hosted the Open Championship more than 20 times and is consistently voted among the top five golf courses in the world. 01620 842123 www.muirfield.org.uk **43 D5**

**Royal Musselburgh** *Prestongrange House, Musselburgh, East Lothian.* One of the oldest golf courses in the world, it is a demanding par-70. 01875 810276 www.royalmusselburgh.co.uk **42 F2**

### Perth, Angus, Dundee and Fife

**Balcomie Golf Course** *Fifeness, Crail, Fife.* A beautiful 18-hole links set above the Fife coastline. It was designed by Tom Morris. www.crailgolfingsociety.co.uk 01333 450686 **58 B4**

**Carnoustie** *Dundee City.* The par-72 Championship Course at Carnoustie is among the best-known links courses in the world. The Burnside and Buddon courses form part of the complex. 01241 802270 www.carnoustiegolflinks.co.uk **67 D5**

**Gleneagles** *Auchterarder, Perth and Kinross.* A complex of four courses, the Kings, Queens and Monarch courses and the 9-hole Wee Course. 0800 3893737 www.gleneagles.com **56 A4**

**St Andrews** *Fife.* There are six public golf courses in and around the town: the par-72 Old Course, par-71 New Course, par-72 Jubilee Course, par-70 Eden Course, par-69 Strathtyrum Course and the par-30, 9-hole Balgove course. All except the Balgove course should be booked well in advance to make sure of playing. 01344 466666 www.standrews.com **67 F4**

### South of Scotland

**Royal Troon** *Craigend Road, Troon, South Ayrshire.* A complex of three courses, the testing par-71 Old Course, the par-71 Portland Course and the Par 3 Couse, which is actually a 9-hole par-21 course. 01292 3111555 www.royaltroon.co.uk **17 D5**

**Turnberry** *Westin Turnberry Resort, South Ayrshire.* There are two courses, the famous par-69 Ailsa course and the new par-72 Kintyre course, against the backdrop of Ailsa Craig and the Turnberry lighthouse. 01655 333 991 www.turnberry.co.uk **6 C3**

## Hanggliding and paragliding

### Glasgow and the Clyde

**Cloudbusters Paragliding School** *2 Inchmurrin Drive, Cathkin, Glasgow, City of Glasgow.* Offers lessons in hanggliding and paragliding. 07899 878509 www.cloudbusters.co.uk **28 A2**

### The Highlands

**Highland Hang Gliding and Paragliding Club** *54 Culloden Road, Balloch, Highland.* Hang gliding and paragliding in spectacular surroundings. www.highlandhgpgclub.co.uk **80 D2**

## Horseracing

### Edinburgh and East Central

**Musselburgh Racecourse** *Musselburgh, East Lothian.* Flat racing in summer, National Hunt racing during winter. 0131 6652859 www.musselburgh-racecourse.co.uk **42 F2**

### Glasgow and the Clyde

**Hamilton Park Racecourse** *Hamilton, South Lanarkshire.* Daytime and evening flat meetings take place from April to September. 01698 283806 www.hamilton-park.co.uk **29 C5**

### Perth, Angus, Dundee and Fife

**Perth Racecourse** *Scone Palace Park, Scone, Perth and Kinross.* Jump racing takes place during the summer season. www.perth-races.co.uk 01738 551597 **66 E1**

### South of Scotland

**Ayr Racecourse** *2 Whitletts Road, Ayr, South Ayrshire.* Flat racing takes place from May to October, with National Hunt usually in January, April and November. 01292 264179 www.ayr-racecourse.co.uk **17 E6**

**Kelso Racecourse** *Kelso, Scottish Borders.* National Hunt racing takes place during the winter season – from October to May. www.kelso-races.co.uk 01668 2880800 **24 B3**

## Motorsports

### Glasgow and the Clyde

**Scotkart – Glasgow East** *Westburn Road, Cambuslang, Glasgow, City of Glasgow.* Offers a variety of karting for all ages and abilities. 0141 641 0222 www.scotkart.co.uk **28 A2**

**Scotkart – Glasgow West** *John Knox Street, Clydebank, Glasgow, City of Glasgow.* Offers a variety of karting for all ages and abilities on Scotland's largest karting track. 0141 641 0222 www.scotkart.co.uk **28 A2**

### Perth, Angus, Dundee and Fife

**Knockhill Racing Circuit** *Dunfermline, Fife.* Events at this circuit include British Touring Cars, British Superbikes plus driving experiences and track days. 01383 723337 www.knockhill.com **40 B5**

## Orienteering

### The Highlands

**National Orienteering Centre** *Glenmore Lodge, Aviemore, Highland.* Provides training, maps, equipment and support for all levels. 01479 861374 www.scottish-orienteering.org **72 A3**

## Riding

### Aberdeen and Moray

**Tomintoul Riding Centre** *St Bridget Farm, Tomintoul, Moray.* A variety of treks, from an hour to a day, through Highland scenery. www.highlandhooves.co.uk 01807 580210 **73 A6**

### South of Scotland

**Ayrshire Equitation Centre** *South Mains, Corton Road, Ayr, South Ayrshire.* A variety of hacks and treks is available including Rozelle Park and Ayr's five-mile-long sandy beaches. 01292 266 267 www.ayrequestrian.co.uk **17 E5**

## Rugby

### Edinburgh and East Central

**Edinburgh Rugby** *Edinburgh.* www.edinburghrugby.org **41 F8**

**Murrayfield Stadium** *Murrayfield, Edinburgh, City of Edinburgh.* The home of Scottish Rugby. Guided tours take visitors to the dressing rooms, royal box, hospitality suites dressing rooms and pitch. www.scottishrugby.org 0131 346 5000 **41 F8**

### Glasgow

**Glasgow Warriors** *Glasgow.* www.glasgowwarriors.org **28 A2**

## Watersports

### Argyll, Bute, Stirling, Trossachs

**Loch Lomond Water Ski Club** *Balloch, West Dunbartonshire.* Offers tuition in water skiing and wave boarding. www.lochlomondwaterskiclub.co.uk 01436 860632 **37 D6**

**Tighnabruaich Sailing School** *Tighnabruaich, Argyll and Bute.* Lessons in dinghy sailing and windsurfing in the sheltered waters of the Kyle of Bute. 01700 811717 www.tssargyll.co.uk **54 E2**

### Edinburgh and East Central

**Port Edgar Marina and Sailing School** *Shore Road, South Queensferry, Edinburgh, City of Edinburgh.* Offers a wide variety of sailing courses to suit all abilities. 0131 331 3330 www.portedgar.co.uk **41 F8**

### Perth, Angus, Dundee and Fife

**Splash White-Water Rafting** *Dunkeld Road, Aberfeldy, Perth and Kinross.* White-water rafting with experienced guides, as well as abseiling, bridge swinging and canyoning. 01887 829706 www.rafting.co.uk **65 C6**

### The Highlands

**Loch Insh Watersports Centre** *Kincraig, Highland.* Offers canoeing, sailing and windsurfing, as well as renting boats for fishing on the loch, mountain bikes. Ski instruction is offered on the 160ft dry ski slope. 01540 651272 www.lochinsh.com **72 B3**

**Loch Morlich Watersports Centre** *Glenmore Forest Park, by Aviemore, Highland.* This centre offers sailing, windsurfing and canoeing in the spectacular surroundings of Loch Morlich. www.lochmorlich.com 01479 861221 **72 B4**

**Raasay House** *Raasay House, Raasay, Highland.* Sailing and windsurfing courses for both children and adults as well as kayaking, rock climbing and abseiling. www.raasay-house.co.uk 01478 660266 **77 E5**

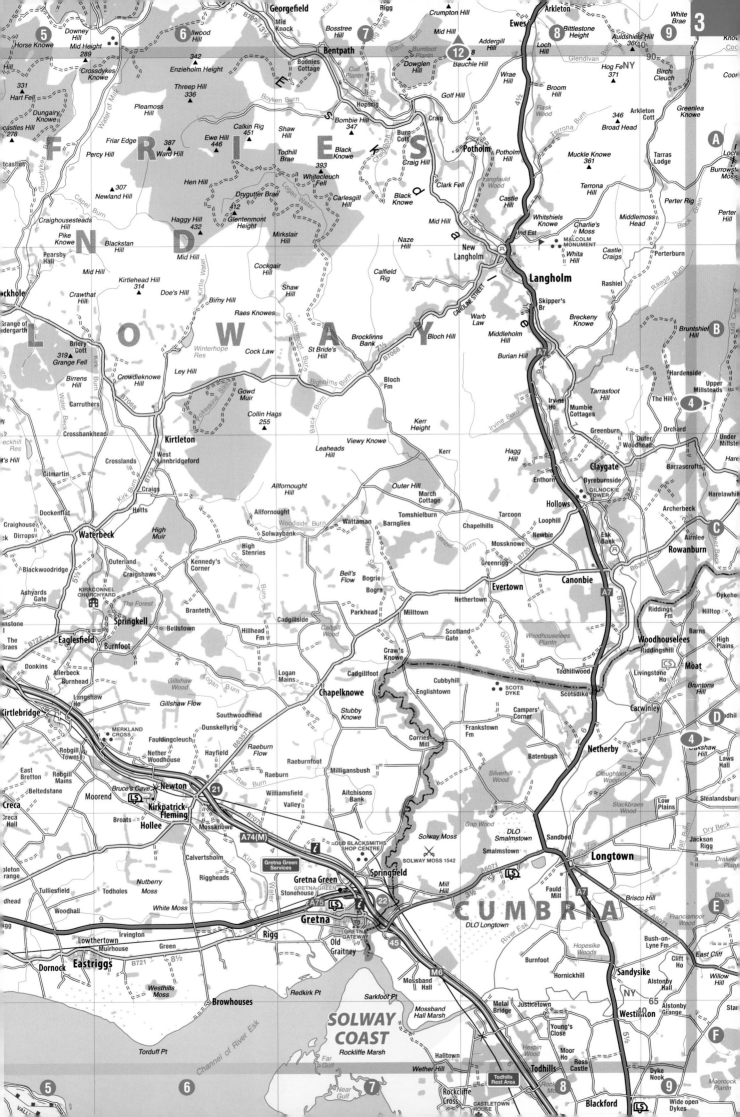

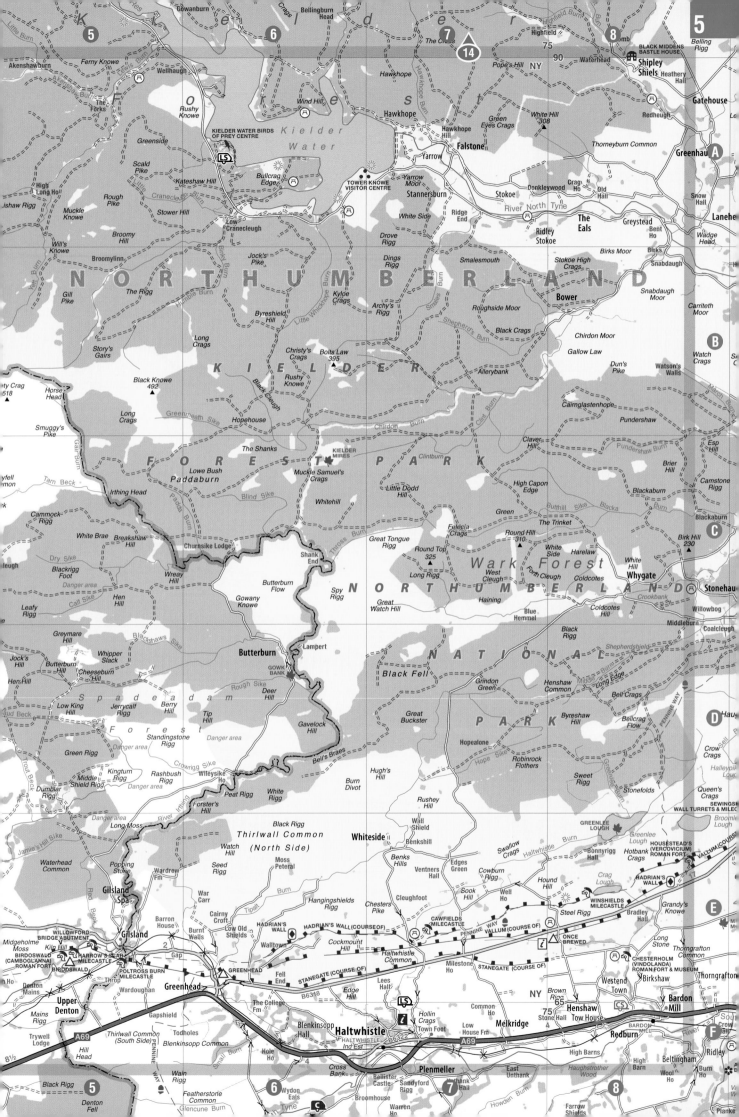

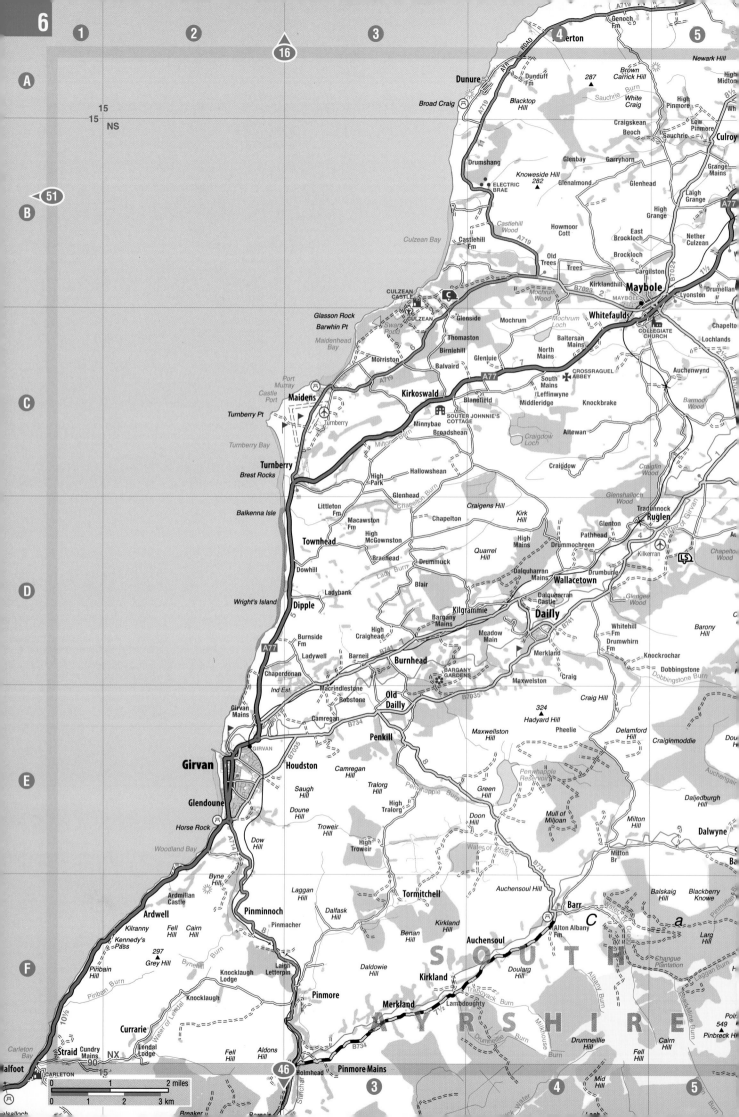

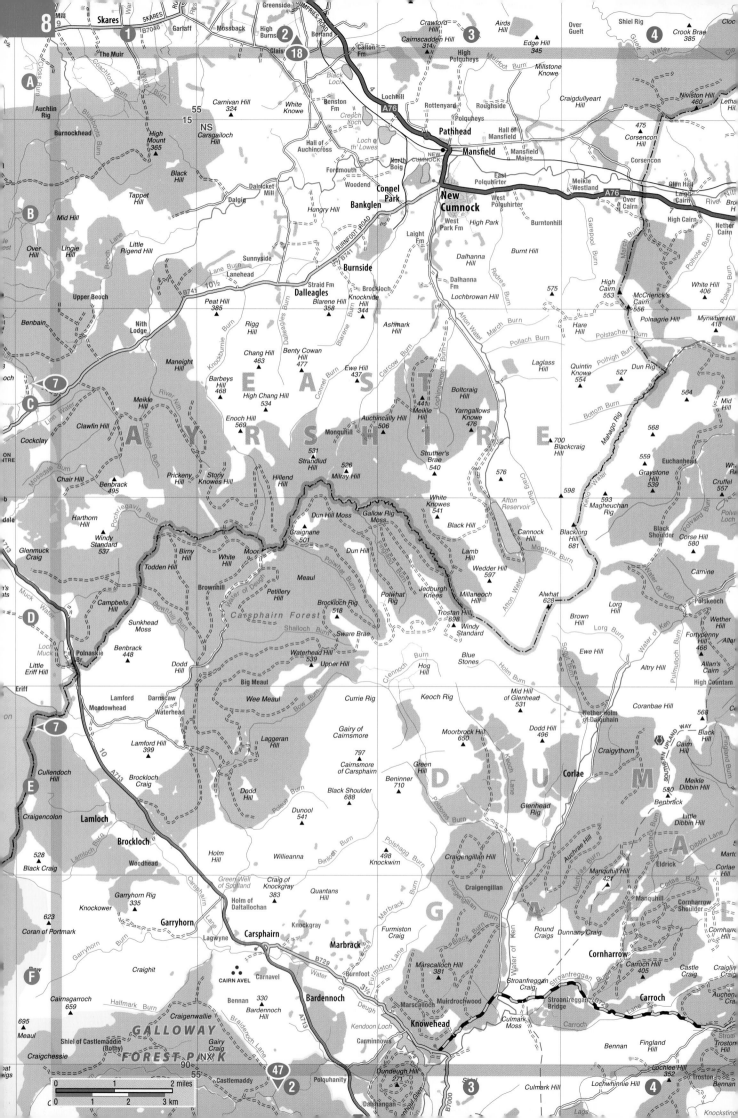

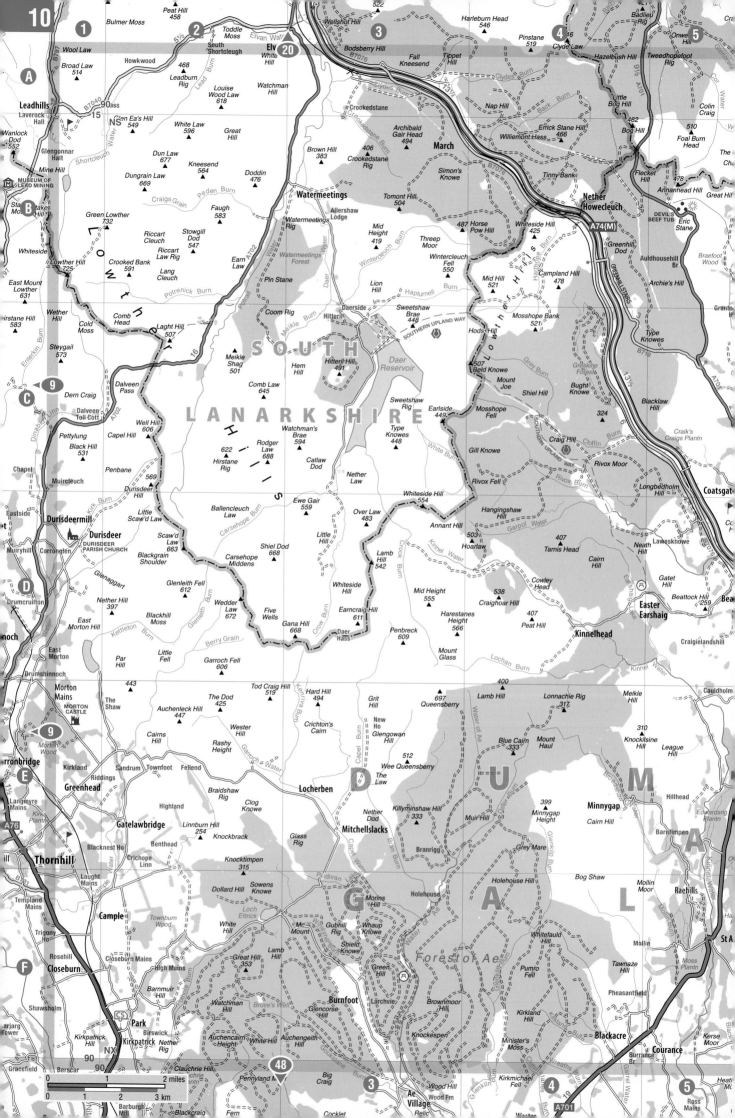

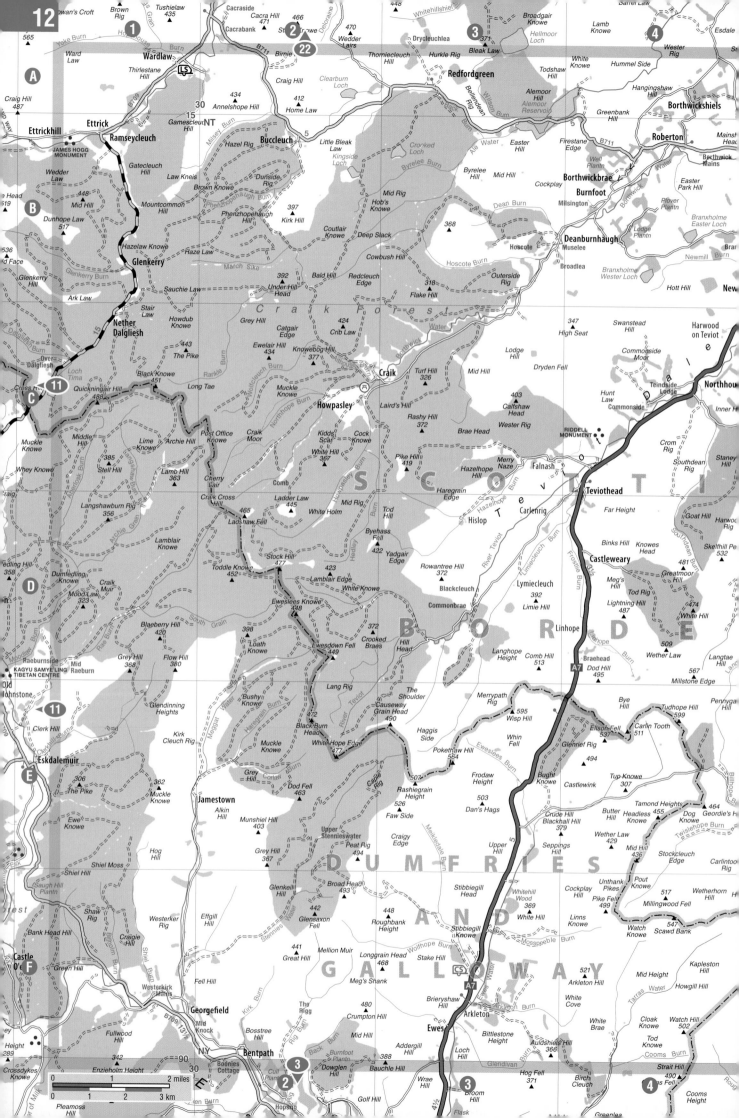

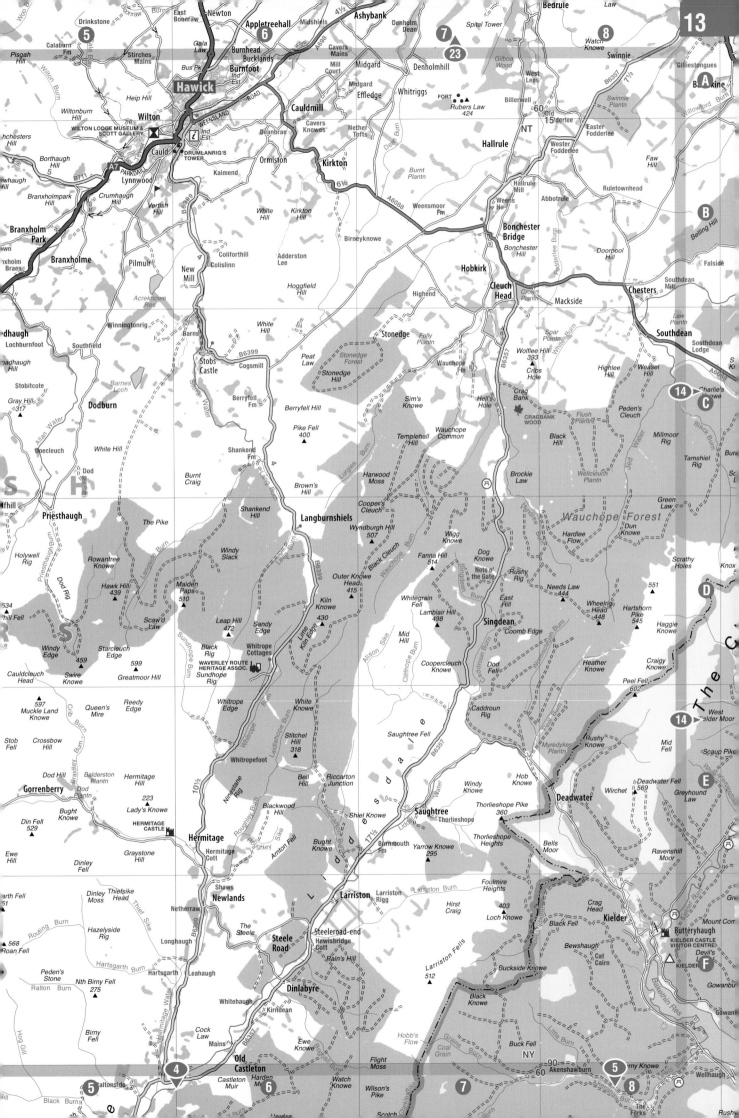

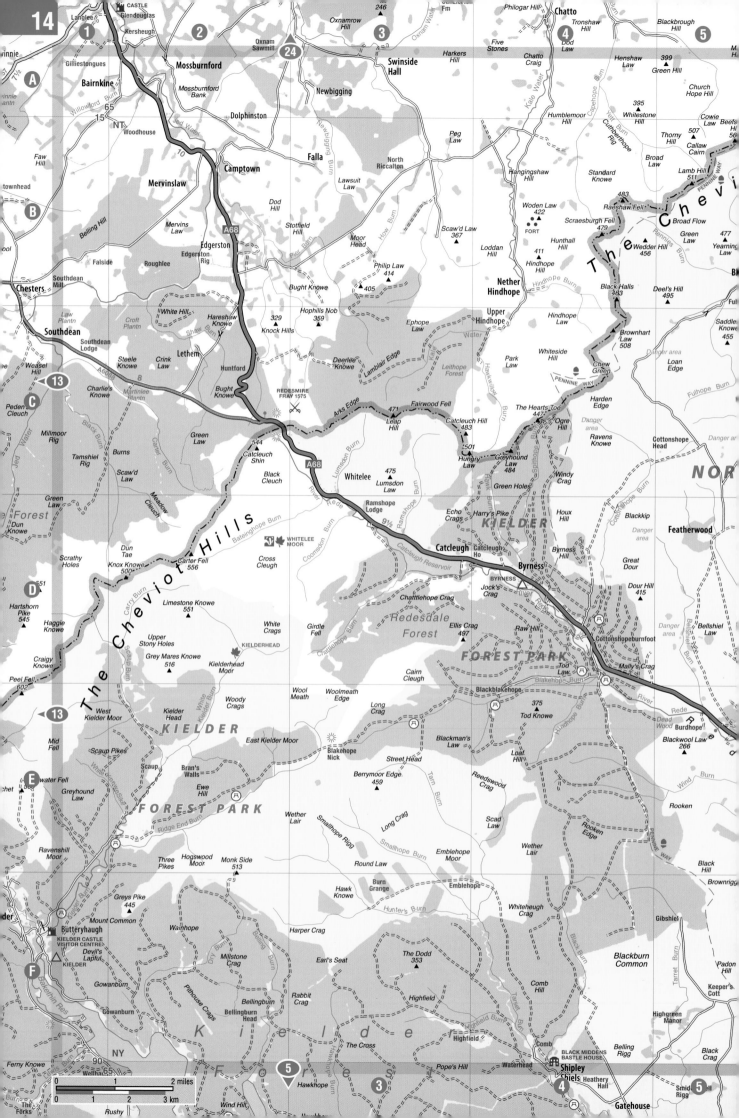

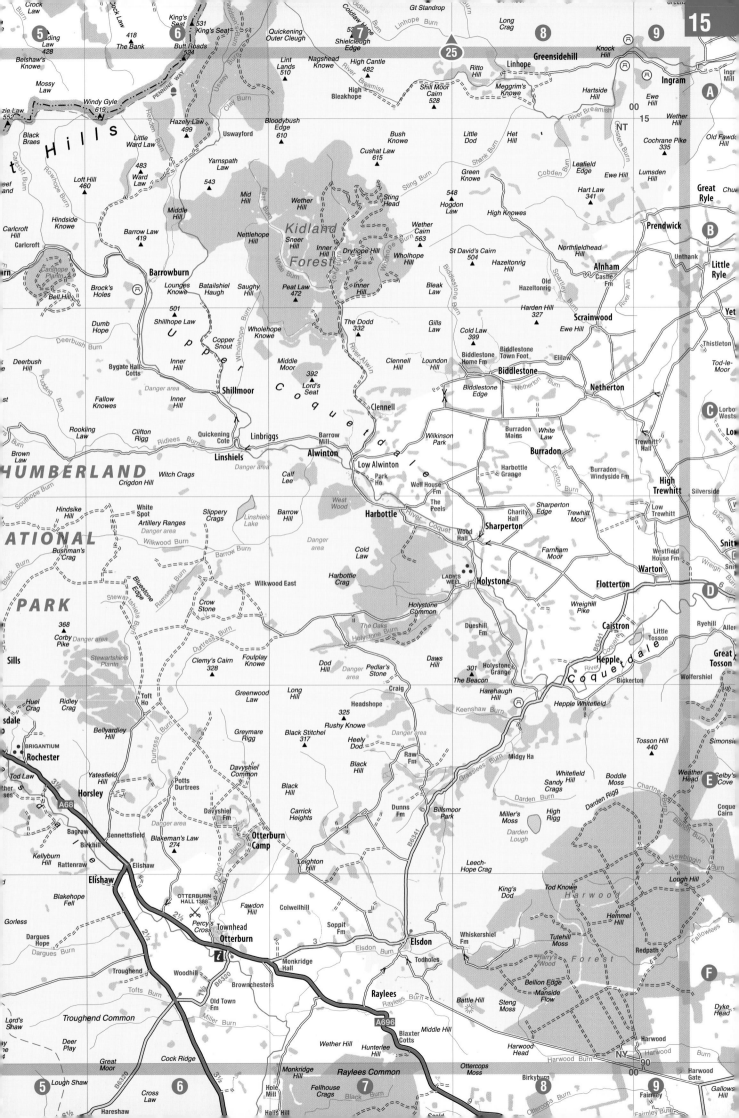

Scart Rock
Montfode
Res
Ashgrove Loch
Wood Fm
Bannoch

A78
Chapelhill
Sharphill
Middlepart
Castlehill
KILWINNING
B714
B785
DALRY RD

**26**

Horse Isle
North Bay
Broad Rock
Ind Est
Dykesmains
**Stevenson**
Retail Pk
KILWINNING ABBEY
**Kilwinni**
B779

**Ardrossan**
ARDROSSAN CASTLE
ARDROSSAN SOUTH BEACH
Ardrossan
1½
GLENCAIRN STREET
Dubbs
A78
Red Burn
Ind Est

**A**

ARDROSSAN HARBOUR
ARDROSSAN TOWN
3½
B780
2½
STEVENSON
2

BRODICK
CAMPBELTOWN
(May-Sept)
South Bay
NORTH AYRSHIRE MUSEUM
**Auchenharvie**

**Saltcoats**
Outer Nebbock
Inner Nebbock
Ind Est
Ind Est

15
40
NS

Bogside Flats

Magnum
SCOTTISH MARITIME MUSEUM
**Fulla**
Retail Pk
GL VE MU

**B**

Beach Park
Irvine Bay
AIR R

*F   I   R   T   H*

**51**
Lappock Rock

Barassie Sands
Stinking Rocks

*O         F*

BAI

Mill Rock

**C**
North Sands
Pan Rocks

*C   L   Y   D   E*
**Troon**
South Bay
South Sands

Seal Roc
Little Cr
Black

Lady Isle

**D**

**51**

**E**
St Nicho
Re
Blac

20
15
NS

Cunnin
Par

Longhill Pt

**F**
**Doonfoot**

Bower Hill
Bracken Bay
HEADS OF AYR FARM PARK
ROBER
BIRTHPLA

A719
Genoch Fm
DUNURE ROAD

**6**
**3**
**Dunure**
**Fisherton**

Dunduff Fm
**4**
287
Brown Carrick Hill
**5**
High Midton
High WH

AYR ROAD
Sauchrie Burn

Broad Craig R
B719
Blacktop Hill
White Craig
High Pinmore
Newark Hill

0      1      2 miles
0    1    2    3 km

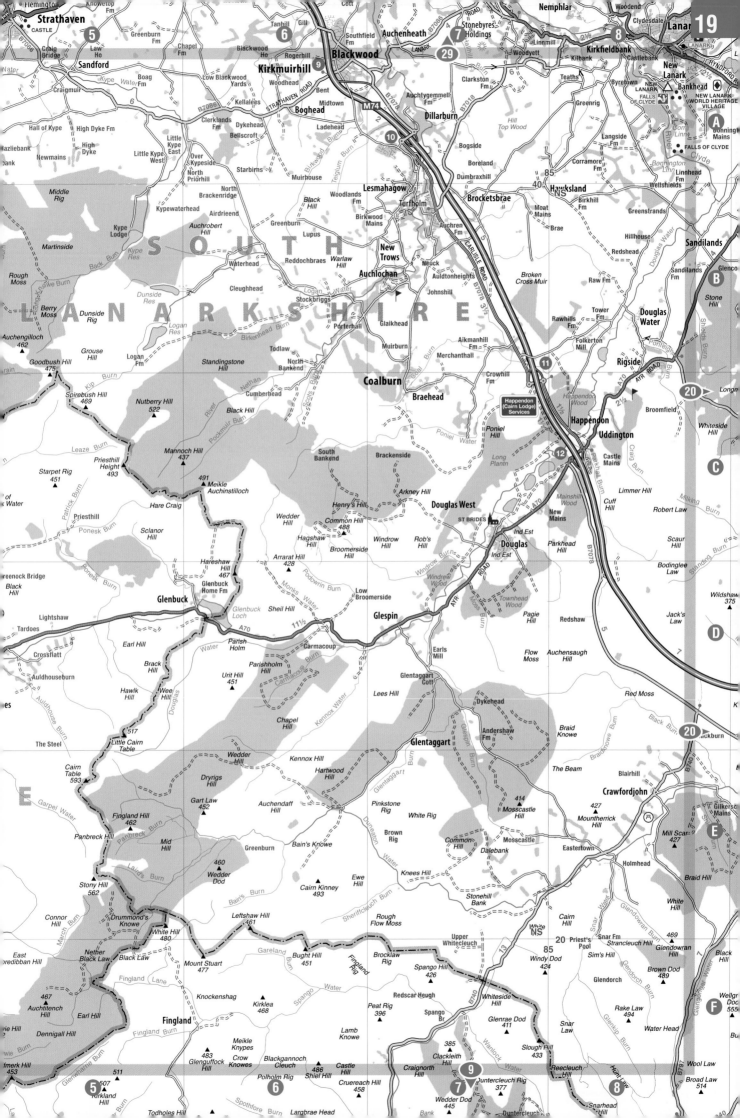

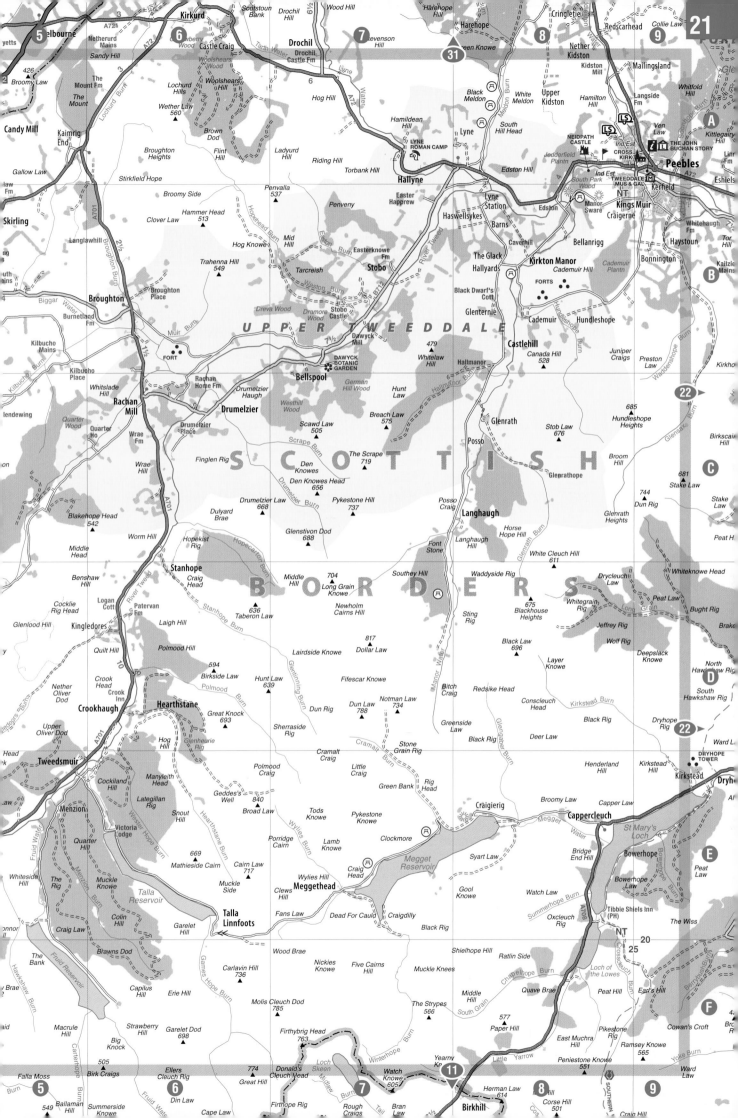

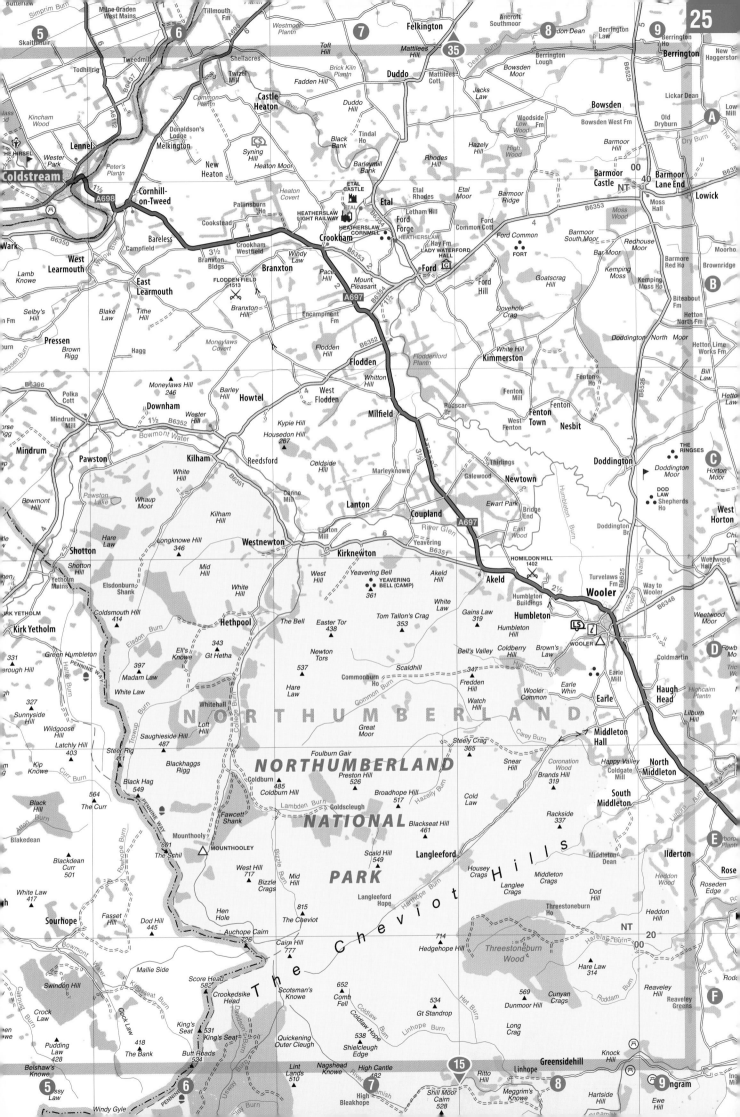

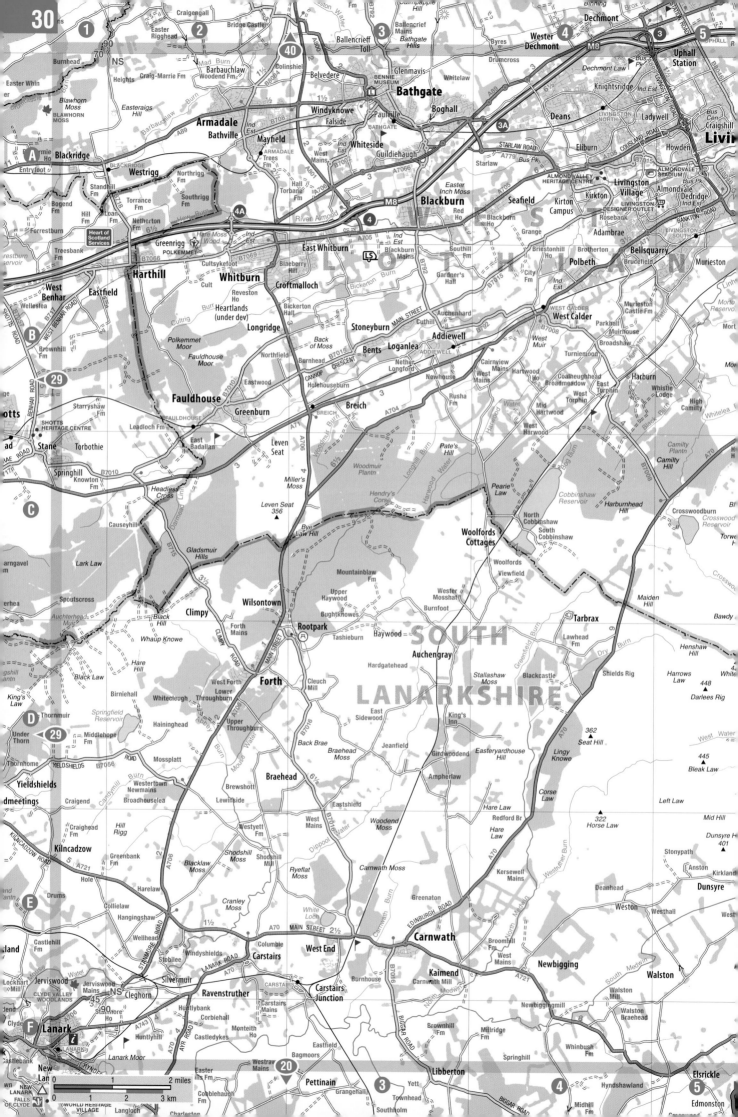

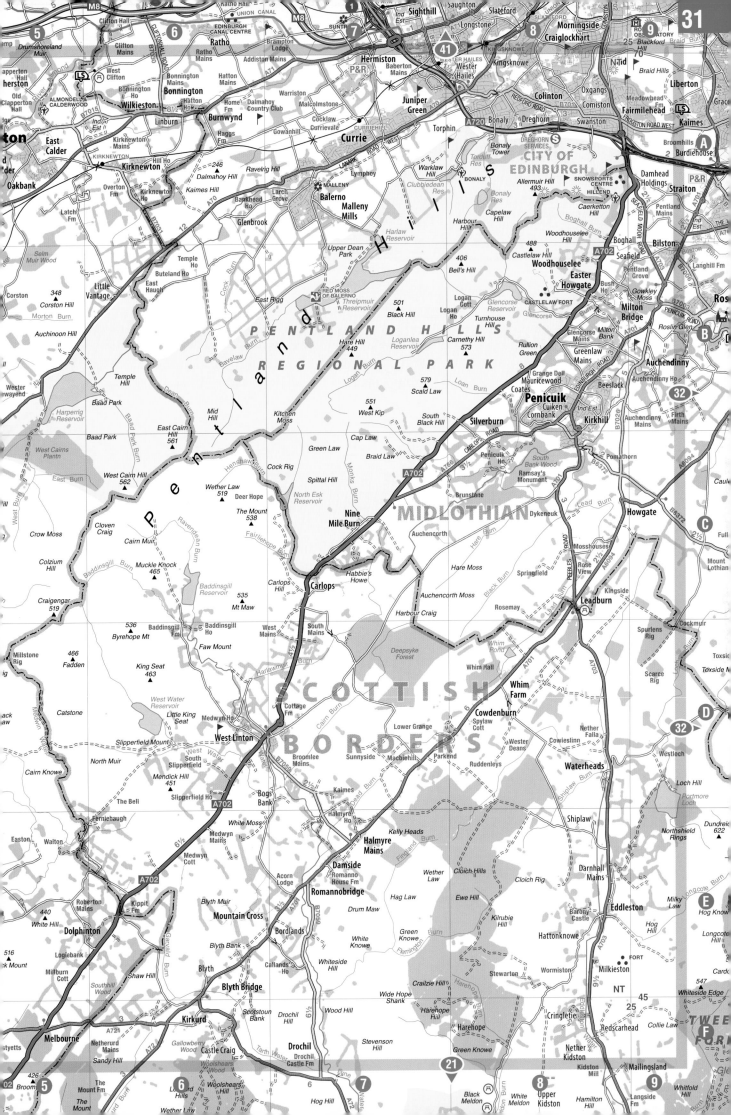

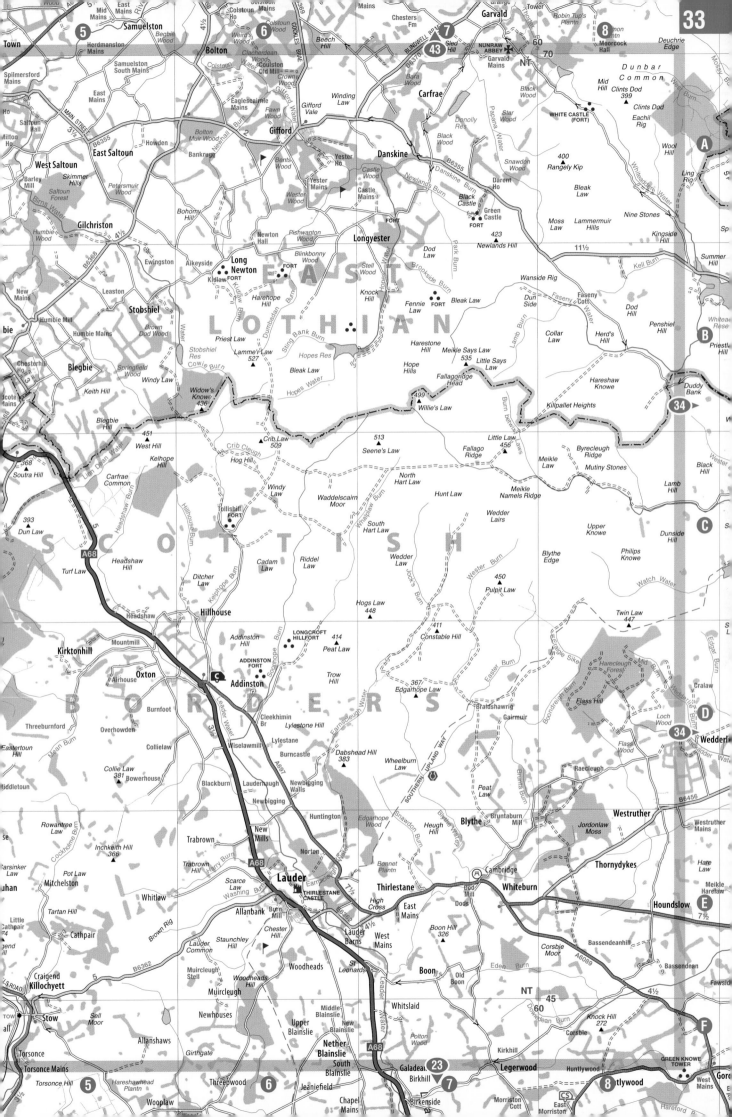

A

00
85
NT

B

**S E A**

C

D

Fast Castle
Head    Wheat Stack
Meikle Poo Craig    Telegraph
Hirst Rocks    Hill    FAST
CASTLE

Oatlee Hill

Dowlaw Burn    St Abb's Head

**Lumsdaine**    ST ABB'S HEAD

Coldingham Loch    SETTLEMENT    Horsecastle Bay

A1107    Coldingham    Lumsdaine    Mire Loch
Common    Moor    Cross    Moorside    Bell
Cambus    9½    Moor    Law    Plantn    Hill    Stoney Bay
Wood    Ho    Buskinburn    **Northfield**
Ho
Bell    Long Latch    Coldingham    **St Abbs**
Hill    Moor    St Abb's Haven
el    Drone    B6438 1½    Coldingham Bay
Hill    **Huxton**    SCHOOL    ROAD    COLDINGHAM    Yellow Craig
on    SANDS
rns    Temple    PRIORY
Hall    Callercove Pt    Hairy
Atton    Three Burn    Press    Abbey    **Coldingham**    Ness
Cott    Grange    Castle    Park    EYEMOUTH
Dalks    Press    Abbey Burn    MUSEUM
Law    Mains    Hallydown    i
Green    Grange    2½    A1107    **Eyemouth**
Wood    Plantn    Gallows    Ale Water
**Houndwood**    Law    Ind    Scout Pt
Mount    North    Est    Horse Head
A1    Alban    **Blackhill**    **Cairncross**    Wood    Fancove Head
Heugh    Breeches
Horseley    Head    Littledean    Rock
Hill    Howburn    Fox    Fm    Ayton
e Water    MAIN STREET    Covert    Aytonwood    Mains
2    A1    Ho    2½
B6437    **Reston**    East    3    **Burnmouth**
Greenburn    B6438    Loanside    Reston Mill    **AYTON**
Plantn    **Ayton**    CASTLE    Ross    Ross Pt
**Auchencrow**    Berrybank    Ayton Hill    NT
Peelwalls    19°    Chester    60
Ho    Cocklaw    Hill    00
Auchencrow    Bowie's    35
Mains    Plantn    **Prenderguest**    Peelwalls
Billiemains    Causeway Bank    Horn Burn    Millerton    Lamberton
Hill    Moor

E

F

5    6    7    8    9

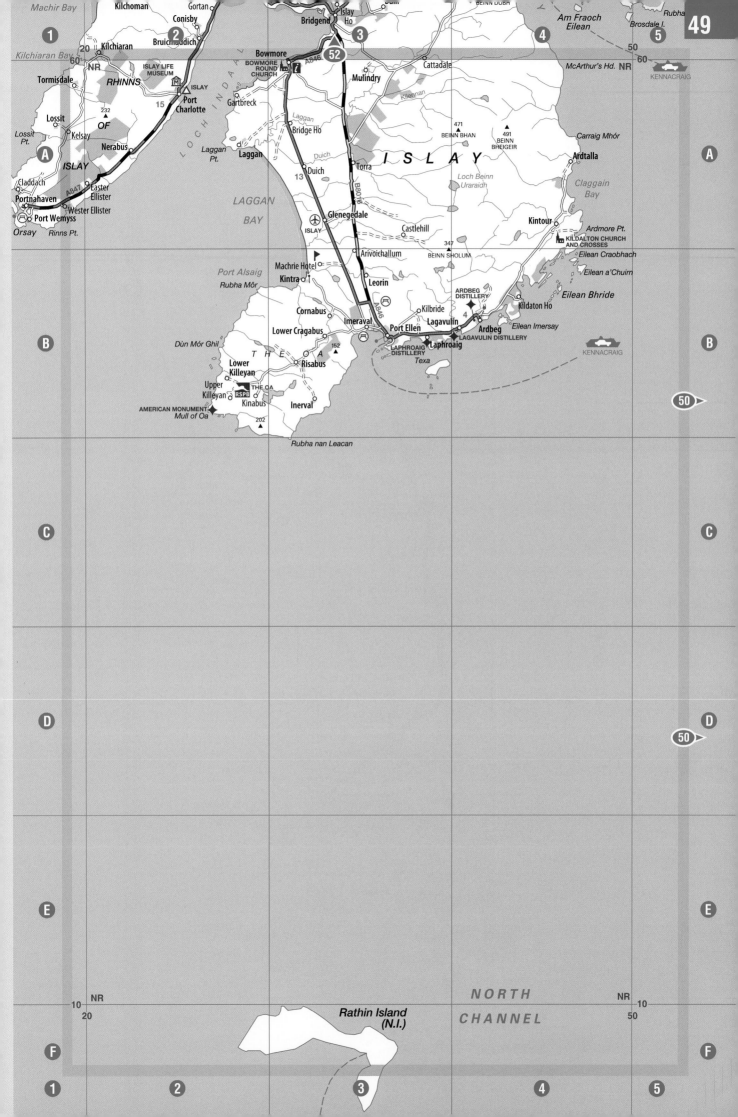

Rubh Ardalanish

① ② ③ ④

△ 60    △ 61

A

Torran Rocks

10
10
NM

B

*Dubh Artach*

Rubh'a'Geadha

*Kiloran Bay*    **Balnahard**

Uragaig

KILORAN GARDENS
**Kilchattan**    **Kiloran**
136
**COLONSAY**    Scalasaig
*Loch Staosnaig*

C

B8086

B8087

B8085
**Ardskenish**    **Garvard**
Rubha Dubh
**Balerominhor**

PRIORY
*Dubh Eilean*    ✝
**Oronsay**

*Eilean nan Ron*

D

(Summer Only)

Rubha a'Mhail

Rubha Bholsa

△ 364
SGARBH
BREAC

*Nave Island*

E

*Ardnave Pt.*

**Bunnahabhain**
BUNNAHABHAIN
DISTILLERY
*Loch a Chnuic
Bhric*

*Carraig Bhan*    **Ardnave**
316
Cnocbreac

Kilnave
*An Clachan*    **Gortantaoid**

Garra
Eallabus
Killinallan

**Sanaigmore**    *Loch Gruinart*

SOUND OF ISLAY

**Caol Ila**

CAOL ILA DISTILLERY

**Port Askaig**
B8018
Leckgruinart
FINLAGGAN
CENTRE
**Feolin Ferry**

**Braigo**
LOCH
GRUINART
*Loch
Finlaggan*
**Keills**

Smaull
**Carnduncan**
LOCH GRUINART NATURE
RESERVE VISITORS CENTRE
RSPB

A846
*Gleann Ulb*

**Ballinaby**
**Aoradh**
*Loch Cam*
**Ballygrant**

B8017
**Craigens**
A846

*Saligo Bay*    Saligo
Tighnacachla
*Loch
Ballygrant*

Balole
8

*Loch
Gorm*
**Kilmeny**

**Coull**
**Lyrabus**
*Esknish*
Lossit Lodge

*Coul Pt.*
I    S    L    A    Y
Foreland
Ho
Knockfearoch

**Sunderland**
B8018
Camas an
Staca

A847
**Blackrock**    **Redhouses**
△ 267
BEINN DUBH

*Machir Bay*
Gortan
**Daill**
*Am Fr
Eile*

**Kilchoman**
Conisby
**Islay
Ho**
**Bridgend**

NR
10

**Kilchiaran**
**Bruichladdich**

*Kilchiaran Bay*
*Loch
Indaal*
**Bowmore**

ISLAY LIFE
MUSEUM
49    A846
Cattadale
McA

60
**RHINNS**
②    △ ISLAY    ③

0    2    4 miles
OF
Gartbreck

0    2    4    6 km
Tormisdale
**ISLAY**
15
**Port
Charlotte**
232

④

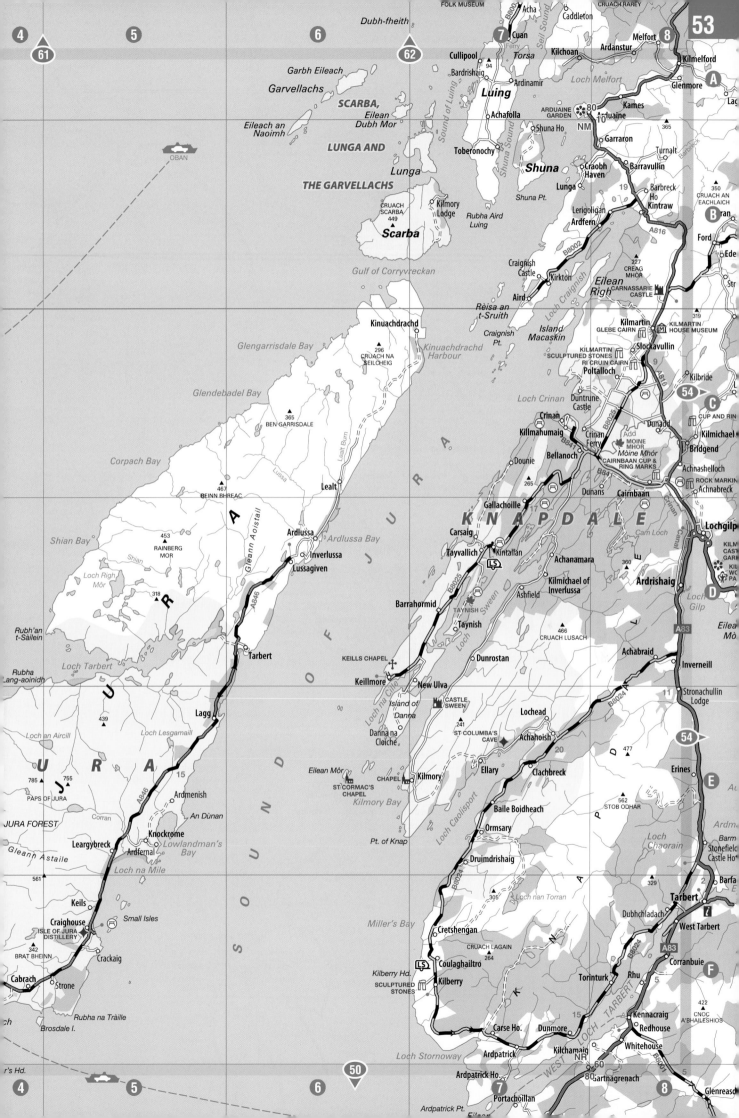

⑤ ⑥ ⑦ ⑧

Ⓐ

10
10
NP

Ⓑ

Ⓒ

Ⓓ

44 45

Ⓔ

Barns Ness

⚓Skateraw

Thorntonloch

Reed Pt.

DUNGLASS
COLLEGIATE
CHURCH

Cove

Cockburnspath

Siccar Pt.

Wheat Stack
🏰FAST CASTLE

🦋 ST ABB'S HEAD

45

St. Abb's Head

Ecclaw

A1107

245▲

Lumsdaine

Coldingham
Moor

12

Northfield

St Abbs

B6438

SOUTHERN
UPLAND WAY

Grantshouse

Huxton

Coldingham

Ale Water

St. Abb's Haven

COLDINGHAM PRIORY

Nether
Monynut

Houndwood

12

Cairncross

Eye Water

i

🅼 EYEMOUTH MUSEUM

Eyemouth

Ⓕ

SCOTTISH BORDERS

A6112

262▲

AYTON
CASTLE

Abbey
St. Bathans

Auchencrow

B6438

Reston

A1

Ayton🏰

B6355

NU
60
10

EDINSHALL
BROCH 12

B6438

B6437

B6355

Prenderguest

21

Burnmouth

⑤ ⑥ ⑦ ⑧

Lintlaw

B6355

Lamberton
Beach

Preston

Lamberton

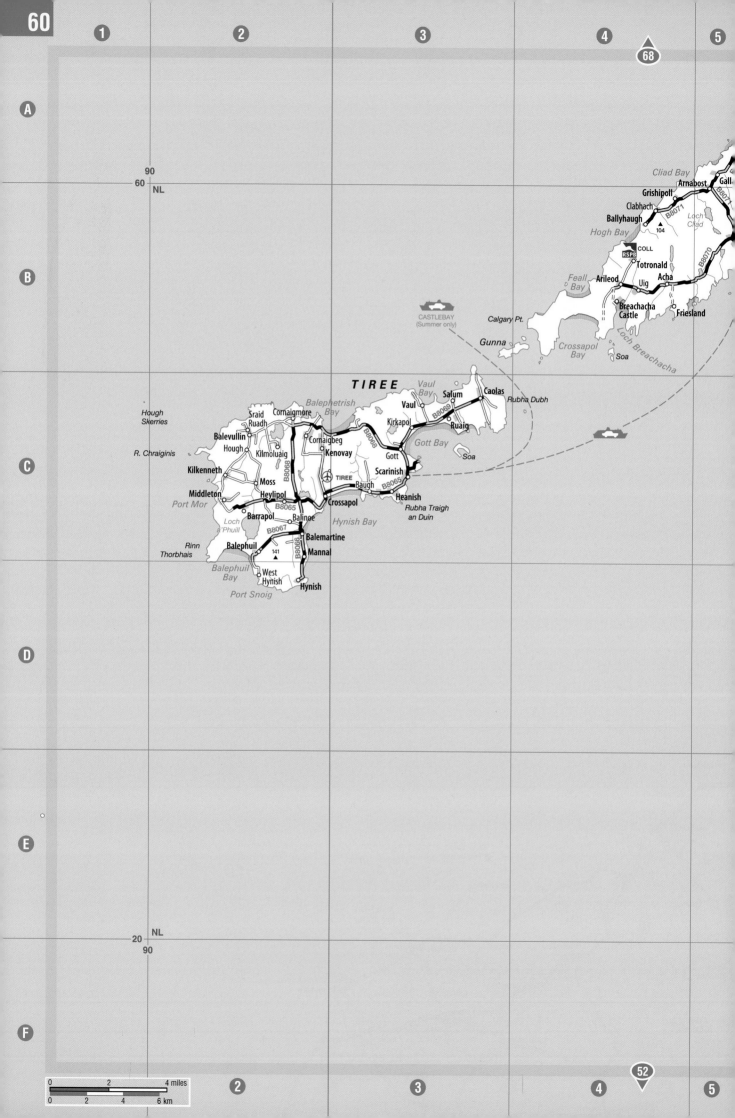

**TIREE**

Cliad Bay
Arnabost
Gall
Grishipoll
Clabhach
Ballyhaugh
*Loch Chad*
104
*Hogh Bay*
COLL
RSPB
Totronald
*Feall Bay*
Arileod
Uig
Acha
*Loch Breachacha*
Breachacha Castle
Friesland
CASTLEBAY
(Summer only)
Calgary Pt.
*Crossapol Bay*
Soa
Gunna

*Vaul Bay*
Caolas
Salum
*Rubha Dubh*
Vaul
Kirkapol
Ruaig
Hough Skerries
Sraid Ruadh
Cornaigmore
*Balephetrish Bay*
*Gott Bay*
Balevullin
Cornaigbeg
Soa
Hough
Kilmoluaig
Kenovay
Gott
R. Chraiginis
Scarinish
Kilkenneth
Moss
TIREE
Baugh
Middleton
Heylipol
Crossapol
Heanish
*Port Mor*
B8065
*Rubha Traigh an Duin*
Barrapol
Balinoe
*Hynish Bay*
*Loch a'Phuill*
B8067
Balemartine
Rinn Thorbhais
Balephuil
141
Mannal
*Balephuil Bay*
West Hynish
Hynish
*Port Snoig*

B8068
B8071
B8070
B8068
B8066

68
52

0    2    4 miles
0   2   4   6 km
90
60
NL
20
90
NL

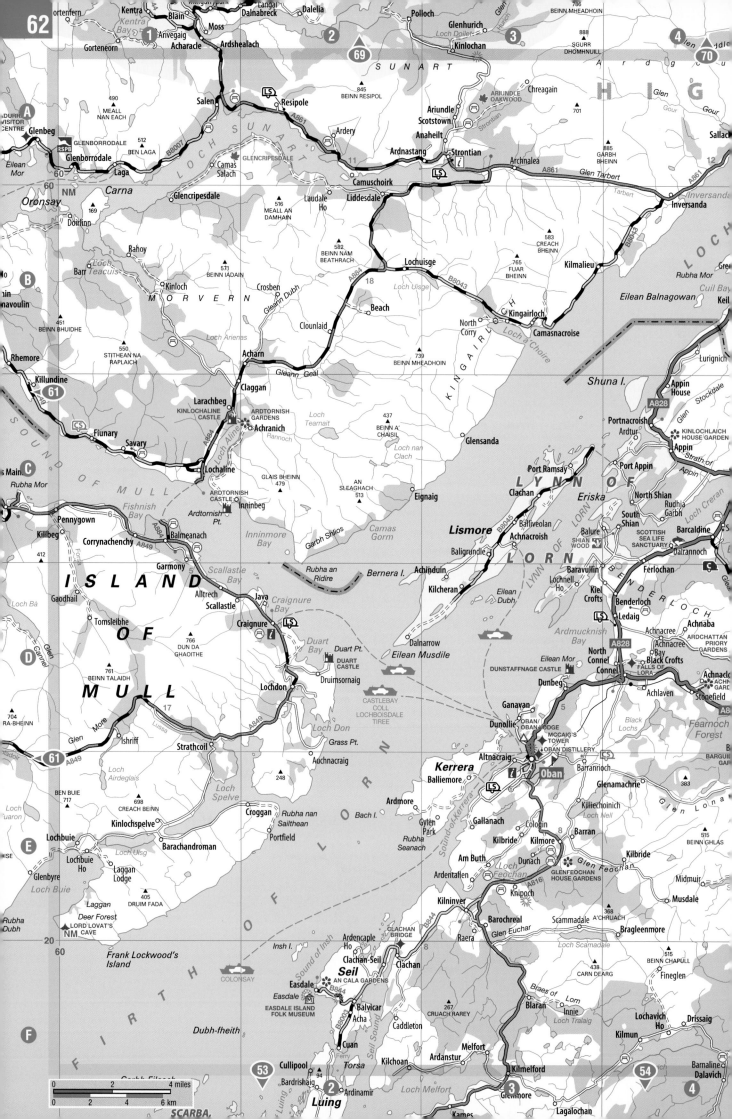

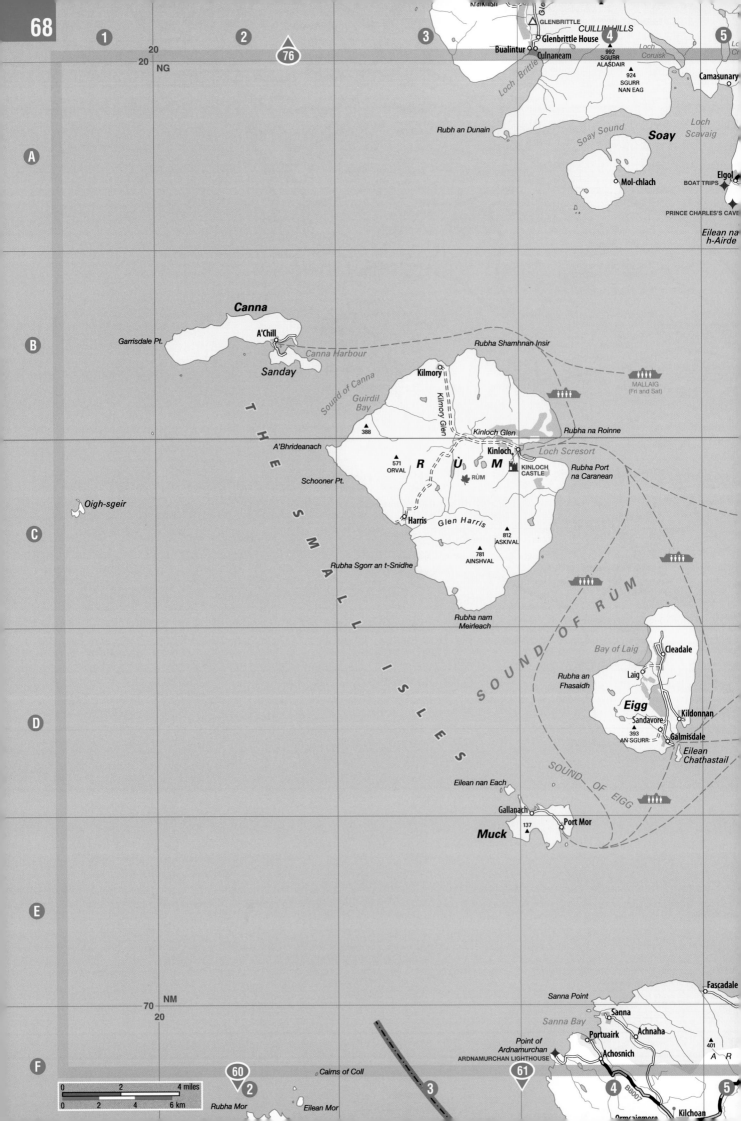

1    2    76    3    4    5

20
20
NG

Kraiknish
GLENBRITTLE
CUILLIN HILLS
Glenbrittle House
Bualintur    Culnaneam
992
SGURR
ALASDAIR
924
SGURR
NAN EAG
Camasunary

Loch
Coruisk

Rubh an Dunain
Soay Sound
Soay
Loch
Scavaig

**A**

Mol-chlach
BOAT TRIPS
Elgol

PRINCE CHARLES'S CAVE

Eilean na
h-Airde

*Canna*

Garrisdale Pt.
A'Chill
Canna Harbour
Rubha Shamhnan Insir

*Sanday*

**B**

Sound of Canna
Kilmory
MALLAIG
(Fri and Sat)

Guirdil
Bay
Kilmory Glen

388
Kinloch Glen
Rubha na Roinne

A'Bhrideanach
571
ORVAL
R    Ù    M
Kinloch
Loch Scresort

RÙM
KINLOCH
CASTLE
Rubha Port
na Caranean

Schooner Pt.

Oigh-sgeir

**C**

Harris
Glen Harris
812
ASKIVAL

Rubha Sgorr an t-Snidhe
781
AINSHVAL

S    O    U    N    D
O    F    R    Ù    M

Rubha nam
Meirleach

Bay of Laig
Cleadale

Rubha an
Fhasaidh
Laig

*Eigg*
Kildonnan

**D**

Sandavore
393
AN SGURR
Galmisdale

Eilean
Chathastail

SOUND
OF
EIGG

Eilean nan Each

Gallanach
Port Mor

*Muck*
137

T    H    E        S    M    A    L    L        I    S    L    E    S

**E**

70
NM
20

Fascadale

Sanna Point

Sanna Bay
Sanna
Achnaha

Portuairk

Point of
Ardnamurchan
ARDNAMURCHAN LIGHTHOUSE
Achosnich
401
A    R

B8007

**F**

0        2        4 miles
0    2    4    6 km

60    2    Cairns of Coll    3    61    4    5

Rubha Mor        Eilean Mor        Ormsaigmore    Kilchoan

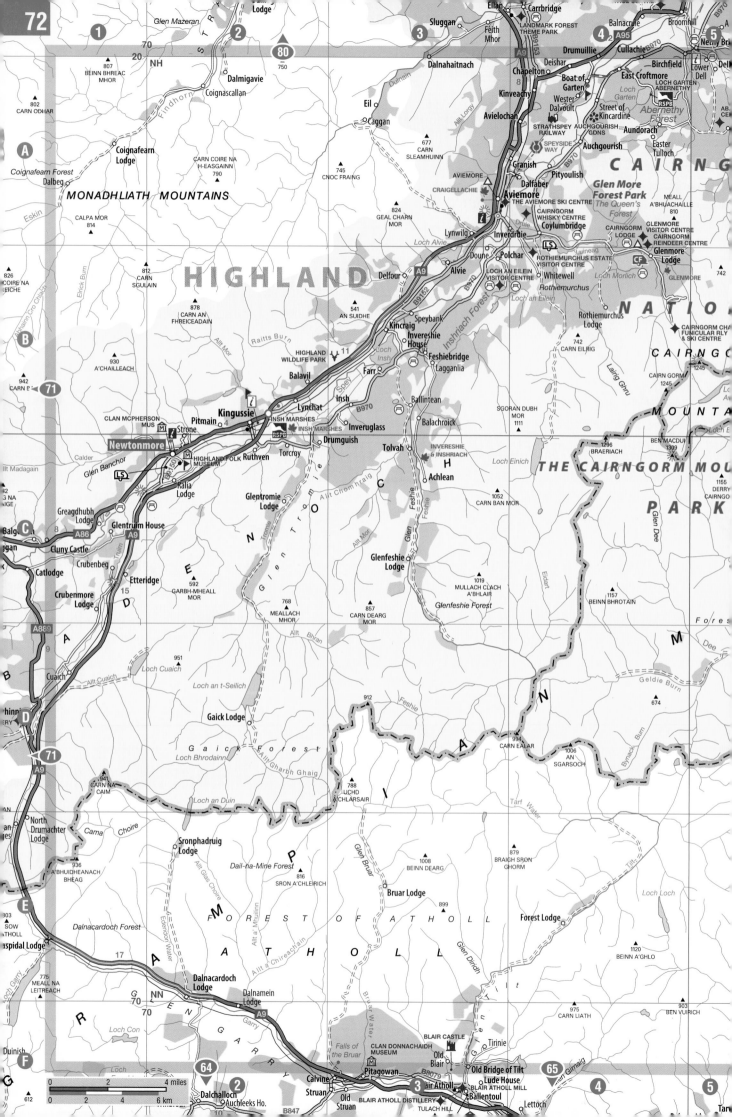

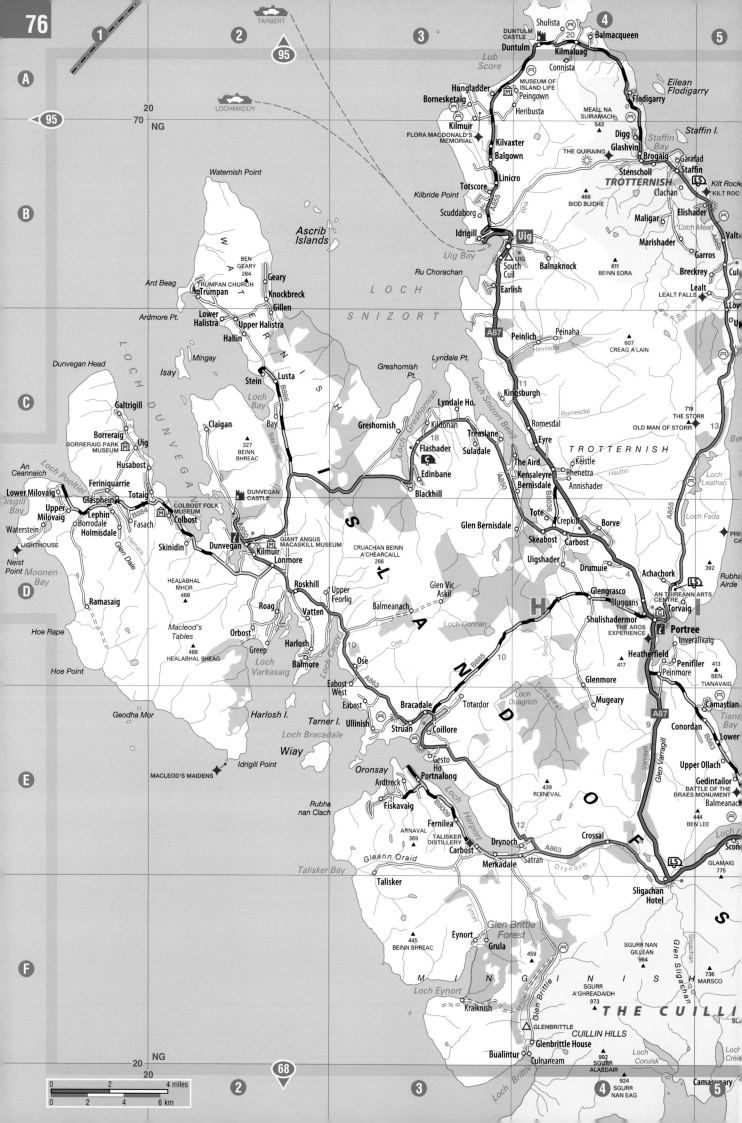

LOCH GAIRLOCH
Charlestown
Bodantionail
7 Port Henderson   Aird
B8056   Badachro
Leacnasaide   Ke
84
8
A832
420

Opinan
Shieldaig   Kerry   A
Eilean Subhainn
Loch Aslan

South Erradale
Loch Clàir
Loch.Bad an Sgalaig
Abhainn a' Gharbh Choire

VICTORIA FALLS
90   NG
70
Tallad le

Redpoint
Erradale
Dubh Loch

Loch Gaineamhach
Flowerdale   Forest
Loch na h-Oidhche

Craig
Shieldaig
875
BAOSBHEINN
Forest
B

624
BEINN BHREAC
Loch a'Bhealaich

Rubha nam Brathairean
aknock
er Tote
er Tote

Rubha na Fearn
Fearnmore

Fearnbeg
Arinacrinachd
Upper Diabaig
Alligin Shuas
985
BEINN ALLIGIN

Reaulay
Cuaig
Kenmore
Loch a' Chracaich
Ardheslaig
Lower Diabaig
Rechullin
Torridon Forest
78
LIATH
17

Island of Rona
125
Abhainn Chuaig
Allt na h-Eirigh
Inveralligin
Torridon Ho.
Fasag
TORRIDON
C

Eilean Garbh
Callakille
Upper Loch Torridon
Balgy
TORRIDON VISITOR CENTRE
Annat

Eilean Tigh   Garbh Eilean
Lonbain
493
CROIC-BHEINN
Shieldaig
A896
Ben-damph Forest

rreraig Bay
An Caol
Loch a' Sguirr
626
BEINN A'CHLACHAIN
Loch Gaineamhach
Loch Lundie
BEN SHIELDAIG
439
902
BEINN DAMH
993
MAOL CHEAN-DEA

Holm I.
254
Eilean Fladday
Loch-nan Eun
Glenshieldaig Forest
513
Kinloch Damph
Loch Coultrie
D

na h Glaise
Manish Pt.
Torran
CHAPEL OF ST MAELRUBHA
Hartfield
Applecross Forest
896
BEINN BHAN
Couldoran S
Tullich
3

NCE CHARLES'S VE
Loch Arnish
Arnish
Applecross Ho.
RASSAL ASHWOOD
Rassal Tornapress
14
Kirkton

Brochel
BROCHEL CASTLE
Applecross Bay
Milton
Applecross
G
H
A
N
D
A896

G
ISLAND OF RAASAY
385
Camusteel
Camusterrach
BEALACH NA BA
Sanachan
Glen Mor
Lochcarron

Glame
Ard-dhubh
Culduie
710
MEALL GORM
Russel
Ardaroch
Slumbay
78
A89U

Balmeanach
Balachuirn
443
DUN CAAN
Ardban
Toscaig
Achintraid
CARN NAN IOMAIREAN
E

Holoman Bay
Rubha na'Leac
Eilean na Bà
Loch Kishorn
STROME CASTLE
395
Ardnarff

vaig
vaig
Oskaig
RAASAY
Reraig Cot
Stromemore
Ardaneaskan
Stromeferry

Ollach
Raasay Ho.
Clachan
RAASAY OUTDOOR CENTRE
North Fearns
Kishorn I.
LOCH CARRON

The Braes
Narrows
Inverarish
Uags
Crowlin Islands
An Dubh-aird
Plockton
Achmore

Peinchorran
East Suisnish
Eyre
Eyre Point
Eilean Mór
Black Is.
Duirinish
CRAIG HIGHLAND FARM
Braeintra
Sallachy

Sligachan
Longay
Port Cam
Drumbuie
Achnandarach
Gleann Udalain
Loch Long
Ca

Moll
Corran a Chan Uachdaraich
Scalpay
Erbusaig
Badicaul
Balmacara Square
Allt-nan-sugh

Scalpay Ho.
Guillamon I.
Pabay
Kyle of Lochalsh
CASTLE MOIL
Balmacara
Reraig
Kirkton
Auchtertyre
A87
Conchra
Bundalloch

Luib
Dunan
Caolas Scalpay
Kyleakin
BRIGHTWATER VISITOR CENTRE
LOCHALSH WOODLAND GARDEN
Nostie
Ardelve
Carndu
634

OLD SKYE CROFTER'S HOUSE
CS
A87
Broadford Bay
Waterloo
Lower Breakish
Ashaig
Avernish
Glas Eilean
Dornie
EILEAN DONAN CASTLE

K
570
GLAS BHEINN MHOR
Corry
Broadford
Upper Breakish
Skulamus
SGURR NA COINNICH
739
Ardintoul Pt.
Totaig
Keppoch
F

N HILLS
RED HILLS
732
Old Corry
Glen Arroch
Allt Mòr
KYLERHEA OTTER HAVEN
Ardintoul
Letterfearn
Inverina

928
16
Harrapool
SKYE ENVIRONMENTAL CENTRE
A851
603
BEINN A'CHUIRN
NG

na heach
E
Torrin
B8083
Bernera
Galltair

Faoilean
Kilbride
Glenelg
BERNERA BARRACKS
Scallasaig
Cnoc Fhionn
20
RATAGAN
90

Kirkibost
5
301
Heast
7
69
610
GEN ASLAK
Glenelg Bay
Eilanreach
GLENELG BROCHS
8
Còsag
Shiel Bri

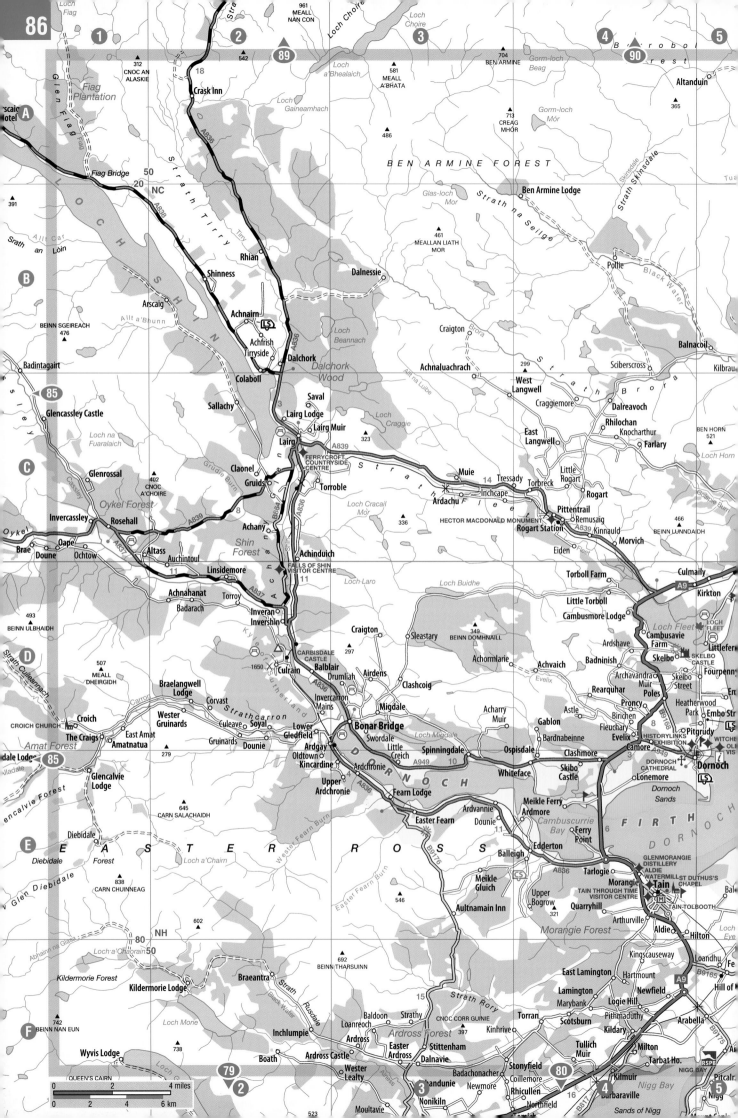

CNOC COIRE
NA PEARNA
Corrichoich
Knockally
Dunbeath
Dunbeath Bay

5
6
7
8
Ramscraigs
DUNBEATH CASTLE

Abhainn na Frithe
90
CNOC AN
EIREANNAICH
705
MORVEN
91
517

Bórrobol
Lodge
A897
Sulsgill Burn
Wag
Borgue

17
626
SCARABEN
Newport

STRATH
Langwell Forest
Aultibea
Ceann Leathad
nam Bò
A

EAG NAM FIADH
387
Kildonan Burn
555
CREAG
SCALABSDALE
Langwell Ho.
Langwell Water
Berriedale
20
20

Craggie
Kildonan Lodge
BAILE AN ÒR GOLDRUSH SITE
BEINN DUBHAIN
422
BADBEA CLEARANCE VILLAGE
ND

Burn
OF
414
Helmsdale
Ousdale

Craggie Burn
KILDONAN
Torrish
Kilphedir
A897
Ord Point

345
ELDRABLE
HILL
417
Marrel
HELMSDALE
Navidale

West
Helmsdale
TIMESPAN HERITAGE CENTRE
B

628
BEINN
DHORAIN
592
Gartymore
East
Helmsdale
Helmsdale

Glen Sletdale
Glen Loth
Portgower

Lothmore

Gordonbush
11
Kilmote

Brora
538
COL-BHEINN
Lothbeg
Crakaig

Carrol
A9
Lothbeg Pt.

Kintradwell
C

Achrimsdale
East Clyne
West Clyne
Clynelish
CLYNELISH
DISTILLERY
Dalchalm

Fanich
Brora

377
AGAR FEOSAIG
Doll

Backies
Uppat
Dunrobin Mains
9
n Brora

DUNROBIN CASTLE
MUSEUM & GARDENS

Golspie
D

ONE
ST OFFICE
CENTRE

R T
Tarbat Ness
TARBAT NESS LIGHTHOUSE
Wilkhaven

hiteness
nds
Hilton

TARBAT DISCOVERY
CENTRE
Bindal
E

Portmahomack
Seafield
Rockfield

Inver
Arboll
Tarrel

Lochslin
Wester
Arboll
Toulvaddie
Geanies House

agall
Lower
Pitkerrie
NJ

Rhynie
ation
B9165
80
20

Fearn
B9166
Cadboll

ARN
BEY
Hilton of Cadboll

ans of Tullich
Balintore
F

Broomton
SHANDWICK STONE

Chapelhill
Shandwick

Port an Righ
5
80
6
7
81
8
Covesea
LOSSIEMOUTH FISHERIES
& COMMUNITY MUSEUM

King's Cave
Skerries
Stotfield

Covesea

CAPE WRATH

Kearvaig

SGRI
BHE

Geodha Ruadh na Fola

Insho

*Bay of Keisgaig*

Loch
Keisgaig

Geodha Ruadh

▲
457
FASHVEN

*Am Balg*

Sandwood
Loch

▲
423
BÉINN DEARG

Rubh'an Fhir Léithe

▲
485
CREAG
RIABHACH

Loch na
Gainimh

Strath Shinary

Sheigra
Balchrick
Blairmore
Dróman    Oldshore Beg
Oldshoremore

▲
521
FARRMHEALL

Eilean Roin Mor

Loch Clash
Kinlochbervie
Badcall
B801    Inshegra
Achriesgill

Gualin Ho.

*Bagh Loch an Roin*

Rhivichie

Achlyness

L. na Claise
Carnaich

Loch Dughaill

Ceathramh Garbh
Ardmore Pt.
Rubha Ruadh

Rhiconich

GANU M
908
Foinav

Ardmore    Portlevorchy
Skerricha

Fanagmore
Tarbet

**NORTH-WEST SUTHER**

Loch Laxford

Loch a'Garbh-
bhaid Mór~

*Handa Island*

Foindle

Sound of Handa

Loch nam
Brac

Laxford Bridge

A894

Badnabay

▲
787
ARKLE

*Scourie Bay*

Scourie More
Rubh'Aird an t-Sionnaich

Scourie

Gorm Loch

Laxford

A838

Lochstack Lodge

Loch Stack

Upper Badcall    Lower Badcall

719
BEN STACK

Strath Stack

Airdachuilir

*Badcall Bay*

18

BEINN AUSKAIRD
386

Achfary

332

*Eil. a'Bhreitheimh*

Duartbeg
Rubha a'Mhucard

Loch
Crocach

R E A Y    F O R

Lochmore Lodge

*Meall Mór*

A894

Calbha
Mór

Duartmore
Bridge

Duartmore
Forest

Loch na Creige
Duibhe

Calbha
Beag

*Eddrachillis Bay*

Loch a'Chairn Bhàin

Kylestrome

Loch an Leathaid
Bhuáin

547
Forest

Point of Stoer

R. nan Còsan

Culkein
Drumbeg

Loch Nedd

Ardvár

Kyleku

Glendhu

Cirean Geardail

Eilean Chrona

161

Oldany
Island

Kylesku

Glendhu

Gleann

*Loch Glendhu*

Dubh

Rubha
Stoér
Cluas Deas

Culkein

*Clashnessie
Bay*

Oldany

Unapool

530
BEINN AIRD
DA LOCH

Achnacarnin

Drumbeg

B869

7

Clashmore

Clashnessie

Nedd
Glenleraig

Newton

Loch
Glencoul

Glen Coul

Loch
an'Eirc

Balchladich
Rienachait

13

Loch
Poll

8

Gleann Leireag

808
QUINAG

NC
00
30

Stoer

Rubh'a'
Mhill Dheirg

*Bay of Stoer*

Loch
Crocach

Loch an
Leothaid

5

EAS COUL AULIN
WATERFALL

BEINN
776

Clachtoll

Lochassynt Lodge

A894

BEINN UIDHE
740

75

Gorm Loch

R. Leum
melvich

84

2

85

Skiàg Bridge

Rhicarn

Little
Assynt

A837

Inver

Achmelvich
ACHMELVICH

0    2    4 miles
0    2    4    6 km

NC
80
00

1    2    3    4    5

A

B

C

D

E

F

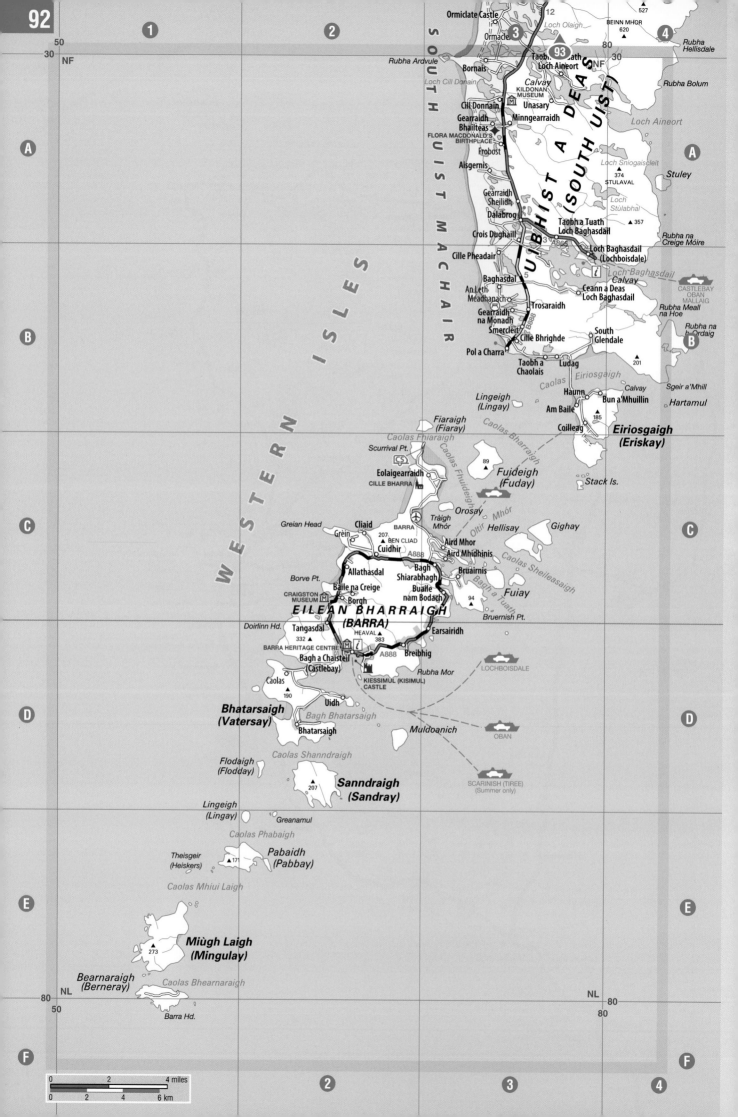

**SOUTH UIST MACHAIR**

**WESTERN ISLES**

Ormiclate Castle
Ormacleit
Loch Olaigh
BEINN MHOR
620
527
Rubha Hellisdale

Rubha Ardvule
Bornais
Taobh a Tuath
Loch Aineort
KILDONAN MUSEUM
Calvay
Rubha Bolum
Loch Cill Donain
Cill Donnain
Unasary
Loch Aineort
Gearraidh Bhailteas
Minngearraidh
FLORA MACDONALD'S BIRTHPLACE
Frobost
Aisgernis
Loch Sniogaiscleit
374 STULAVAL
Stuley

Gearraidh Sheilidh
Dalabrog
Taobh a Tuath Loch Baghasdail
357
Rubha na Creige Móire

Crois Dughaill
A865
Loch Baghasdail (Lochboisdale)
Cille Pheadair
Baghasdal
Calvay
CASTLEBAY OBAN MALLAIG
An Leth Meadhanach
Ceann a Deas Loch Baghasdail
Rubha Meall na Hoe
Gearraidh na Monadh
Trosaraidh
Smercleit
B888
South Glendale
Rubha na h Ordaig
Cille Brighde
Pol a Charra
Taobh a Chaolais
Ludag
201
Caolas Eiriosgaigh
Lingeigh (Lingay)
Haun
Calvay
Sgeir a'Mhill
Am Baile
Bun a'Mhuillin
Hartamul
Coilleag
185
**Eiriosgaigh (Eriskay)**

Fiaraigh (Fiaray)
Scurrival Pt.
Caolas Bharraigh
Caolas Fhiaraigh
89
Fuideigh (Fuday)
Stack Is.
Eolaigearraidh
CILLE BHARRA

Greian Head
Cliaid
Grèin
BARRA
207 BEN CLIAD
Cuidhir
Tràigh Mhór
Orosay
Oitir Mhór
Hellisay
Gighay
Aird Mhor
A888
Aird Mhidhinis
Caolas Sheileasaigh
Allathasdal
Bagh Shiarabhagh
Bruairnis
Baile na Creige
Bagh a Tuath
Fuiay
Borve Pt.
CRAIGSTON MUSEUM
Borgh
Buaile nam Bodach
94
**EILEAN BHARRAIGH (BARRA)**
Doirlinn Hd.
Bruernish Pt.
Tangasdal
HEAVAL 383
Earsairidh
332
BARRA HERITAGE CENTRE
Breibhig
A888
Bagh a Chaisteil (Castlebay)
Rubha Mor
LOCHBOISDALE
Caolas
KIESSIMUL (KISIMUL) CASTLE
190
Uidh
**Bhatarsaigh (Vatersay)**
Bagh Bhatarsaigh
Muldoanich
OBAN
Bhatarsaigh
Flodaigh (Flodday)
Caolas Shanndraigh
207
**Sanndraigh (Sandray)**
SCARINISH (TIREE) (Summer only)
Lingeigh (Lingay)
Greanamul
Caolas Phabaigh
Theisgeir (Heiskers)
Pabaidh (Pabbay)
171
Caolas Mhiui Laigh
**Miùgh Laigh (Mingulay)**
273
Bearnaraigh (Berneray)
Caolas Bhearnaraigh
NL 80 50
Barra Hd.

0 2 4 miles
0 2 4 6 km

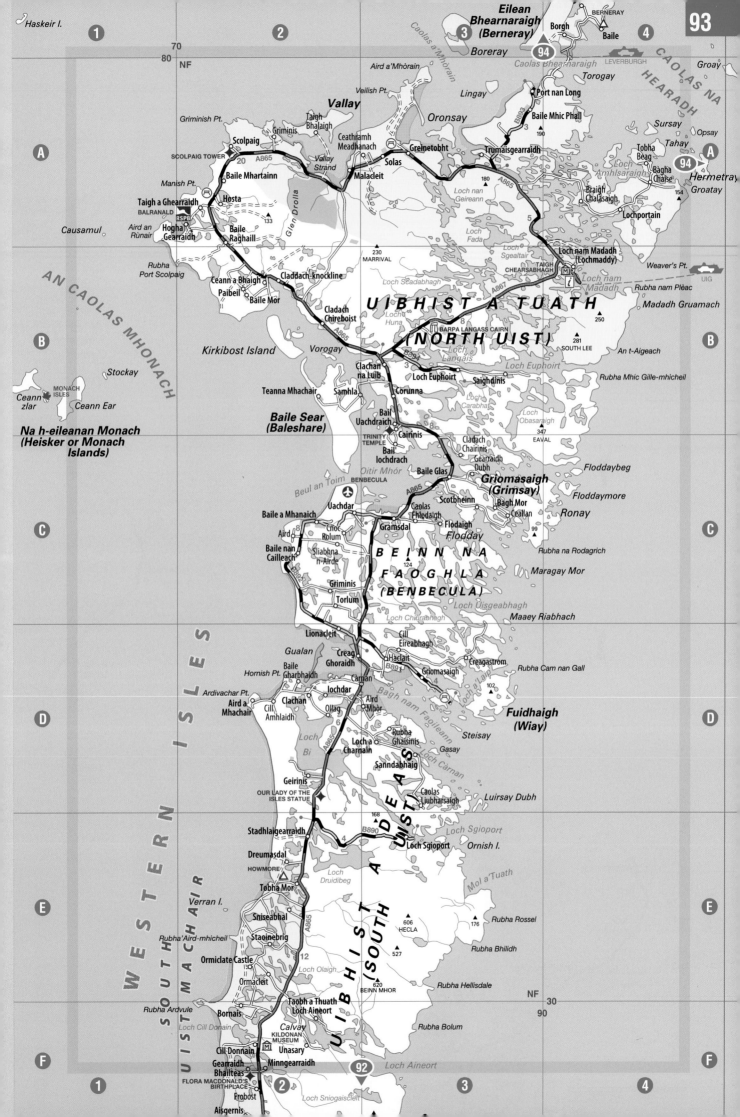

Morsgail
Forest

Beiniseabhal

Strandabhat

Tabost
KERSHADER    13
Marbhig
Calbost

LEWIS,

96

Ceann
Tarabhaigh
A859    6
Airidh a
Bhruaich
Ceann
Shiphoirt
97

Taobh a' Ghlinne
Grabhair
B8060

Loch
nan
Eilean

Taobh a' Ghlinne
Grabhair

Loch Odhairn
Kebock Head

A

STULAVAL
579

Aird an
Troim

Sgiacleit

Tom an
Fhuadain

Orasaigh
Leumrabhagh

40    10

659
ULLAVAL

Aline Lodge
Seaforth I.

Aird a' Mhulaidh
Scaladal

PARK
OR
PAIRC

Eisgean

Loch Shanndabhat

NB

Srianach

UISGNAVAL
MORE
729

CLISHAM
799

17

572
BEINN MHOR

Loch Shell or Loch Sealg

Eilean Iubhard

CEANN A TUATH NA
HEARADH

A859

Maraig

449

470
CRIONAIG

Mol Truisg

B

13

Miabhag
Bun Abhainn
Eadarra

Eilean
Anabaich

Loch Shiphoirt

Loch Claidh

Gob Rubh'Uisenis
Rubha Bhrollum

Loch Bhrollum

559

Old Whaling Station

RHENIGIDALE

Loch
an
Tairbeart

Rubha
a'Bhaird

CAOLAS NAN EILEAN

Cul na
h-Aird

Reinigeadal

Garbh
Eilean

UIST

Isay

Aird Asaig
3

Leacainn

Taobh
Siar

Oban Beag

Urgha

Loch Trollamarig

Na h-Eileanan Mòra
(Shiant Islands)

Eilean Mhuire

436

Urgha

Eilean an Tighe

BEN LUSKENTYRE

467

Tairbeart
(Tarbert)

Direcleit

Carragraich

Caolas Scalpaigh
Carnach

Sgeotasaigh

Rudha Crago

South Harris
Forest

A859

Miabhag

Scalpay

Eilean
Scalpaigh
(Scalpay)

C

A HEARADH
(HARRIS)

Drinisiadar

Kennacley

Ceann
a Bhàigh

Plocropol Pt.

386

Aird Mhighe

Greosabhagh

Plocrapol

WESTERN

Liceasto
Leac a Li
Collam
Cliuthar

Scadabhagh

Rubha
Bhocaig

Beacrabhaic

Caolas
Stocinis

Loch Greosabhagh

ideabhagh

Manais

Stockinish I.

Cuidhtinis

Loch Fleoideabhagh

ISLES

D

oirseam
eabhagh

arabay I.

Loch Fionnsbhagh

Fladda-chùain

Eilean Trodday

Rubha Hunish

Rubha na h-Aiseig

Shulista

Balmacqueen

DUNTULM
CASTLE

20

Duntulm

Kilmaluag

Connista

E

Lub
Score

Hungladder
Bornesketaig

MUSEUM OF
ISLAND LIFE

Peingown
Heribusta

TR

55

MEALL NA
SUIRAMACH

Flodigar

Digg

Kilmuir

FLORA MACDONALD'S
MEMORIAL

Kilvaxter
Balgown

45

543

THE QUIRAING

Glashvin
Brog

Stenscholl

Waternish Point

Linicro

466
BIOD BUIDHE

Kilbride Point

Totscore

A855

TROTTERNISH

F

Ascrib
Islands

LOCHMADDY

Scuddaborg

Idrigill

Uig

Uig Bay

Ru
Chorachan

South
Cuil

UIG

Baln ck

611
BEINN EDRA

Marish

Earlish

4    5    6    BEN
LARY
284

Geary
Knockbreck

7

Ard Beag
TRUMPAN CHURCH
Trumpan

76

LOCH
SNIZORT

8

1
2
3
4
5
A
B
C
D
E
F
90
70
NA
20
WESTERN ISLES
Bàgh Dhail Beag
SHAW
Siabo
GEARRANNAN BLACKHOUSE VILLAGE
GARENIN
Dail Be
Dail Mor
Na Gearrannan
Borghastan
Carlab
Campay
Loch Chàrlabhaigh
DUN CARLOWAY BROCH
Dun Charlabhaigh
Ciribhig
Floday
Little Bernera
Harsgeir
Bostadh
IRON AGE HOUSE
Crothair
An Galan Uigeach
AN CAOLAS
Tobson
Pabay Mor
Loch Ròg an Ear
Tolastadh a Chaolais
Aird Uig
Vacsay
BERNERA
Bhalasaigh
Breacleit
Bhaltos
Bàgh Fhiabhaig
Cnip
Great Bernera
A858
205
Cliobh
Vuia Mór
Circebost
Barraglom
Keava
Miabhig
Rìof
Tacleit
Timsgearraidh
Uigen
Loch Ròg
Iarsiadar
Tobhtarol
Eilean Kearstay
Cradhlastadh
B8011
Vuia Beag
Crulabhig
Calanais
Ard More Mangersta
Cairisiadar
Floday
Lundal
CALANAIS STANDING STONES
Càrnais
Eadar Dha Fhadhail
Linsiad
Mangurstadh
SUAINAVAL
429
Geisiadar
B8059
Loch Smuaiseabhat
Loch Suaineabhal
256
Aird Fenish
Ungisiadar
B801
Loch Tungabhat
Einacleite
Aird Brenish
Islibhig
574
MEALISVAL
Loch Ròg
Scaliscro
Loch Grunabhat
Giosla
B8011
Breanais
Giosla
Loch Chaolartan
Loch Fuaroil
19
Loch Airigh na h-Airde
Mealasta
397
BEINN MHEADHONACH
Mealasta Island
Caolas an Eilein
Loidse Mhorsgail
Loch Morsgail
Loch Cro Criosdaig
Loch Coirigerod
Tamanabhagh
Loch Tamanabhaigh
Loch Beiniseabhal
LOCH LANGABHAT
Morsgail Forest
Loch Bòdabhat
Ceà
Tarabha
Loch Tealasabhaigh
Loch Reasort
Kearstay
94
Bràighe Mòr
Scarp
Loch Crabhadail
Abhainn Bhe
Uladail
95
0
2
4 miles
6 km

E D A Y

Eday Sound

Ness

Holm of Huip

Huip Ness

7

5
Banks
Skaill
ST MAGNUS CHURCH

Mae Ness
Km Holm
Side

6
Backaland
101
South Side
Sandybank
Stenaquoy
Veness

100

Links Ness
Odie
STRONSAY

Papa Stronsay

8

80

30

HY

Seal Skerrie
War Ness

Egilsay
Onziebust

Huip Sound
Whitehall Village

Grice Ness

B9064
Brinian

Muckle Green Holm

Linga Holm

St Catherine's Bay

Mill Bay

Odness

A

CUBBIE'S ROO'S CASTLE AND ST MARY'S CHAPEL
Hawn
Wyre
Pt. of the Graand

North Taing

Wardhill

Everbay
STRONSAY

Rousay Sound

S T R O N S A Y

Grobister

Odin Bay

Gairsay Sound
Sweyn Holm

Rothiesholm

Bay of Holland

Dishes
Kirbister
Burgh Hd.

UST
102
Gairsay

The Galt
Ness of Ork

Rothiesholm Hd.

Holland

Lamb Hd.

Veantrow Bay

Burroughston

Greenli Ness

Tor Ness

Bay of Houseby

Edmonstone

Bay of Linton

Auskerry Sound

B9058

Auskerry

Shapinsay
MILL DAM SHAPINSAY
RSPB

Haughland

F I R T H

Balfour Mains
Crossgate
64
B9059

Taing
BALFOUR CASTLE
Balfour

Helliar Holm
Newlot

B

de Firth
Car Ness
Haco's Ness

Shapinsay Sound

ABERDEEN LERWICK

Work
ORKNEY MUSEUM

Rerwick Hd.

ORTAK VISITOR CENTRE
Craigiefield

Yinstay
Linksness

Mull Hd.

Kirkwall
ST MAGNUS CATHEDRAL
Berstane

Hall of Tankerness

Den Wick

capa
Inganess Bay

The Ness

KIRKWALL
HIGHLAND PARK DISTILLERY
KIRKWALL

Deer Sound

North Halley
43

Tradespark
Whitecleat

Deerness
Skaill

Sandside Bay

A961
Longtownmail

Grindigar

Roana Bay

N
10
Toab
Sebay

Gritley

capa Bay
7
100

Braebuster

Pt. of Ayre

Foubister

B9050

B9051

C

A

D
North Dawn
NORWOOD MUSEUM

Upper Sanday

Newark Bay

Corn Holm

Hardbreck
B9052

Copinsay

OW
y of Sandoyne
Howequoy Hd.
St Mary's
ITALIAN CHAPEL
Braehead

Lamb Holm

Cornquoy

Rose Ness

Glims Holm

Holm Sound

SSIL AND VINTAGE CENTRE
Echnaloch Bay
Northtown

da
Hillside
Burray
A961

Burray Ness

Water Sound
Burray Village
Southtown

St. Margaret's Hope
14
Grimness
B9044

Rumley Pt.

D

B9043
Brandyquoy
Papley

Grim Ness

wall
Aikers

Newark Bay

lwick
Lythes
118

SOUTH RONALDSAY

kquoy
A961
Linklater

Wind Wick

Halcro Hd.

das Ho.
Cleat

E

wick
B9041
Brough
Liddel

TOMB OF THE EAGLES AND BRONZE AGE HOUSE
Old Hd.

h Ness

F I R T H

ND

80

80

Muckle Skerry

F

Pentland Skerries

5
6
7
8

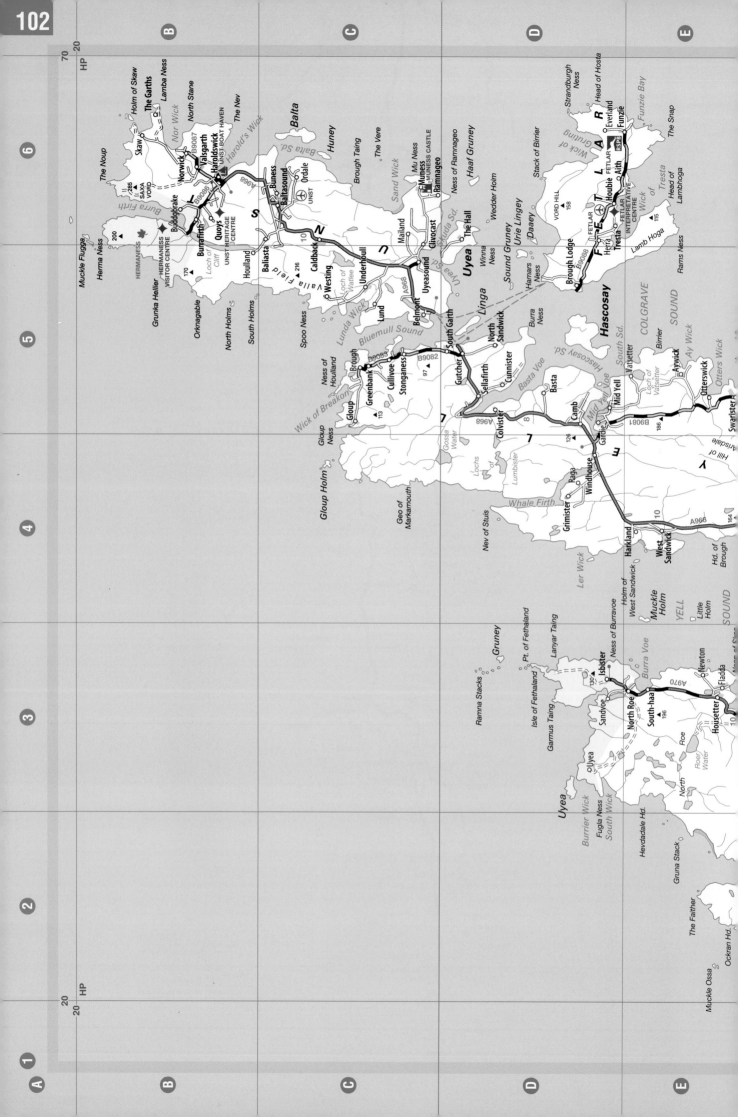

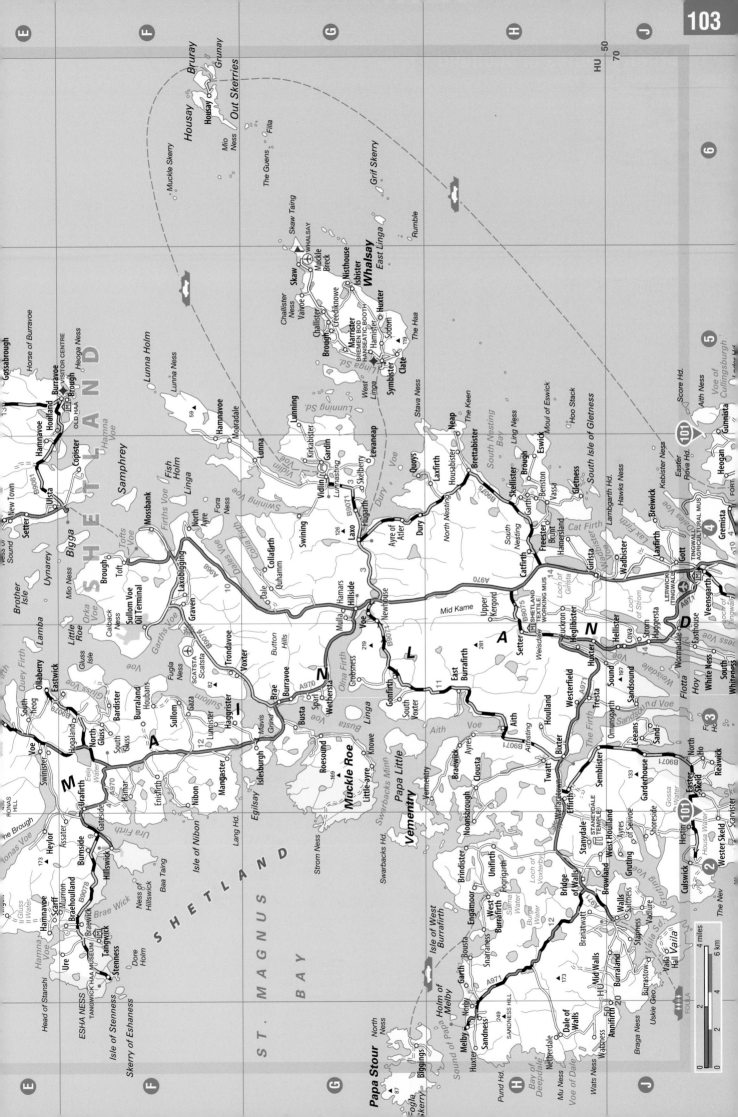

# Main ferry routes in Scotland

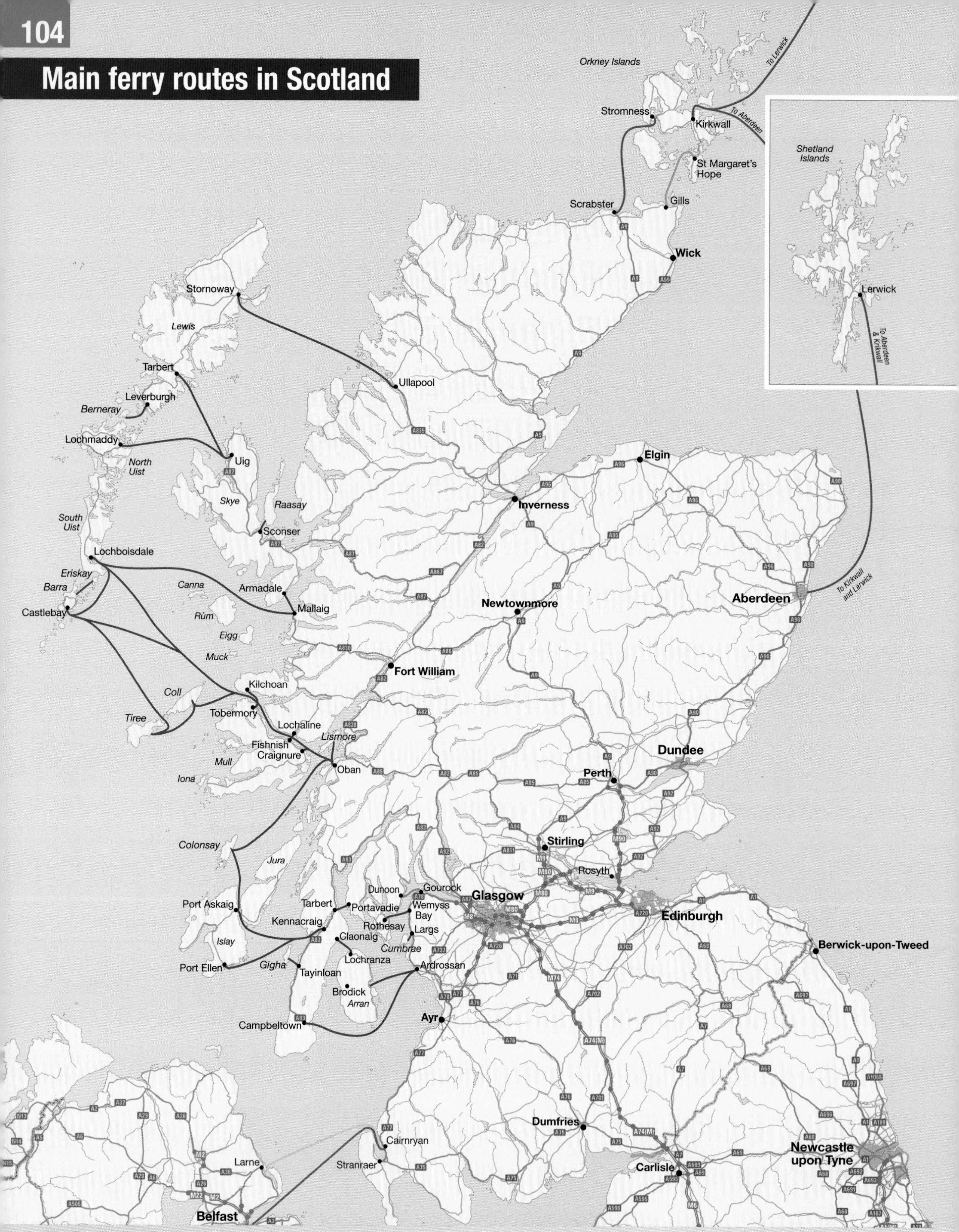

*Orkney Islands*

Stromness
Kirkwall
St Margaret's Hope
Scrabster
Gills
Wick

*To Lerwick*
*To Aberdeen*

*Shetland Islands*

Lerwick

*To Aberdeen & Kirkwall*

Stornoway
*Lewis*
Tarbert
Leverburgh
*Berneray*
Lochmaddy
*North Uist*
Uig
*Skye*
*Raasay*
Sconser
Ullapool
Elgin
Inverness
*South Uist*
Lochboisdale
*Eriskay*
*Barra*
Castlebay
*Canna*
Armadale
Mallaig
Newtownmore
Aberdeen
*To Kirkwall and Lerwick*
*Rùm*
*Eigg*
*Muck*
Kilchoan
Fort William
*Coll*
Tobermory
Lochaline
*Lismore*
Dundee
*Tiree*
Fishnish
Craignure
Oban
Perth
*Iona*
*Mull*
Stirling
Rosyth
*Colonsay*
*Jura*
Dunoon
Gourock
Glasgow
Edinburgh
Port Askaig
Tarbert
Portavadie
Wemyss Bay
Largs
Berwick-upon-Tweed
Kennacraig
Rothesay
*Islay*
*Cumbrae*
Claonaig
Port Ellen
*Gigha*
Lochranza
Ardrossan
Tayinloan
Brodick
*Arran*
Ayr
Campbeltown
Dumfries
Cairnryan
Newcastle upon Tyne
Larne
Stranraer
Carlisle
Belfast

**Caledonian MacBrayne**
www.calmac.co.uk
0800 066 5000

**Northlink Ferries**
www.northlinkferries.co.uk
0845 6000 449

**Orkney Ferries**
www.orkneyferries.co.uk
01856 872 044

**P&O Irish Sea**
www.poferries.com
0800 130 0030

**Pentland Ferries**
www.pentlandferries.co.uk
0800 688 8998

**Shetland Islands Council**
www.shetland.gov.uk/ferries
01595 693535

**Stenaline**
www.stenaline.co.uk
08447 70 70 70

**Western Ferries**
www.western-ferries.co.uk
01369 704452

# Town plans

## Town plan symbols

| | |
|---|---|
| ▬▬▬ | **Motorway** |
| ▬▬▬ | **Primary route** – dual/single carriageway |
| ▬▬▬ | **A road** –dual/single carriageway |
| ▬▬▬ | **B road** – dual/single carriageway |
| ───→ | **Minor through road, one-way street** |
| ▬ ▬ ▬ | **Pedestrian roads** |
| ▬▬▬ | **Shopping streets** |
| ┄┄┄┄ | **Railway** |
| ┼┼┼🚋 City Hall | **Tramway with tram stop** |
| ▬ | **Railway or bus station** |
| ▭ | **Shopping precinct or retail park** |
| ▭ | **Park** |
| Ⓗ | **Hospital** |
| Ⓟ | **Parking** |
| ⛨ | **Police station** |
| PO | **Post office** |
| ♿ | **Shopmobility** |
| ⊖ Bank ● West St | **Underground or metro station** |
| ▲ | **Youth hostel** |

## Tourist information

| | |
|---|---|
| ✝ | **Abbey or cathedral** |
| 🏛 | **Ancient monument** |
| 🐟 | **Aquarium** |
| 🖼 | **Art gallery** |
| 🦅 | **Bird garden** |
| 🏛 | **Building of public interest** |
| 🏰 | **Castle** |
| ⛪ | **Church of interest** |
| 🎬 | **Cinema** |
| ❀ | **Garden** |
| ⚓ | **Historic ship** |
| 🏠 | **House** |
| 🏡 | **House and garden** |
| 🏛 | **Museum** |
| ✦ | **Other place of interest** |
| 🚂 | **Preserved railway** |
| ⌖ | **Railway station** |
| 🗿 | **Roman antiquity** |
| 🎭 | **Theatre** |
| | **Tourist information centre** |
| 𝒊 | open all year |
| 𝒊 | summer only |
| 🐘 | **Zoo** |

## Aberdeen

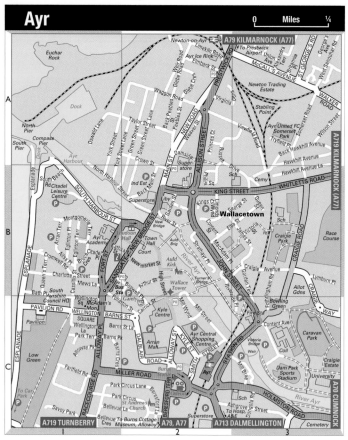

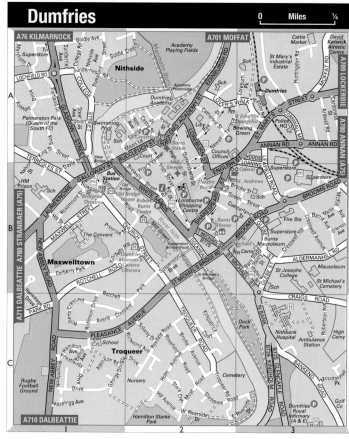

## Ayr

## Dumfries

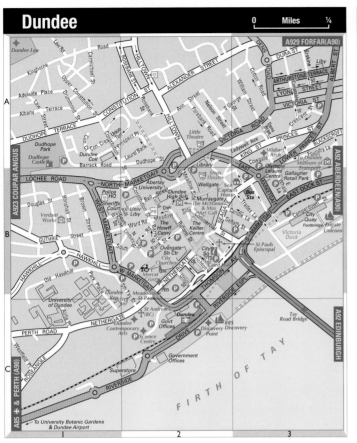

**Dundee**

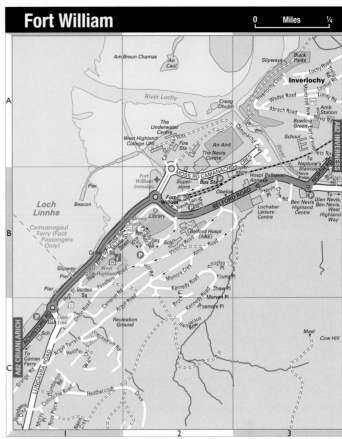

**Fort William**

## Dundee

| | | | |
|---|---|---|---|
| Abertay University . B2 | Drummond St . . . . . A1 | Ladywell Ave . . . . . . A3 | Roseangle . . . . . . . . C1 |
| Adelaide Pl . . . . . . . A1 | Dudhope Castle ▦ . A1 | Laurel Bank . . . . . . A2 | Rosebank St . . . . . . A2 |
| Airlie Pl . . . . . . . . . C1 | Dudhope St . . . . . . A2 | Law Rd . . . . . . . . . A1 | RRS Discovery ⚓ . . C2 |
| Albany Terr . . . . . . A1 | Dudhope Terr . . . . . A1 | Law St . . . . . . . . . A1 | St Andrew's ✝ . . . . C2 |
| Albert St . . . . . . . . A3 | Dundee ⇌ . . . . . . . C2 | Library . . . . . . . A2/A3 | St Pauls |
| Alexander St . . . . . A2 | Dundee | Library and Steps | Episcopal ✝ . . . . B3 |
| Ann St . . . . . . . . . . A2 | Contemporary | Theatre ▦ . . . . . A2 | Science Centre ✦ . C2 |
| Arthurstone Terr . A3 | Arts ✦ . . . . . . . . . C2 | Little Theatre ▦ . . A2 | Seagate . . . . . . . . B2 |
| Bank St . . . . . . . . . B2 | Dundee High | Lochee Rd . . . . . . . B1 | Sheriffs Court . . . . B1 |
| Barrack Rd . . . . . . . A1 | School . . . . . . . . B2 | Lower Princes St . . B2 | Shopmobility . . . . . B2 |
| Barrack St . . . . . . . B2 | Dundee Law ✦ . . . . A1 | Lyon St . . . . . . . . . A3 | South George St . . . A2 |
| Bell St . . . . . . . . . . B2 | Dundee | McManus Museum | South Marketgait . . B3 |
| Blackscroft . . . . . . A3 | Repertory ▦ . . . . C2 | and Art Gallery, | South Tay St . . . . . B2 |
| Blinshall St . . . . . . B1 | Dunhope Park . . . . A1 | The ☖ . . . . . . . . B2 | South Ward Rd . . . . B2 |
| Brown St . . . . . . . . B1 | Dura St . . . . . . . . . A3 | Meadow Side . . . . . B2 | Tay Road Bridge ✦ . C3 |
| Bus Station . . . . . . B3 | East Dock St . . . . . B3 | Meadowside | Thomson Ave . . . . . A3 |
| Caird Hall . . . . . . . B2 | East Marketgait . . . B3 | St Pauls 🛆 . . . . . B2 | Trades La . . . . . . . B3 |
| Camperdown St . . . B3 | East Whale La . . . . B3 | Mercat Cross ✦ . . . B2 | Union St . . . . . . . . B2 |
| Candle La . . . . . . . . B3 | Erskine St . . . . . . . A3 | Murraygate . . . . . . B2 | Union Terr . . . . . . . A1 |
| Carmichael St . . . . A3 | Euclid Cr . . . . . . . . B2 | Nelson St . . . . . . . A2 | University Library . . B2 |
| City Churches 🛆 . . B2 | Forebank Rd . . . . . A2 | Nethergate . . . . B2/C1 | University of |
| City Quay . . . . . . . B3 | Foundry La . . . . . . A3 | North Lindsay St . . . B2 | Dundee . . . . . . . . B1 |
| City Sq . . . . . . . . . B2 | Frigate Unicorn ⚓ . B3 | North Marketgait . . B2 | Upper Constitution |
| Commercial St . . . . B2 | Gallagher | Old Hawkhill . . . . . B1 | St . . . . . . . . . . . . A1 |
| Constable St . . . . . A3 | Retail Park . . . . . B3 | Olympia Leisure | Verdant Works ☖ . . B1 |
| Constitution Cres . . A1 | Gellatly St . . . . . . B3 | Centre . . . . . . . B3 | Victoria Dock . . . . . B3 |
| Constitution Ct . . . . A1 | Government | Overgate Shopping | Victoria Rd . . . . . . A2 |
| Constitution St . A1/B2 | Offices . . . . . . . . C2 | Centre . . . . . . . B2 | Victoria St . . . . . . . A3 |
| Cotton Rd . . . . . . . A3 | Guthrie St . . . . . . . B1 | Park Pl . . . . . . . . . B1 | Ward Rd . . . . . . . . B1 |
| Courthouse Sq . . . . B1 | Hawkhill . . . . . . . . B1 | Perth Rd . . . . . . . . C1 | Wellgate . . . . . . . . B2 |
| Cowgate . . . . . . . . A3 | Hilltown . . . . . . . . A2 | Police Station | West Bell St . . . . . . B1 |
| Crescent St . . . . . . A3 | Howff Cemetery, | ▣ . . . . . . . . . A2/B1 | West |
| Crichton St . . . . . . B2 | The . . . . . . . . . . B2 | Post Office ▣ . . . . B2 | Marketgait . . . B1/B2 |
| Dens Brae . . . . . . . A3 | Information Ctr ▣ . B2 | Princes St . . . . . . . A3 | Westfield Pl . . . . . . B1 |
| Dens Rd . . . . . . . . A3 | Keiller Shopping | Prospect Pl . . . . . . A2 | William St . . . . . . . A3 |
| Discovery Point ✦ . C2 | Centre . . . . . . . . B2 | Reform St . . . . . . . B2 | Wishart Arch ✦ . . . A3 |
| Douglas St . . . . . . . B1 | Keiller Ctr, The . . . B2 | Riverside Dr . . . . . . C2 | |
| | King St . . . . . . . . . A3 | Riverside | |
| | Kinghorne Rd . . . . A1 | Esplanade . . . . . . C2 | |

## Fort William

| | | | |
|---|---|---|---|
| | Cow Hill . . . . . . . . . C3 | Information Ctr ▣ . A3 | Nevis Rd . . . . . . . . . A3 |
| Abrach Rd . . . . . . . A3 | Creag Dhubh . . . . . A2 | Inverlochy Ct . . . . . A3 | Nevis Terr . . . . . . . B2 |
| Achintore Rd . . . . . C1 | Croft Rd . . . . . . . . . B3 | Kennedy Rd . . . B2/C2 | North Rd . . . . . . . . B3 |
| Alma Rd . . . . . . . . B2 | Douglas Pl . . . . . . . B2 | Library . . . . . . . . . B2 | Obelisk . . . . . . . . . B2 |
| Am Breun Chamas . A2 | Dudley Rd . . . . . . . B2 | Lime Tree | Parade Rd . . . . . . . B2 |
| Ambulance Station A3 | Dumbarton Rd . . . . C1 | Gallery ✦ . . . . . . C1 | Police Station ▣ . . C1 |
| An Aird . . . . . . . . . A3 | Earl of Inverness | Lochaber Leisure | Post Office ▣ . . A3/B2 |
| Argyll Rd . . . . . . . . C1 | Rd . . . . . . . . . . . A3 | Centre . . . . . . . B3 | Ross Pl . . . . . . . . . C1 |
| Argyll Terr . . . . . . . C1 | Fassifern Rd . . . . . B1 | Lochiel Rd . . . . . . . A3 | St Andrews 🛆 . . . . B2 |
| Bank St . . . . . . . . . B2 | Fire Station . . . . . . A2 | Lochy Rd . . . . . . . . A3 | Shaw Pl . . . . . . . . . B2 |
| Belford Hospital Ⓗ B2 | Fort William ⇌ . . . . B2 | Lundavra Cres . . . . C1 | Station Brae . . . . . B2 |
| Ben Nevis Highland | Fort William | Lundavra Rd . . . . . C1 | Superstore . . . . . . B3 |
| Centre . . . . . . . . B3 | (Remains) ✦ . . . . B2 | Lundy Rd . . . . . . . . A3 | Treig Rd . . . . . . . . A3 |
| Black Parks . . . . . . A3 | Glasdrum Rd . . . . . C1 | Mamore Cr. . . . . . . B2 | Underwater |
| Braemore Pl . . . . . C2 | Glen Nevis Pl . . . . . B3 | Mary St. . . . . . . . . B2 | Centre, The . . . . . A2 |
| Bruce Pl . . . . . . . . C1 | Gordon Sq . . . . . . . B1 | Middle St . . . . . . . B1 | Union Rd . . . . . . . . C1 |
| Bus Station . . . . . . B2 | Grange Rd . . . . . . . C1 | Montrose Ave . . . . . A3 | Victoria Rd. . . . . . . B2 |
| Camanachd Cr . A3/B2 | Heathercroft Dr . . . C1 | Moray Pl . . . . . . . . C1 | Wades Rd . . . . . . . A3 |
| Cameron Rd . . . . . C1 | Heather Croft Rd . . C1 | Morven Pl . . . . . . . C2 | West Highland 🛆 . . B1 |
| Cameron Sq. . . . . . B1 | Henderson Row . . . C2 | Moss Rd . . . . . . . . B2 | West Highland |
| Carmichael Way . . . A2 | High St . . . . . . . . . B1 | Nairn Cres . . . . . . . C1 | College UHI . . . . . A2 |
| Claggan Rd . . . . . . B3 | Hill Rd. . . . . . . . . . B2 | Nevis Bridge . . . . . B3 | Young Pl . . . . . . . . B2 |
| Connochie Rd . . . . C1 | Hospital Belhaven | Nevis Centre, The . . A2 | |
| | Annexe . . . . . . . . B3 | | |

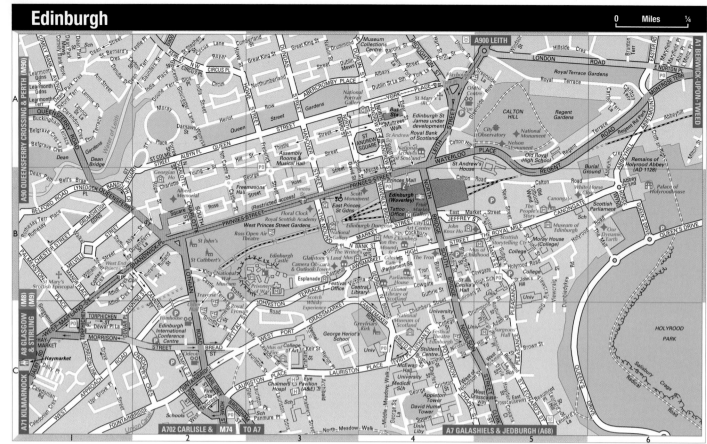

# Glasgow

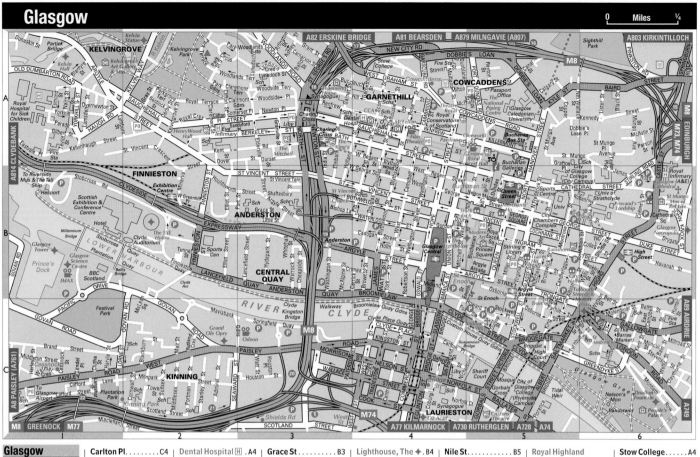

0 — Miles — ¼

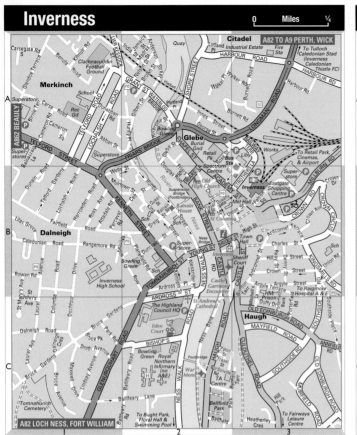

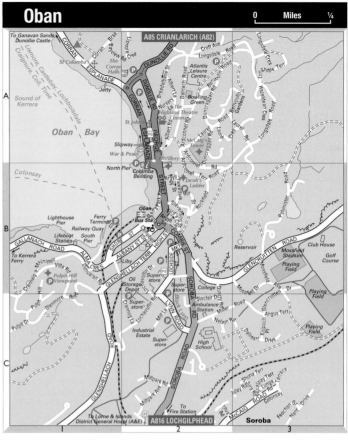

## Inverness

| | |
|---|---|
| Abban St. | A1 |
| Academy St | B2 |
| Alexander Pl | B2 |
| Anderson St. | A2 |
| Annfield Rd | C3 |
| Ardconnel St. | B3 |
| Ardconnel Terr | B3 |
| Ardross Pl | B2 |
| Ardross St | B2 |
| Argyle St | B3 |
| Argyle Terr | B3 |
| Attadale Rd | B1 |
| Ballifeary La | C2 |
| Ballifeary Rd | C1/C2 |
| Balnacraig La | A1 |
| Balnain House ✦ | B2 |
| Balnain St | B2 |
| Bank St | B2 |
| Bellfield Park | C2 |
| Bellfield Terr | C3 |
| Benula Rd | A1 |
| Birnie Terr | A1 |
| Bishop's Rd | C2 |
| Bowling Green | A2 |
| Bowling Green | B2 |
| Bowling Green | C2 |
| Bridge St | B2 |
| Brown St | A2 |
| Bruce Ave | C1 |
| Bruce Gdns | C1 |
| Bruce Pk | C1 |
| Burial Ground | A2 |
| Burnett Rd | A3 |
| Bus Station | B3 |
| Caledonian Rd | B1 |
| Cameron Rd | A1 |
| Cameron Sq. | A1 |
| Carse Rd. | A1 |
| Carsegate Rd South | A1 |
| Castle Garrison Encounter ✦ | B2 |
| Castle Rd | B2 |
| Castle St | B3 |
| Celt St | B2 |

| | |
|---|---|
| Chapel St | A2 |
| Charles St | B3 |
| Church St | B2 |
| Clachnacuddin Football Ground | A1 |
| Columba Rd | B1/C1 |
| Crown Ave | B3 |
| Crown Circus | B3 |
| Crown Dr | B3 |
| Crown Rd | B3 |
| Crown St | B3 |
| Culduthel Rd | C3 |
| Dalneigh Cres | C1 |
| Dalneigh Rd | C1 |
| Denny St. | B3 |
| Dochfour Dr | B1/C1 |
| Douglas Row | B2 |
| Duffy Dr | C3 |
| Dunabban Rd | A1 |
| Dunain Rd | B1 |
| Duncraig St | B2 |
| Eastgate Shopping Centre | B3 |
| Eden Court ♿📷 | C2 |
| Fairfield Rd | B1 |
| Falcon Sq. | B3 |
| Fire Station | A3 |
| Fraser St | B2 |
| Fraser St | C2 |
| Friars' Bridge | A2 |
| Friars' La | B2 |
| Friars' St | A2 |
| George St | A2 |
| Gilbert St | A2 |
| Glebe St | A2 |
| Glendoe Terr | A1 |
| Glenurquhart Rd | C1 |
| Gordon Terr | B3 |
| Gordonville Rd | C2 |
| Grant St | A2 |
| Greig St | B2 |
| Harbour Rd | A3 |
| Harrowden Rd | B1 |
| Haugh Rd | C2 |
| Heatherley Crescent | C3 |
| High St | B3 |

| | |
|---|---|
| Highland Council HQ, The | C2 |
| Hill Park | C3 |
| Hill St | B3 |
| HM Prison | B3 |
| Huntly Pl | A2 |
| Huntly St | B2 |
| India St | A2 |
| Industrial Estate | A3 |
| Information Ctr ℹ | B2 |
| Innes St | B2 |
| Inverness ⇌ | B3 |
| Inverness High School | B1 |
| Inverness Museum 🏛 | B2 |
| Jamaica St. | A2 |
| Kenneth St. | B2 |
| Kilmuir Rd | A1 |
| King St | B2 |
| Kingsmills Rd | B3 |
| Laurel Ave | B1/C1 |
| Library | A3 |
| Lilac Gr. | B1 |
| Lindsay Ave | C1 |
| Lochalsh Rd | A1/B1 |
| Longman Rd | A3 |
| Lotland Pl | A2 |
| Lower Kessock St. | A1 |
| Madras St. | A2 |
| Market Hall | B2 |
| Maxwell Dr | C1 |
| Mayfield Rd | C3 |
| Millburn Rd | B3 |
| Mitchell's La | C3 |
| Montague Row | B2 |
| Muirfield Rd | C3 |
| Muirtown St | B1 |
| Nelson St | A2 |
| Ness Bank | C2 |
| Ness Bridge | B2 |
| Ness Walk | B2/C2 |
| Old Edinburgh Rd | C3 |
| Park Rd. | C1 |
| Paton St. | C2 |
| Perceval Rd | B1 |

| | |
|---|---|
| Planefield Rd | B2 |
| Police Station 🏛 | A3 |
| Porterfield Bank | C3 |
| Porterfield Rd. | C3 |
| Portland Pl | A2 |
| Post Office 📮 | A2/B1/B2 |
| Queen St | B2 |
| Queensgate | B2 |
| Railway Terr | A3 |
| Rangemore Rd | C1 |
| Reay St. | B3 |
| Riverside St. | A2 |
| Rose St | A2 |
| Ross Ave. | B1 |
| Rowan Rd. | B1 |
| Royal Northern Infirmary 🏥 | C2 |
| St Andrew's Cathedral † | C2 |
| St Columba 🏛 | B2 |
| St John's Ave. | C1 |
| St Mary's Ave. | C1 |
| Sheriff Court | B3 |
| Shore St. | A2 |
| Smith Ave. | C1 |
| Southside Pl | C3 |
| Southside Rd. | C3 |
| Spectrum Centre | B2 |
| Strothers La | B3 |
| Superstore | A1/B2 |
| TA Centre | C2 |
| Telford Gdns | B1 |
| Telford Rd | A1 |
| Telford St. | A1 |
| Tomnahurich Cemetery | C1 |
| Tomnahurich St | B2 |
| Town Hall | B3 |
| Union Rd | B3 |
| Union St | B3 |
| Walker Pl | A2 |
| Walker St | A2 |
| War Memorial ✦ | C2 |
| Waterloo Bridge | A2 |
| Wells St | B1 |
| Young St. | B2 |

## Oban

| | |
|---|---|
| Aird's Cres | B2 |
| Albany St | B2 |
| Albert La | A2 |
| Albert Rd | A2 |
| Alma Cres | B1 |
| Ambulance Station | C2 |
| Angus Terr | C3 |
| Ardconnel Rd | A2 |
| Ardconnel Terr | A2 |
| Argyll Sq | B2 |
| Argyll St | B2 |
| Atlantis Leisure Centre | A2 |
| Bayview Rd | A1 |
| Benvoulin Rd | A2 |
| Bowling Green | A2 |
| Breadalbane St | A2 |
| Bus Station | B2 |
| Campbell St. | B2 |
| College | B2 |
| Colonsay Terr | C3 |
| Columba Building | B2 |
| Combie St | B2 |
| Corran Brae | A1 |
| Corran Esplanade | A1/A2 |

| | |
|---|---|
| Corran Halls, The 🎭 | A2 |
| Court | B2 |
| Crannaig-a-Mhinister | B1 |
| Crannog La | C2 |
| Croft Ave | A2 |
| Dalintart Dr | C3 |
| Dalriach Rd | A2 |
| Distillary ✦ | B2 |
| Drummore Rd | C2 |
| Duncraggan Rd. | A2 |
| Dunollie Rd | A1 |
| Dunuaran Rd. | B1 |
| Feochan Gr | C3 |
| Ferry Terminal | B1 |
| Gallanach Rd. | B1 |
| George St. | A2 |
| Glencruitten Dr | C3 |
| Glencruitten Rd | B3 |
| Glenmore Rd. | C1 |
| Glenshellach Rd | C1 |
| Glenshellach Terr. | B2 |
| Hazeldean Cres | A3 |
| High St | C2 |
| Highland Theatre Cinema, The 🎬 | A2 |
| Industrial Estate. | C2 |

| | |
|---|---|
| Information Ctr ℹ | B2 |
| Islay Rd | C3 |
| Jacob's Ladder ✦ | B2 |
| Jura Rd | C3 |
| Knipoch Pl. | C3 |
| Laurel Cres | A2 |
| Laurel Rd | A2/A3 |
| Library | B1 |
| Lifeboat Station | B1 |
| Lighthouse Pier | B1 |
| Lismore Cres | A2 |
| Lochavullin Dr | B2 |
| Lochavullin Rd | C2 |
| Lochside St | C2 |
| Longsdale Cres. | A3 |
| Longsdale Rd | A2/A3 |
| Longsdale Terr | A2 |
| Lunga Rd | C3 |
| Lynn Rd | C2 |
| Market St | B2 |
| McCaig Rd | C3 |
| McCaig's Tower ✦ | A2 |
| Mill La | B2 |
| Miller Rd | C2 |
| Millpark Ave | C2 |
| Millpark Rd | C2 |
| Mossfield Ave | B3 |
| Mossfield Dr | B3 |
| Mossfield Stadium | B3 |

| | |
|---|---|
| Nant Dr | C3 |
| Nelson Rd | C2 |
| North Pier | B2 |
| Nursery La | A2 |
| Oban ⇌ | B2 |
| Police Station 🏛 | B2 |
| Polvinister Rd | A2 |
| Post Office 📮 | A2/B2 |
| Pulpit Dr. | C1 |
| Pulpit Hill. | C1 |
| Pulpit Hill Viewpoint ✦ | B1 |
| Quarry Rd. | C2 |
| Queen's Park Pl | B2 |
| Railway Quay. | B1 |
| Rockfield Rd | C2 |
| St Columba's † | A1 |
| St John's † | A2 |
| Scalpay Terr | C3 |
| Shore St. | C3 |
| Shuna Terr. | C3 |
| Sinclair Dr | C3 |
| Soroba Rd | B2/C2 |
| South Pier | B1 |
| Stevenson St. | B2 |
| Tweedale St. | B2 |
| Ulva Rd. | C2 |
| Villa Rd. | B1 |
| War & Peace 🏛 | A2 |

# Perth

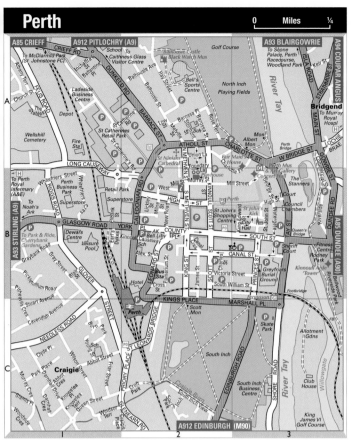

# St Andrews

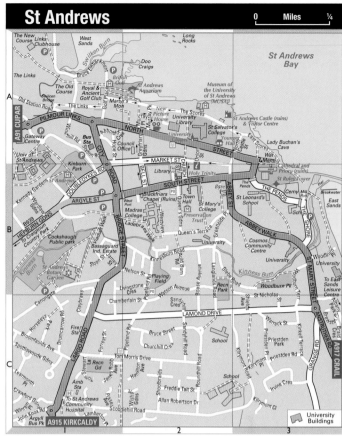

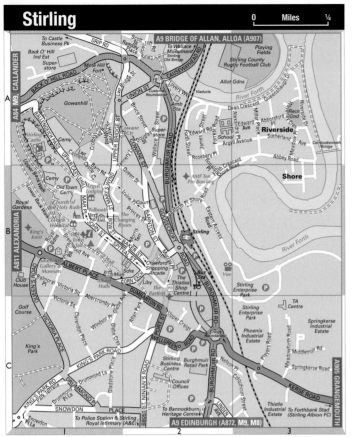

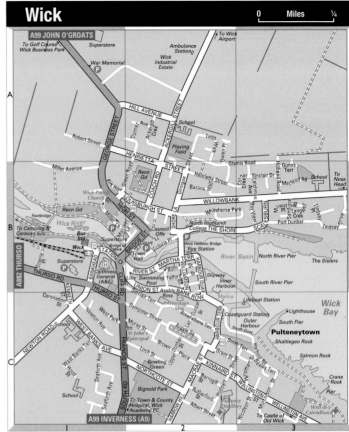

## Stirling

Abbey Rd . . . . . . . . . A3
Abbotsford Pl . . . . . A3
Abercromby Pl . . . . C1
Albert Halls ☻ . . . . . B1
Albert Pl . . . . . . . . . B1
Alexandra Pl . . . . . . A3
Allan Park . . . . . . . . C2
Ambulance
  Station . . . . . . . . A2
AMF Ten Pin
  Bowling ✦ . . . . . . B2
Argyll Ave. . . . . . . . A3
Argyll's Lodging ✦ B1
Back O' Hill
  Industrial Estate. . A1
Back O' Hill Rd. . . . A1
Baker St . . . . . . . . . B2
Ballengeich Pass . . A1
Balmoral Pl . . . . . . . B1
Barn Rd . . . . . . . . . B1
Barnton St . . . . . . . B2
Bastion, The ✦ . . C2
Bow St . . . . . . . . . . B1
Bruce St . . . . . . . . . A2
Burghmuir
  Retail Park. . . . . . C2
Burghmuir
  Rd . . . . . . A2/B2/C2
Bus Station . . . . . . B2
Cambuskenneth
  Bridge . . . . . . . . . A3
Castle Ct. . . . . . . . . B1
Causewayhead Rd . A2
Cemetery. . . . . . . . A1
Changing Room,
  The ☻ . . . . . . . . B1
Church of the
  Holy Rude ♠ . . . . B1
Clarendon Pl . . . . . C1
Club House . . . . . . B1

Colquhoun St . . . . . C3
Corn Exchange . . . B2
Council Offices. . . . C2
Court . . . . . . . . . . . B2
Cowane Ctr ☻ . . . . A2
Cowane St . . . . . . . A2
Cowane's
  Hospital ☎ . . . . . B1
Crawford Shopping
  Arcade . . . . . . . . B2
Crofthead Rd. . . . . A1
Dean Cres . . . . . . . A3
Douglas St . . . . . . . A2
Drip Rd . . . . . . . . . A1
Drummond La . . . . C1
Drummond Pl . . . . . C1
Drummond Pl La. . . C1
Dumbarton Rd . . . . C2
Eastern Access Rd . B2
Edward Ave . . . . . . A3
Edward Rd . . . . . . . A2
Forrest Rd . . . . . . . A2
Fort . . . . . . . . . . . . A1
Forth Cres . . . . . . . B2
Forth St . . . . . . . . . A2
Gladstone Pl . . . . . C1
Glebe Ave. . . . . . . . C1
Glebe Cres . . . . . . . C1
Golf Course . . . . . . C1
Goosecroft Rd. . . . . B2
Gowanhill . . . . . . . A1
Greenwood Ave . . . B1
Harvey Wynd . . . . . A1
Information Ctr ☑ . . B1
Irvine Pl . . . . . . . . . B2
James St . . . . . . . . A2
John St . . . . . . . . . B1
Kerse Rd. . . . . . . . . C3
King's Knot ✦ . . . . . B1
King's Park . . . . . . . C1
King's Park Rd. . . . . C1
Laurencecroft Rd . . A2

Leisure Pool . . . . . . B2
Library . . . . . . . . . . B2
Linden Ave. . . . . . . C2
Lovers Wk . . . . . . . A2
Lower Back Walk . . B1
Lower Bridge St . . . A2
Lower Castlehill . . . A1
Mar Pl . . . . . . . . . . B1
Meadow Pl. . . . . . . A3
Meadowforth Rd . . C3
Middlemuir Rd . . . . C3
Millar Pl . . . . . . . . . A3
Morris Terr . . . . . . . B2
Mote Hill . . . . . . . . A1
Murray Pl . . . . . . . . B2
Nelson Pl . . . . . . . . C2
Old Town
  Cemetery. . . . . . . B1
Old Town Jail ✦ . . . B1
Park Terr . . . . . . . . C1
Phoenix Industrial
  Estate . . . . . . . . . C3
Players Rd . . . . . . . C3
Port St . . . . . . . . . . C2
Post Office. . . . . . . B2
Princes St . . . . . . . B2
Queen St . . . . . . . . B2
Queen's Rd . . . . . . . C1
Queenshaugh Dr . . A3
Ramsay Pl . . . . . . . A2
Riverside Dr . . . . . . A3
Ronald Pl . . . . . . . . A1
Rosebery Pl . . . . . . A2
Royal Gardens. . . . . B1
Royal Gdns . . . . . . . B1
St Mary's Wynd . . . B1
St Ninian's Rd . . . . C2
Scott St . . . . . . . . . A2
Seaforth Pl . . . . . . . B2
Shore Rd . . . . . . . . B2
Smith Art Gallery &
  Museum ☖☖ . . . . B1

Snowdon Pl. . . . . . . C1
Snowdon Pl La . . . . C1
Spittal St . . . . . . . . B2
Springkerse
  Industrial Estate. . C3
Springkerse Rd. . . . C3
Stirling Business
  Centre . . . . . . . . . C2
Stirling Castle ☖ . . A1
Stirling County
  Rugby Football
  Club . . . . . . . . . . A3
Stirling Enterprise
  Park . . . . . . . . . . B3
Stirling Old Bridge. A2
Stirling Station ≋ . B2
Superstore . . . . A1/A2
Sutherland Ave. . . . A3
TA Centre. . . . . . . . C3
Tannery La. . . . . . . A1
Thistle Industrial
  Estate. . . . . . . . . C3
Thistles Shopping
  Centre, The . . . . . B2
Tolbooth ✦ . . . . . . B1
Town Wall . . . . . . . B1
Union St. . . . . . . . . A2
Upper Back Walk . . B1
Upper Bridge St . . . A1
Upper Castlehill . . . B1
Upper Craigs . . . . . C2
Victoria Pl . . . . . . . C1
Victoria Rd. . . . . . . B1
Victoria Sq. . . . . . B1/C1
Vue ☷ . . . . . . . . . . B2
Wallace St . . . . . . . A2
Waverley Cres. . . . . A3
Wellgreen Rd . . . . . C1
Windsor Pl. . . . . . . C1
YHA ▲ . . . . . . . . . . B1

## Wick

Ackergill Cres . . . . A2
Ackergill St . . . . . . A2
Albert St. . . . . . . . . C2
Ambulance Station A2
Argyle Sq . . . . . . . . C2
Assembly Rooms . . C2
Bank Row. . . . . . . . C2
Bankhead . . . . . . . . B1
Barons Well . . . . . . B2
Barrogill St . . . . . . C2
Bay View. . . . . . . . . B3
Bexley Terr . . . . . . . C2
Bignold Park . . . . . C3
Bowling Green . . . . C2
Breadalbane Terr. . C2
Bridge of Wick . . . . B1
Bridge St . . . . . . . . B2
Brown Pl . . . . . . . . C1
Burn St . . . . . . . . . C2
Bus Station . . . . . . B2
Caithness General
  Hospital (A&E) Ⓗ. B1
Cliff Rd . . . . . . . . . B1
Coach Rd . . . . . . . . C2
Coastguard
  Station . . . . . . . . C3
Corner Cres. . . . . . C3
Coronation St . . . . C1
Council Offices. . . . B2
Court . . . . . . . . . . . C2
Crane Rock . . . . . . C3
Dempster St . . . . . C2
Dunnet Ave . . . . . . A2

Fire Station . . . . . . B2
Francis St. . . . . . . . C1
George St . . . . . . . . A1
Girnigoe St . . . . . . B2
Glamis Rd. . . . . . . . B2
Gowrie Pl . . . . . . . . B1
Grant St . . . . . . . . . C2
Green Rd . . . . . . . . B2
Gunns Terr. . . . . . . B3
Harbour Quay . . . . B2
Harbour Rd . . . . . . C3
Harbour Terr . . . . . C2
Harrow Hill . . . . . . C2
Henrietta St. . . . A2/B2
Heritage
  Museum ☖ . . . . . C2
High St . . . . . . . . . B2
Hill Ave . . . . . . . . . A2
Hillhead Rd . . . . . . B3
Hood St . . . . . . . . . C1
Huddart St . . . . . . . C2
Kenneth St. . . . . . . C1
Kinnaird St . . . . . . C2
Kirk Hill . . . . . . . . . B1
Langwell Cres . . . . B3
Leishman Ave . . . . B3
Leith Walk . . . . . . . A2
Library . . . . . . . . . . B2
Lifeboat Station . . . C3
Lighthouse . . . . . . . C3
Lindsay Dr . . . . . . . B3
Lindsay Pl . . . . . . . B3
Loch St . . . . . . . . . C2
Louisburgh St . . . . B2
Lower Dunbar St. . . C2

Macleay La. . . . . . . B1
Macleod Rd . . . . . . B3
MacRae St . . . . . . . C2
Martha Terr . . . . . . B2
Miller Ave. . . . . . . . B1
Miller La. . . . . . . . . B1
Moray St. . . . . . . . . C2
Mowat Pl . . . . . . . . B3
Murchison St. . . . . C3
Newton Ave . . . . . . C1
Newton Rd . . . . . . . C1
Nicolson St . . . . . . C3
North Highland
  College. . . . . . . . B2
North River Pier . . . B3
Northcote St . . . . . C2
Owen Pl . . . . . . . . . A2
Police Station 🛆 . . B1
Port Dunbar . . . . . . B3
Post Office 🖃 . . B2/C2
Pulteney
  Distillery ✦ . . . . . C3
River St. . . . . . . . . . B2
Robert St . . . . . . . . A1
Rutherford St . . . . . C2
St John's
  Episcopal ♠. . . . . C2
Sandigoe Rd . . . . . B3
Scalesburn . . . . . . B3
Seaforth Ave . . . . . C1
Shore La. . . . . . . . . B2
Shore, The . . . . . . . B2
Sinclair Dr . . . . . . . B3
Sinclair Terr . . . . . . C2
Smith Terr . . . . . . . C3

South Pier . . . . . . . C3
South Quay . . . . . . C3
South Rd . . . . . . . . C1
South River Pier . . . B3
Station Rd . . . . . . . B2
Superstore . . . . . A1/B2
Swimming Pool . . . B2
Telford St. . . . . . . . B1
Thurso Rd . . . . . . . B1
Thurso St. . . . . . . . B1
Town Hall . . . . . . . . B2
Union St. . . . . . . . . B2
Upper Dunbar St. . . C2
Vansittart St . . . . . B2
Victoria Pl . . . . . . . B2
War Memorial . . . . A1
Well of
  Cairndhuna ✦ . . . C3
Wellington Ave . . . C3
Wellington St . . . . . C3
West Banks Ave . . . C1
West Banks Terr . . . C1
West Park . . . . . . . C1
Whitehorse Park . . B2
Wick Harbour
  Bridge . . . . . . . . . B2
Wick Industrial
  Estate. . . . . . . . . A2
Wick Parish
  Church ♠ . . . . . . . B1
Wick Station ≋ . . . B1
Williamson St . . . . B1
Willowbank. . . . . . . B2

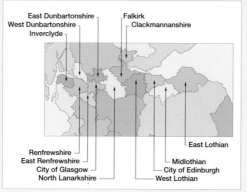

# Index to road maps

## How to use the index

### Example

**Benmore Lodge** Highland **85** B7

— grid square
— page number
— county or unitary authority

Barrmill 27 D6
Barrock 91 A6
Barrock Ho. 91 B6
Barrowburn 15 B6
Barry 67 D5
Barshare 18 F2
Barthol Chapel 83 E5
Basta 102 D5
Batavaime 64 D2
Bathgate 30 A3
Bathville 30 A2
Bauds of Cullen 82 B1
Baugh 60 C3
Bay 76 C2
Beach 62 B2
Beachans 81 D5
Beacharr 50 B2
Beacrabhaic 95 C5
Bealach 63 B4
Bealach Maim 54 D2
Beancross 40 E2
Beansburn 17 B7
Beaquoy 98 A4
Bearnus 61 C6
Bearsden 38 F1
Beattock 11 D5
Beaufort Castle 79 D7
Beauly 79 D7
Bedrule 23 F8
Beeslack 31 B8
Beeswing 48 C2
Beitearsaig 94 A3
Beith 27 D5
Beleybridge 58 A3
Belhaven 44 C2
Belhelvie 75 A6
Belhinnie 82 F1
Bellabeg 73 A8
Bellamore 46 A4
Bellanoch 53 C7
Bellanrigg 21 B8
Bellaty 66 B2
Bellehiglash 81 E6
Bellfield 17 B7
Belliehill 67 A5
Belloch 50 C2
Bellochantuy 50 C2
Bellsbank 7 D8
Bellshill 29 B5
Bellside 29 C7
Bellsmyre 37 E7
Bellspool 21 B7
Bellsquarry 30 A4
Bellyeoman 41 C6
Belmaduthy 79 C8
Belmont
 Shetland 102 C5
 South Ayrshire 17 E5
Belnacraig 73 A8
Belnagarrow 81 D8
Belses 23 D7
Belston 17 E6
Beltingham 5 F8
Belts of Collonach 74 C3
Belvedere 30 A3
Bemersyde 23 C7
Ben Alder Lodge 71 F7
Ben Armine Lodge 86 B4
Benbuie 9 E5
Ben Casgro 97 E7
Benderloch 62 D4
Bendronaig Lodge 78 E2
Benfield 47 C5
Benholm 75 F5
Benmore
 Argyll and Bute 36 D1
 Stirling 64 E2
Benmore Lodge
 Argyll and Bute 61 D8
 Highland 85 B7
Bennan 51 D5
Bennane Lea 46 A2
Bennetsfield 80 C1
Benslie 17 A5
Benston 103 H4
Bent 74 E3
Benthoul 75 B5
Bentpath 12 F2
Bents 30 B3
Benvie 66 D3
Beoraidbeg 69 C6
Berefold 83 E6
Bernera 77 F8
Bernice 36 B1
Bernisdale 76 C4
Berriedale 87 A8
Berrington 35 F9
Berryhillock 82 B2
Berstane 99 B5
Berwick-upon-
 Tweed 35 D8
Bethelnie 83 E4
Bettyhill 90 B1
Bewcastle 4 D4
Bewlie 23 D7
Bewlie Mains 23 D7
Bhalasaigh 96 D4
Bhaltos 96 D3
Bhatarsaigh 92 D2
Bhlàraidh 71 A5
Biddlestone 15 C8
Bieldside 75 B5
Biggar 20 B4
Biggar Road 29 B6
Biggings 103 G1
Bighouse 90 B2
Bigram 56 B1
Big Sand 84 F1
Bigswell 98 B4
Bigton 101 D2
Bilbster 91 C6
Bilston 32 B1
Bimbister 98 B4
Bindal 87 E6
Bingham 42 F2
Binniehill 39 F8
Birchburn 51 D5
Birchfield 80 F4
Birdfield 54 C2
Birdston 38 E4
Birgham 24 B4
Birichen 86 D4
Birkenbog 82 B2
Birkenhills 82 D4
Birkenshaw
 North Lanarkshire 28 B4
 South Lanarkshire 29 E6
Birkenside 23 A7
Birkhall 73 C8
Birkhill
 Angus 66 D3
 Scottish Borders 11 A8
 Scottish Borders 23 A7
Birkshaw 5 E8
Birnam 65 C8
Birniehill 28 D3
Birse 74 C2
Birsemore 74 C2
Bishopbriggs 38 F3
Bishop Kinkell 79 C7
Bishopmill 81 B7
Bishopton
 Dumfries & Galloway 47 E6
 Renfs 37 F7
Bixter 103 H3
Blackacre 10 F4
Blackadder West 35 D5
Blackbraes 75 A5
Blackburn
 Aberdeenshire 75 A5
 Aberdeenshire 82 E2
 West Lothian 30 A3
Blackcastle 32 C4
Blackchambers 75 A4
Black Clauchrie 46 A4
Black Corries Lodge 63 B7
Blackcraig 48 A1
Blackcraigs 74 D2
Black Crofts 62 D4
Blackdog 75 A6
Blackdykes 43 D7
Blackford
 Dumfries & Galloway 2 B3
 Perth and Kinross 56 B3
Blackgate 67 B4
Blackhall
 Aberdeenshire 74 C3
 Edinburgh 41 F8
 Renfs 27 B8
Blackhaugh 22 B4
Blackhill
 Aberdeenshire 83 C7
 Aberdeenshire 83 D7
 Aberdeenshire 83 E7
 Highland 76 C3
Blackhillock 82 D1
Blackhills
 Highland 80 C4
 Moray 81 C7
Blacklaw 82 C3
Blacklunans 66 A1
Black Mount 63 C7
Blackness
 Aberdeenshire 74 C3
Blackness *continued*
 Falkirk 40 E5
Blackpark 47 C5
Blackpool Gate 4 C3
Blackridge 30 A1
Blackrock 52 F3
Blackshaw 2 E1
Blacktop 75 B5
Blackwaterfoot 50 D4
Blackwater Lodge 81 F8
Blackwood 29 F6
Bladnoch 47 D6
Blaich 70 E2
Blain 69 F6
Blainacraig Ho. 74 C2
Blair 42 B2
Blair Atholl 65 A6
Blairbeg 51 C6
Blairburn 40 C3
Blairdaff 74 A3
Blair Drummond 56 C2
Blairdryne 74 C4
Blairglas 37 C5
Blairgorm 81 F5
Blairgowrie 66 C1
Blairhall 40 C4
Blairhill 29 A5
Blairingone 40 A3
Blairland 26 E5
Blairlinn 39 F6
Blairlogie 39 A7
Blairlomond 54 C4
Blairmore
 Argyll and Bute 36 D2
 Highland 88 C3
Blairnamarrow 73 A7
Blairquhosh 38 D1
Blair's Ferry 54 F2
Blairskaith 38 E2
Blakelaw 24 C4
Blandy 89 C8
Blanefield 38 E2
Blanerne 35 C5
Blantyre 28 C4
Blar a'Chaorainn 70 F3
Blaran 62 F3
Blarghour 63 F4
Blarmachfoldach 70 F2
Blarnalearoch 85 D5
Blebocraigs 66 F4
Blegbie 33 B5
Blervie Castle 81 C5
Blindburn 15 B5
Blingery 91 D7
Bloomfield 23 E7
Bluecairn 23 A6
Blughasary 85 C5
Blyth 31 E6
Blyth Bridge 31 E6
Blythe 33 E7
Blythswood 27 A9
Boarhills 67 F5
Boath 86 F2
Boat of Garten 72 A4
Boblainy 79 E6
Bochastle 56 B1
Bodantionail 84 F1
Boddam
 Aberdeenshire 83 D8
 Shetland 101 E2
Bodiechell 83 D4
Bogallan 79 C8
Bogbrae 83 E7
Bogend
 Scottish Borders 34 E4
 South Ayrshire 17 C6
Bogentory 74 B4
Boghall
 Midlothian 31 A8
 West Lothian 30 A3
Boghead
 Aberdeenshire 74 C3
 South Lanarkshire 19 A6
Bogmoor 81 B8
Bogniebrae
 Aberdeenshire 82 D2
 Aberdeenshire 82 D3
Bograxie 74 A4
Bogs 82 F2
Bogs Bank 31 D7
Bogside 29 D7
Bogton 82 C3
Bogtown 82 B2
Bogue 47 A8
Bohenie 71 D4
Bohuntine 71 D4
Bohuntinville 71 D4
Boirseam 95 D4
Boleside 23 C5
Bolshan 67 B6
Bolton 43 F6
Boltonfellend 4 E2
Bombie 48 D1
Bonaly 31 A8
Bonar Bridge 86 D3
Bonawe 63 D5
Bonchester Bridge 13 B7
Bonhill 37 E6
Bonjedward 24 E2
Bonkle 29 C7
Bonnavoulin 61 B8
Bonnington
 Edinburgh 31 A6
 Scottish Borders 21 B9
Bonnybank 58 B1
Bonnybridge 39 D7
Bonnykelly 83 C5
Bonnyrigg and
 Lasswade 32 A2
Bonnyton
 Aberdeenshire 82 E3
 Angus 66 D3
 Angus 67 B6
 East Ayrshire 17 B7
Bonskeid House 65 A6
Boon 33 E7
Boquhan 38 C1
Bordlands 31 E7
Boreland
 Dumfries & Galloway 11 F7
 Dumfries & Galloway 47 C5
 Fife 42 B2
 Stirling 64 D3
Boreland of
 Southwick 48 C3
Borestone 39 B6
Borgh
 Western Isles 92 C2
 Western Isles 94 D3
Borghasdal 94 D4
Borghastan 96 C5
Borgie 89 C8
Borgue
 Dumfries & Galloway 47 E8
 Highland 87 A8
Bornais 92 A3
Bornesketaig 76 A3
Borness 47 E8
Borreraig 76 C1
Borrobol Lodge 87 A5
Borrodale 76 D1
Borrohill 83 C6
Borrowfield 75 C5
Borrowston 91 D7
Borrowstoun Mains 41 D4
Borthwick 32 C3
Borthwickbrae 12 B4
Borthwickshiels 12 A4
Borve 76 D4
Borve Lodge 94 C4
Bostadh 96 C4
Bothwell 29 C5
Bothy 71 E4
Bottacks 79 B6
Bottomcraig 66 E3
Boultenstone 74 A1
Bourtreehill 17 B5
Bousd 61 A5
Bousta 103 H2
Bovain 64 D3
Bow
 Orkney 98 D4
 Scottish Borders 23 A5
Bowden 23 C7
Bower
 Highland 91 B6
 Northumberland 5 B8
Bowerhope 21 E9
Bowermadden 91 B6
Bowershall 41 B5
Bowertower 91 B6
Bowhill
 Fife 41 A8
 Scottish Borders 22 D4
Bowhouse 48 C4
Bowhousebog or
 Liquo 29 C8
Bowismiln 23 E6
Bowling 37 F8
Bowmore 49 A3
Bow of Fife 57 A8
Bowrie-fauld 67 C5
Bowsden 25 A8
Bowshank 23 A5
Bowside Lodge 90 B2
Boyndie 82 B3
Boysack
 Angus 67 C5
 Angus 67 C6
Braal Castle 91 B5
Brabster 91 B7
Bracadale 76 E3
Bracara 69 C7
Bracklamore 83 C5
Brackletter 70 D3
Brackley 50 B3
Brackloch 85 A5
Braco 56 B3
Bracobrae 82 C2
Braco Castle 56 A3
Braco Park 83 B6
Bracorina 69 C7
Brae
 Dumfries & Galloway 48 B2
 Highland 84 E2
 Highland 85 C8
 Shetland 103 G3
Braeantra 86 F2
Braebuster 99 C5
Braedownie 73 E7
Braeface 39 D6
Braefield 79 E6
Braefindon 79 C8
Braegrum 65 E8
Braehead
 Dumfries &
 Galloway 47 D6
 Orkney 99 C6
 Orkney 100 B2
 South Ayrshire 17 E5
 South Lanarkshire 19 C7
 Stirling 39 B7
Braehead of Lunan 67 B6
Braehoulland 103 F2
Braehour 91 C4
Braehungie 91 E5
Braeintra 77 E8
Braelangwell Lodge 86 D2
Braemar 73 C6
Braemore
 Highland 85 F5
 Highland 91 E4
Brae of Achnahaird 84 B4
Brae of Boquhapple 56 B1
Braepark 41 E7
Brae Roy Lodge 71 C5
Braeside 36 E3
Braes of Enzie 81 C8
Braes of Ullapool 85 D5
Braeswick 100 C4
Braevallich 54 B2
Braewick
 Shetland 103 F2
 Shetland 103 H3
Bragar 97 C5
Brageenmore 62 E4
Braid 41 F8
Braidfauld 28 B3
Braids 50 B3
Braidwood 29 E7
Braigh Chalasaigh 93 A4
Braigo 52 F2
Braingortan 54 E3
Branatwatt 103 H2
Branault 69 F5
Branchill 81 C5
Branchton 36 E3
Branderburgh 81 A7
Brandyquoy 99 D5
Branshill 40 B1
Branxholme 13 B5
Branxholm Park 13 B5
Branxton 25 B6
Brathens 74 C3
Braulen Lodge 78 E4
Brawl 90 B2
Brawlbin 90 C4
Breachacha Castle 60 B4
Breacleit 96 D4
Breakachy 79 D6
Breanais 96 E2
Breascleit 96 D5
Brechin 67 A5
Breckan 98 C3
Breck of Cruan 98 B4
Breckrey 76 B5
Breibhig
 Western Isles 92 D2
 Western Isles 97 D7
Breich 30 B3
Breiwick 103 J4
Bremirehoull 101 D3
Brenachoile Lodge 55 B7
Brenchoillie 54 B3
Brettabister 103 H4
Brewlands Bridge 66 A1
Briach 81 C5
Brideswell 82 E2
Bridge-End 101 C2
Bridgefoot
 Aberdeenshire 74 B1
 Angus 66 D3
Bridge Ho. 49 A3
Bridgelands 23 C5
Bridgend
 Aberdeenshire 74 A2
 Aberdeenshire 82 E2
 Angus 74 F2
 Argyll and Bute 50 C3
 Argyll and Bute 52 F3
 Argyll and Bute 54 C1
 Fife 58 A1
 Highland 79 C5
 Inverclyde 36 E4
 Moray 81 E8
 North Lanarkshire 38 F4
 West Lothian 40 E4
Bridgend of
 Lintrathen 66 B2
Bridgeness 40 D4
Bridge of Alford 74 A2
Bridge of Allan 39 A6
Bridge of Avon
 Moray 81 E6
 Moray 81 F6
Bridge of Awe 63 E5
Bridge of Balgie 64 C3
Bridge of Cally 66 B1
Bridge of Canny 74 C3
Bridge of Craigisla 66 B2
Bridge of Dee 48 D1
Bridge of Don 75 A6
Bridge of Dun 67 B6
Bridge of Dye 74 D3
Bridge of Earn 66 F1
Bridge of Ericht 64 B3
Bridge of Feugh 74 C4
Bridge of Forss 90 B4
Bridge of Gairn 73 C8
Bridge of Gaur 64 B3
Bridge of Lyon 64 C5
Bridge of Muchalls 75 C5
Bridge of Muick 73 C8
Bridge of Oich 71 B5
Bridge of Orchy 63 D7
Bridge of Waith 98 B3
Bridge of Walls 103 H2
Bridge of Weir 27 A6
Bridgeton 28 B3
Brightons 40 E2
Brig o'Turk 55 B8
Brims 98 E3
Brims Castle 90 A4
Brinacory 69 C7
Brindister
 Shetland 101 C3
 Shetland 103 H2
Brinian 100 D2
Brinmore 80 F1
Broadfield 37 F5
Broadford 77 F6
Broadhaugh 12 C4
Broadhaven 91 C7
Broadley 81 B8
Broadleys 83 B5
Broadmeadows 22 C4
Broadrashes 82 C1
Broadsea 83 B6
Brochel 77 D5
Brochroy 63 D5
Brocketsbrae 19 B7
Brockhill 22 E3
Brocklehirst 2 D2
Brockloch 8 E1
Brodick 51 C6
Brodie 80 C4
Brodiesord 82 B2
Brogaig 76 B4
Brookfield 27 B7
Brooklands 48 B2
Broom 28 C1
Broomfield 83 E6
Broomhill
 Highland 80 F4
 Scottish Borders 23 D5

Geisiadar 96 D4
Gellyburn 65 D8
Gelston 48 D1
Geocrab 95 C5
Georgefield 12 F1
Gergask 71 C8
Germiston 28 A3
Gesto Ho 76 E3
Gibbshill 48 B1
Gibshill 36 F5
Giffnock 28 C2
Gifford 33 A6
Giffordland 26 E4
Giffordtown 57 A7
Gilchriston 33 A5
Gillen 76 C2
Gillesbie 11 F7
Gillock 91 C6
Gills 91 A7
Gilmanscleuch 22 E2
Gilmerton
  Edinburgh 32 A1
  Perth and Kinross 65 E6
Gilmourton 18 A4
Gilsland 5 E5
Gilsland Spa 5 E5
Gilston 32 C4
Giosla 96 E4
Girdle Toll 17 A5
Girlsta 103 H4
Girthon 47 D8
Girvan 6 E2
Glachavoil 54 E3
Glackmore 79 C8
Glack of Midthird 81 D8
Gladsmuir 43 F5
Glaichbea 79 E7
Glame 77 D5
Glamis 66 C3
Glas-allt Shiel 73 D7
Glaschoil 81 E5
Glascorrie
  Aberdeenshire 73 C8
  Perth and Kinross 65 E6
Glasdrum 63 C5
Glasgoforest 75 A5
Glasgow 28 A2
Glashvin 76 B4
Glasnacardoch 69 C6
Glasnakille 69 A5
Glasphein 76 D1
Glassburn 79 E5
Glasserton 47 F6
Glassford 29 E5
Glassgreen 81 B7
Glasslie 57 B7
Glasterlaw 67 B5
Gleanhead 47 A6
Gleann Tholàstaidh 97 C8
Glebe 101 B3
Glecknabae 54 F3
Glen
  Dumfries & Galloway 47 D7
  Dumfries & Galloway 48 B2
Glenallachie 81 D7
Glenalmond College 65 E7
Glenalmond Ho. 65 E7
Glenamachrie 62 E4
Glenample 64 E3
Glenancross 69 C6
Glenapp Castle 46 A2
Glenaros Ho. 61 C8
Glenbarr 50 C2
Glenbeg
  Highland 61 A8
  Highland 80 F5
Glen Bernisdale 76 D4
Glenbervie 74 D4
Glenboig 29 A5
Glenborrodale 62 A1
Glenbranter 54 C4
Glenbreck 20 E5
Glenbrein Lodge 71 A6
Glenbrittle House 76 F4
Glenbrook 31 A6
Glenbuchat Castle 73 A8
Glenbuchat Lodge 73 A8
Glenbuck 19 D6
Glenburn 27 B8
Glenbyre 61 E8
Glencalvie Lodge 86 E1
Glencanisp Lodge 85 A5
Glencaple 48 C3
Glencarron Lodge 78 C2
Glencarse 66 E1
Glencassley Castle 85 C8
Glencat 74 C2
Glenceitlein 63 C6
Glencoe 63 B5
Glencraig 41 A7
Glencripesdale 62 B1
Glencrosh 48 A1
Glendavan Ho. 74 B1
Glendearg 23 B6
Glendevon 57 B4
Glendoebeg 71 B6
Glendoe Lodge 71 B6
Glendoick 66 E2
Glendoll Lodge 73 E7
Glendoune 6 E2
Glenduckie 66 F2
Glendye Lodge 74 D3
Gleneagles Hotel 56 A4
Gleneagles House 56 B4
Glenearn 66 F1
Glenegedale 49 A3
Glenelg 69 A8
Glenernie 80 D5
Glenfarg 57 A6
Glenfarquhar Lodge 74 D4
Glenferness House 80 D4
Glenfeshie Lodge 72 C3
Glenfiddich Lodge 81 E8
Glenfinnan 69 D8
Glenfinnan Lodge 70 D1
Glenfintaig Ho. 70 D4
Glenfoot 66 F1
Glenfyne Lodge 63 F7
Glengap 47 D8
Glengarnock 26 D5
Glengolly 91 B5
Glengorm Castle 61 B7
Glengoulandie 65 B5
Glengrasco 76 D4
Glenhead Farm 66 A2
Glen Ho 22 C1
Glenhoul 47 A8
Glenhurich 69 F8
Glenkerry 12 B1
Glenkiln 48 B2
Glenkindie 74 A1
Glenlair 48 B1
Glenlatterach 81 C6
Glenlee 47 A8
Glenleraig 88 E3
Glenlichorn 56 A2
Glenlicht Ho. 70 A2
Glenlivet 81 F6
Glenlochar 48 C1
Glenlochsie 73 E5
Glenlocksie Lodge 73 E5
Glenloig 51 C5
Glenlomond 57 B6
Glenluce 46 D4
Glenlussa Ho. 50 D3
Glenmallan 36 A4
Glenmark 74 D1
Glenmarkie Lodge 66 A2
Glenmarksie 79 C5
Glenmassan 54 D4
Glenmavis
  North Lanarkshire 29 A5
  West Lothian 30 A3
Glenmayne 23 C5
Glenmeanie 79 C4
Glenmidge 48 A2
Glenmoidart Ho 69 E7
Glen Mor 77 E8
Glenmore
  Argyll and Bute 53 A8
  Argyll and Bute 54 F3
  Highland 76 D4
Glenmore Lodge 72 B4
Glenmoy 66 A4
Glen Nevis House 70 E3
Glennoe 63 D5
Glen of Newmill 82 C1
Glenogil 66 A4
Glenprosen Lodge 73 F7
Glenprosen Village 66 A3
Glenquaich Lodge 65 D6
Glenquiech 66 A4
Glenquithlie 83 B5
Glenrath 21 C8
Glenrazie 47 C5
Glenreasdell Mains 50 A4
Glenree 51 D5
Glenrosa 51 C5
Glenrossal 86 C1
Glenrothes 57 B7
Glensanda 62 C3
Glensaugh 74 E3
Glensburgh 40 D2
Glenshero Lodge 71 C7
Glenshoe Lodge 73 F6
Glen Sluain 54 C3
Glenstockadale 46 C2
Glenstriven 54 E3
Glentaggart 19 D7
Glen Tanar House 74 C1
Glentarkie 57 A6
Glenternie 21 B8
Glentirranmuir 38 B4
Glenton 82 F3
Glentress 22 B1
Glentromie Lodge 72 C2
Glen Trool Lodge 47 A6
Glentrool Village 47 B5
Glentruim House 72 C1
Glenuaig Lodge 78 D3
Glenuig 69 E6
Glenure 63 C5
Glenurquhart 80 B2
Glen Vic Askil 76 D3
Glenview 63 E6
Glen Village 39 E8
Glespin 19 D7
Gletness 103 H4
Gloup 102 C5
Glutt Lodge 90 E3
Gobernuisgach
  Lodge 89 D6
Gobernuisgeach 90 E3
Gobhaig 94 B4
Gogar 41 F7
Goirtean
  a'Chladaich 70 E2
Gollanfield 80 C3
Golspie 87 C5
Golval 90 B2
Gometra Ho. 61 C6
Gonfirth 103 G3
Gorbals 28 B2
Gord 101 D3
Gordon 24 A1
Gordonbush 87 C5
Gordonsburgh 82 B1
Gordonstoun 81 B6
Gordonstown
  Aberdeenshire 82 C2
  Aberdeenshire 82 E4
Gorebridge 32 B2
Gorgie 41 F8
Gorrachie 82 C4
Gorrenberry 13 E5
Gorseness 98 B5
Gorstan 79 B5
Gorstanvorran 69 E8
Gortan 52 F2
Gortantaoid 52 E3
Gortenacullish 69 D6
Gorteneorn 69 F6
Gortenfern 69 F6
Gortinanane 50 B3
Gossabrough 103 E5
Gott
  Argyll and Bute 60 C3
  Shetland 103 J4
Goukstone 82 C1
Gourdas 83 D4
Gourdon 75 E5
Gourock 36 E3
Govan 28 A2
Govanhill 28 B2
Gowanhill 83 B7
Gowanwell 83 D5
Gowkhall 40 C5
Gowkthrapple 29 D6
Grabhair 95 A7
Gracemount 32 A1
Grahamston 39 D8
Gramsdal 93 C3
Grandtully 65 B7
Grange
  East Ayrshire 17 B7
  Fife 58 B2
  Perth and Kinross 66 E2
Grange Crossroads 82 C1
Grange Hall 81 B5
Grangemouth 40 D2
Grangemuir 58 B3
Grange of Cree 47 D6
Grange of Lindores 66 F2
Grangepans 40 D4
Granish 72 A4
Grantlodge 74 A4
Granton
  Dumfries & Galloway 11 C5
  Edinburgh 41 E8
Grantown 82 C2
Grantown-on-Spey 81 F5
Grantshouse 34 A5
Graplin 47 E8
Graven 103 F4
Greagdhubh Lodge 72 C1
Greamchary 90 E2
Greenan 54 F3
Greenbank
  Falkirk 39 E8
  Shetland 102 C5
Greenburn 30 B2
Greenend 29 B5
Greenfaulds 39 F6
Greenfield
  Glasgow 28 B3
  Highland 63 B4
  Highland 70 B4
Greenfoot 29 A5
Greengairs 39 F6
Greenhall 28 C4
Greenhead
  Dumfries & Galloway 10 E1
  North Lanarkshire 29 D7
  Northumberland 5 E6
  Scottish Borders 23 D5
Greenhill
  Dumfries & Galloway 2 C3
  Falkirk 39 E7
Greenhills
  North Ayrshire 27 D6
  South Lanarkshire 28 D3
Greenholm 18 B1
Greenhouse 23 E7
Greenigoe 98 C5
Greenland 91 B6
Greenland Mains 91 B6
Greenlaw
  Aberdeenshire 82 C3
  Scottish Borders 34 E3
Greenlaw Mains 31 B8
Greenlea 48 D4
Greenloaning 56 B3
Greenmow 101 D3
Greenock 36 E4
Greenock West 36 E4
Greenrigg 30 B2
Greens 4 A2
Greensidehill 15 A8
Greenwells 23 C7
Greeny 98 A3
Greep 76 D2
Grèin 92 C2
Greinetobht 93 A3
Gremista 101 B3
Greosabhagh 95 C5
Greshornish 76 C3
Gretna 3 E7
Gretna Green 3 E7
Greyrigg 2 A2
Greystead 5 A8
Greystone
  Aberdeenshire 74 C1
  Aberdeenshire 82 E3
  Angus 67 C5
  Dumfries & Galloway 48 B3
Griais 97 C7
Grianan 97 D7
Grimbister 98 B4
Griminis
  Western Isles 93 A2
  Western Isles 93 C2
Grimister 102 D4
Grimness 99 D5
Grindigar 99 C6
Grindiscol 101 C3
Grindon 35 F7
Griomasaigh 93 D3
Griomsidar 97 E6
Grishipoll 60 B4
Gritley 99 C6
Groam 79 D7
Grobister 100 D4
Grobsness 103 G3
Grogport 50 B4
Grotaig 79 F6
Grougfoot 40 E4
Grudie 79 B5
Gruids 86 C2
Gruinard House 84 D3
Gruinards 86 D2
Grula 76 F3
Gruline 61 C8
Gruline Ho. 61 D8
Grumbeg 89 E8
Grunasound 101 C2
Gruting 103 J2
Grutness 101 F3
Gualachulain 63 C6
Gualin Ho. 88 C5
Guardbridge 66 F4
Guay 65 C8
Guesachan 69 E8
Guildiehaugh 30 A3
Guildtown 66 D1
Guisachan 79 F5
Guith 100 C3
Gulberwick 101 C3
Gullane 43 D5
Gunnista 101 B4
Gutcher 102 D5
Guthrie 67 B5
Gylen Park 62 E3
Gyre 98 C4


## H


Hackland 98 A4
Hackness 98 D4
Haclait 93 D3
Hadden 24 B4
Haddington 43 F6
Haddoch 82 D2
Haggbeck 4 D2
Haggersta 103 J3
Haggrister 103 F3
Haggs 39 E6
Haghill 28 A3
Haimer 91 B5
Hairmyres 28 D3
Halbeath 41 C6
Halcro 91 B6
Halkburn 23 A5
Halket 27 D7
Halkirk 91 C5
Halleaths 2 B2
Hallglen 40 E1
Halliburton 34 E2
Hallin 76 C2
Hall of Clestrain 98 C3
Hall of Tankerness 99 C6
Hallrule 13 B7
Halls 44 D2
Hallyards 21 B8
Hallyburton House 66 D2
Hallyne 21 A7
Halmyre Mains 31 E7
Haltwhistle 5 F7
Ham
  Highland 91 A6
  Shetland 101 H5
Hamar 103 F3
Hamarhill 100 C3
Hamars 103 G4
Hametoun 101 H5
Hamilton 28 C4
Hamister 103 G5
Hamnavoe
  Shetland 101 C2
  Shetland 103 E2
  Shetland 103 E4
  Shetland 103 F4
Hangingshaw
  Dumfries & Galloway 2 A3
  Scottish Borders 22 C3
Hansel Village 17 C6
Happendon 19 C8
Harbottle 15 D7
Harburn 30 B4
Hardbreck 99 C5
Hardgate
  Aberdeenshire 75 B4
  Dumfries & Galloway 48 C2
  West Dunbartonshire 37 F9
Hardiston 57 C5
Harehope 31 F8
Hareleeshill 29 D6
Hareshaw 29 B7
Harestanes 38 F4
Harkland 102 E4
Harlaw Ho. 82 F4
Harleyholm 20 B2
Harlosh 76 D2
Haroldswick 102 B6
Harpsdale 91 C5
Harrapool 77 F6
Harrier 101 G5
Harrietfield 65 E7
Harris 68 C3
Harrow 91 A6
Hartfield 77 D7
Harthill 30 B2
Hartmount 86 F4
Hartwood 29 C7
Hartwoodburn 23 D5
Harvieston 38 C2
Harwood on Teviot 12 C4
Hassendean 23 E6
Haster 91 C7
Hastigrow 91 B6
Haswellsykes 21 B8
Hatston 99 B5
Hatterseat 83 F6
Hatton
  Aberdeenshire 83 E7
  Angus 67 D5
  Moray 81 C6
Hattonburn 74 B4
Hatton Castle 82 D4
Hattoncrook 83 F5
Hattonknowe 31 E8
Hatton of Fintray 75 A5
Haugh 17 D8
Haugh Head 25 D9
Haugh-head 22 B2
Haughland 99 B6
Haugh of Glass 82 E1
Haugh of
  Kilnmaichlie 81 E6
Haugh of Urr 48 C2
Haughs of Clinterty 75 A5
Haulkerton 74 E4
Haunn
  Argyll and Bute 61 C6
  Western Isles 92 B3
Hawick 13 A6
Hawkhope 5 A7
Hawksland 19 B7
Hawn 100 D2
Hayfield 42 B1
Hayhill 7 A8
Hayhillock 67 C5
Hayshead 67 C6
Hayston 38 F3
Haystoun 21 B9
Hayton 75 B6
Haywood 30 D3
Hazelbank 29 E7
Hazelton Walls 66 E3
Head of Muir 39 D7
Heads 29 E5
Headshaw 23 E5
Headwell 41 C5
Heanish 60 C3
Hearthstane 21 D6
Heast 69 A6
Heathcot 75 B5
Heatherfield 76 D4
Heatherwood Park 86 D5
Heatherybanks 82 D4
Heathfield 17 E6
Heathhall 48 B3
Heck 2 B2
Heddle 98 B4
Heglibister 103 H3
Heights of Brae 79 B7
Heights of
  Kinlochewe 78 B2
Heilam 89 B6
Heiton 24 C3
Helensburgh 36 D4
Hellister 103 J3
Helmburn 22 E3
Helmsdale 87 B7
Hempriggs House 91 D7
Henshaw 5 F8
Heogan 101 B3
Hepple 15 D8
Heribusta 76 A4
Heriot 32 D3
Hermiston 41 F7
Hermitage 13 E6
Heronsford 46 A3
Herra 102 D6
Herston 98 D5
Hestinsetter 101 B1
Hestwall 98 B3
Hethersgill 4 E2
Hetherside 4 E1
Hethpool 25 D6
Heugh-head 73 A8
Heylipol 60 C2
Heylor 103 E2
Higham 66 F2
High Banton 39 D5
High Blantyre 28 C4
High Bonnybridge 39 E7
Highbridge 70 D3

Sparl 103 G3
Spean Bridge 70 D4
Speybank 72 B3
Spey Bay 81 B8
Speybridge 81 F5
Speyview 81 D7
Spillardsford 83 C7
Spinningdale 86 E3
Spittal
Dumfries & Galloway 47 D5
East Lothian 43 E5
Highland 91 C5
Northumberland 35 D9
Stirling 38 C1
Spittalfield 66 C1
Spittal of Glenmuick 73 D8
Spittal of Glenshee 73 E6
Spott 44 C2
Springboig 28 B4
Springburn 28 A3
Springfield
Argyll and Bute 54 E3
Dumfries & Galloway 3 E7
Fife 57 A8
Highland 80 B1
Moray 81 C5
Springhill
East Renfrewshire 27 C9
North Lanarkshire 29 C8
Springholm 48 C2
Springkell 3 C6
Springside 17 B6
Springwells 11 F5
Sprouston 24 B4
Spynie 81 B7
Sraid Ruadh 60 C2
Srannda 94 D4
Sronphadruig Lodge 72 E2
Stadhlaigearraidh 93 E2
Staffin 76 B4
Stagehall 33 F5
Stain 91 B7
Stair 17 E7
Stairhaven 46 D4
Stamperland 28 C2
Stand 29 A6
Standburn 40 F2
Stane 29 C8
Stanecastle 17 B5
Stanhope 21 D6
Stanley 66 D1
Stannergate 66 D4
Stannersburn 5 A7
Stanydale 103 H2
Staoinebrig 93 E2
Stapleton 4 D3
Stapness 103 J2
Star 57 B8
Stara 98 A3
Staxigoe 91 C7
Steelend 40 B4
Steele Road 13 F6
Steeleroad-end 13 F6
Stein 76 C2
Steinmanhill 82 D4
Stemster 91 B5
Stemster Ho. 91 B5
Stenaquoy 100 C3
Stenhouse
Dumfries & Galloway 9 F7
Edinburgh 41 F8
Stenhousemuir 39 D8
Stenness 103 F2
Stenscholl 76 B4
Stenso 98 A4
Stenton
East Lothian 43 F8
Fife 57 C7
Stepps 28 A4
Stevenston 16 A4
Stewarton
Argyll and Bute 50 E2
East Ayrshire 27 E7
Stichill 24 B3
Stirkoke Ho. 91 C7
Stirling
Aberdeenshire 83 D8
Stirling 39 B6
Stittenham 86 F3
St. Margaret's Hope 99 D5
Stobieside 18 B3
Stobo 21 B7
Stobs Castle 13 C6
Stobshiel 33 B5
Stockiemuir 37 D9
Stoer 88 F2
Stokoe 5 A7
Stonebyres Holdings 29 F7
Stonedge 13 C7
Stonefield
Argyll and Bute 62 D4
South Lanarkshire 28 C4
Stonefield Castle Hotel 54 E1
Stonehaven 75 D5
Stonehouse
Aberdeenshire 83 E5
South Lanarkshire 29 E6
Stonewells 81 B7
Stoneybank 42 F2
Stoneybreck 101 E4
Stoneyburn 30 B3
Stoneyfield 81 C6
Stoneygate 83 E7
Stoneykirk 46 D2
Stoneywood
Aberdeen City 75 A5
Falkirk 39 D6
Stonganess 102 C5
Stonyfield 86 F3
Stormontfield 66 E1
Stornoway 97 D7
Stotfield 81 A7
Stoul 69 C7
Stove
Orkney 100 C4
Shetland 101 D3
Stow 33 F5
Straad 54 F3
Strachan 74 C3
Strachurmore 54 B4
Straid 6 F1
Straith 48 A2
Straiton
Edinburgh 32 A1
South Ayrshire 7 D6
Straloch
Aberdeenshire 83 F5
Perth and Kinross 65 A8
Stranog 75 C5
Stranraer 46 C2
Strath
Highland 84 F1
Highland 91 C6
Strathallan Castle 65 F7
Strathan
Highland 70 C1
Highland 85 A4
Highland 89 B7
Strathan Skerray 89 B8
Strathaven 29 F5
Strathavon Lo. 81 F6
Strathblane 38 E2
Strathcanaird 85 C5
Strathcarron 78 D1
Strathcoil 62 D1
Strathcoul 91 C5
Strathdon 73 A8
Strathellie 83 B7
Strathgarve Lodge 79 B6
Strathkinness 66 F4
Strathmashie House 71 C7
Strathmiglo 57 A7
Strathmore Lodge 91 D5
Strathpeffer 79 C6
Strathrannoch 85 F7
Strathtay 65 B7
Strathvaich Lodge 85 F7
Strathwhillan 51 C6
Strathy
Highland 86 F3
Highland 90 B2
Strathyre 64 F3
Stravithie 58 A3
Street of Kincardine 72 A4
Strichen 83 C6
Strom 103 J3
Stromeferry 77 E8
Stromemore 77 E8
Stromness 98 C3
Stronaba 70 D4
Stronachlachar 55 A7
Stronachullin Lodge 53 E8
Stronchreggan 70 E2
Stronchrubie 85 B6
Strone
Argyll and Bute 36 D2
Argyll and Bute 50 E2
Strone *continued*
Argyll and Bute 53 F5
Highland 70 D3
Highland 72 C2
Highland 79 F7
Inverclyde 36 F4
Stronelairg Lodge 71 B7
Stroneskar 54 B1
Stronmachair 55 B7
Stronmilchan 63 E6
Stronord 47 C6
Stronsaul 54 E4
Strontian 62 A3
Stronvar 64 E3
Stroul 36 D3
Stroupster 91 B7
Struan
Highland 76 E3
Perth and Kinross 65 A6
Strutherhill 29 E6
Struthers 58 B1
Struy 79 E5
Stuartfield 83 D6
Stuckgowan 55 B6
Suainebost 97 A8
Suardail 97 D7
Succoth
Aberdeenshire 82 E1
Argyll and Bute 55 B5
Suckquoy 99 E5
Suddie 80 C1
Suisnish 69 A5
Suladale 76 C3
Sulaisiadar 97 D8
Sulland 100 B3
Sullom 103 F3
Sullom Voe Oil Terminal 103 F3
Sumburgh 101 F3
Summerston 38 F2
Sundaywell 48 A2
Sunderland 52 F2
Sundhope 22 D2
Sunipol 61 B6
Sunnylaw 56 C2
Sutherland Grove 62 C4
Sutors of Cromarty 80 B3
Swanbister 98 C4
Swannay 98 A3
Swanston 31 A8
Swarister 102 E5
Swartland 98 A3
Swiney 91 E6
Swining 103 G4
Swinister
Shetland 101 D3
Shetland 103 E3
Swinnie 13 A8
Swinside Hall 14 A3
Swinside Townfoot 14 A3
Swinton
Glasgow 28 B4
Scottish Borders 35 E5
Swinton Hill 35 E5
Swintonmill 34 E5
Swordale
Highland 79 B7
Highland 86 D3
Swordland 69 C7
Swordly 90 B1
Symbister 103 G5
Symington
Scottish Borders 32 E4
South Ayrshire 17 C6
South Lanarkshire 20 B3
Synton 23 E5
Synton Mains 23 E5
Syre 89 D8
Syster 91 B6


## T


Taagan 78 B2
Tàbost 97 A8
Tabost 97 F6
Tacleit 96 D4
Taigh a Ghearraidh 93 A2
Taigh Bhalaigh 93 A2
Tain
Highland 86 E4
Highland 91 B6
Tairbeart = Tarbert 95 B5
Talisker 76 E3
Talladale 78 A1
Talla Linnfoots 21 E6
Tallaminnoch 7 E7
Talmine 89 B7
Tamanabhagh 96 E3
Tamfourhill 39 D8
Tandlehill 27 B7
Tangasdal 92 D2
Tangwick 103 F2
Tangy 50 D2
Tannach 91 D7
Tannachie 75 D4
Tannadice 66 B4
Tannochside 29 B5
Taobh a Chaolais 92 B3
Taobh a'Ghlinne 95 A7
Taobh a Thuath Loch Aineort 92 A3
Taobh a Tuath Loch Baghasdail 92 A3
Taobh Siar 95 B5
Taobh Tuath 94 D3
Tarbat Ho. 86 F4
Tarbert = Tairbeart 95 B5
Tarbert
Argyll and Bute 50 A2
Argyll and Bute 53 D6
Argyll and Bute 54 F1
Tarbet
Argyll and Bute 55 B6
Highland 69 C7
Highland 88 D3
Tarbolton 17 D7
Tarbrax 30 C4
Tarfside 74 E1
Tarland 74 B1
Tarlogie 86 E4
Tarrel 87 E5
Tarryblake Ho. 82 D2
Tarsappie 66 E1
Tarskavaig 69 B5
Tarves 83 E5
Tarvie
Highland 79 C6
Perth and Kinross 65 A8
Tay Bridge 66 E4
Tayinloan 50 B2
Taymouth Castle 65 C5
Taynish 53 D7
Taynuilt 63 D5
Tayport 66 E4
Tayvallich 53 D7
Tealing 66 D4
Teangue 69 B6
Teanna Mhachair 93 B2
Templand 2 A2
Temple
Glasgow 28 A1
Midlothian 32 C2
Templehall 42 B1
Tenandry 65 A7
Tenston 98 B3
Terpersie Castle 82 F2
Terregles Banks 48 B3
Terryhorn 82 E1
Teuchan 83 E7
Teviothead 12 C4
Tewel 75 D5
Thainston 74 E3
Thankerton 20 B3
The Aird 76 C4
The Balloch 65 F6
The Barony 98 A3
The Bows 56 B2
The Braes 76 E5
The Breck 98 C4
The Craigs 86 D1
The Den 27 D5
The Eals 5 A8
The Flatt 4 C4
The Garths 102 B6
The Glack 21 B8
The Grove 48 B3
The Hall 102 D6
The Inch 42 F1
The Lake 47 E8
The Murray 28 D3
The Neuk 74 C4
The Pole of Itlaw 82 C3
The Riggs 22 C2
The Rink 23 C5
Thirdpart 26 E2
Thirlestane 33 E7
Thomastown 82 E2
Thomshill 81 C7
Thorngrafton 5 E8
Thornhill
Dumfries & Galloway 9 E8
Stirling 56 C1
Thornielee 22 B4
Thornliebank 28 C1
Thornly Park 27 B8
Thornroan 83 E5
Thornton
Angus 66 C3
Fife 57 C7
Northumberland 35 E8
Thorntonhall 28 C2
Thorntonloch 44 D4
Thornton Park 35 E7
Thornydykes 33 E8
Thrashbush 29 A6
Three Bridges 54 A3
Threemiletown 40 E5
Threepwood 23 A6
Thrask 39 B8
Throughgate 48 A2
Thrumster 91 D7
Thundergay 50 B4
Thurso 91 B5
Thurso East 91 B5
Tibbermore 65 E8
Tifty 83 D4
Tigerton 67 A5
Tigh-na-Blair 65 F5
Tighnabruaich 54 E2
Tighnacachla 52 F2
Tighnafiline 84 E2
Tighness 55 B5
Tillathrowie 82 E1
Tillicoultry 40 A2
Tillietudlem 29 E7
Tillyarblet 74 F2
Tillybirloch 74 B3
Tillycorthie 83 F6
Tillydrine 74 C3
Tillyfour 74 A2
Tillyfourie 74 A3
Tillygarmond 74 C3
Tillygreig 83 F5
Tillykerrie 83 F5
Tilly Lo. 74 B2
Tillynaught 82 B2
Timsgearraidh 96 D3
Tingon 103 E2
Tingwall 98 A4
Tinwald 48 A4
Tipperty
Aberdeenshire 82 B3
Aberdeenshire 83 F6
Tiraghoil 61 E6
Tirinie 72 F3
Tiroran 61 E7
Tirryside 86 B2
Toab
Orkney 99 C6
Shetland 101 E2
Tobermory 61 B8
Toberonochy 53 B7
Tobha Beag 93 A4
Tobha Mor 93 E2
Tobhtarol 96 D4
Tobson 96 D4
Tocher 82 E3
Toddlehills 83 D7
Todhill 66 D4
Todlachie 74 A3
Todrig 22 F4
Toft 103 F4
Tofts 91 B7
Tokavaig 69 A6
Tolastadh a Chaolais 96 D4
Tolastadh bho Thuath 97 C8
Tollie 79 C7
Toll of Birness 83 E7
Tolm 97 D7
Tolvah 72 C3
Tomaknock 65 E6
Tom an Fhuadain 95 A7
Tomatin 80 F3
Tombreck 80 E1
Tombui 65 B6
Tomchrasky 70 A4
Tomdoun 70 B3
Tomich
Highland 79 F5
Highland 80 A1
Tomich House 79 D7
Tomintoul
Aberdeenshire 73 C6
Moray 73 A6
Tomnaven 82 E1
Tomnavoulin 81 F7
Tomsleibhe 62 D1
Tonderghie 47 F6
Tongland 47 D8
Tongue 89 C7
Torbeg 50 D5
Torboll Farm 86 D4
Torbothie 30 C1
Torbreck 86 C4
Torbrex 39 B6
Torbush 29 C7
Torcroy 72 C2
Tore 79 C8
Torgyle 71 A5
Torinturk 53 F8
Torlum 93 C2
Torlundy 70 E3
Tormisdale 49 A1
Tormitchell 6 F3
Tormore
Highland 69 B6
North Ayrshire 50 C4
Tornagrain 80 D2
Tornahaish 73 B7
Tornapress 77 D8
Tornaveen 74 B3
Torness 79 F7
Torphichen 40 F3
Torphin 31 A8
Torphins 74 B3
Torquhan 32 E4
Torra 49 A3
Torran
Argyll and Bute 54 B1
Highland 77 D5
Highland 86 F4
Torrance 38 F3
Torrans 61 E7
Torranyard 27 F6
Torridon 78 C1
Torridon Ho. 77 C8
Torries 74 A3
Torrin 77 F5
Torrisdale 89 B8
Torrisdale Castle 50 C3
Torrisdale-Square 50 C3
Torrish 87 B6
Torroble 86 C2
Torroy 86 D2
Torry
Aberdeen City 75 B6
Aberdeenshire 82 E1
Torryburn 40 C4
Torsonce 33 F5
Torsonce Mains 33 F5
Torterston 83 D7
Torthorwald 48 B4
Torvaig 76 D4
Torwood 39 D7
Torwoodlee Mains 23 B5
Toscaig 77 E7
Totaig
Highland 76 C2
Highland 77 F8
Totardor 76 E3
Tote 76 D4
Totegan 90 B2
Totronald 60 B4
Totscore 76 B3
Toulvaddie 87 E5
Tournaig 84 E2
Toux 83 C6
Toward 26 A1
Tow House 5 F8
Towie
Aberdeenshire 74 A1
Aberdeenshire 82 F2
Aberdeenshire 83 B5
Towiemore 81 D8
Townend 37 E7
Townhead
Dumfries & Galloway 47 E8
North Lanarkshire 29 A5
Northumberland 15 F6
South Ayrshire 6 D3
Town-head 54 F3
Townhead of Greenlaw 48 C1
Townhill 41 C6
Town Yetholm 24 D5
Trabboch 17 E7
Trabrown 33 E6
Tradespark
Highland 80 C3
Orkney 99 C5
Traigh Ho 69 C6
Tranent 42 F4
Trantlebeg 90 C2